THE **BEAT,**
THE **SCENE,**
THE **SOUND**

THE BEAT, THE SCENE, THE SOUND

A DJ'S JOURNEY THROUGH THE RISE, FALL, AND REBIRTH OF HOUSE MUSIC IN NEW YORK CITY

DJ DISCIPLE AND HENRY KRONK

ROWMAN & LITTLEFIELD
Lanham • Boulder • New York • London

Rowman & Littlefield
Bloomsbury Publishing Inc, 1385 Broadway, New York, NY 10018, USA
Bloomsbury Publishing Plc, 50 Bedford Square, London, WC1B 3DP, UK
Bloomsbury Publishing Ireland, 29 Earlsfort Terrace, Dublin 2, D02 AY28, Ireland
www.bloomsbury.com

First published in the United States of America 2023
Paperback edition published 2025

Copyright © 2023 by The Rowman & Littlefield Publishing Group, Inc.

All rights reserved. No part of this publication may be: i) reproduced or transmitted in any form, electronic or mechanical, including photocopying, recording or by means of any information storage or retrieval system without prior permission in writing from the publishers; or ii) used or reproduced in any way for the training, development or operation of artificial intelligence (AI) technologies, including generative AI technologies. The rights holders expressly reserve this publication from the text and data mining exception as per Article 4(3) of the Digital Single Market Directive (EU) 2019/790.

British Library Cataloguing in Publication Information available

Library of Congress Cataloging-in-Publication Data
Names: DJ Disciple, author. | Kronk, Henry, 1991- author.
Title: The beat, the scene, the sound : a DJ's journey through the rise, fall, and rebirth of house music in New York City / DJ Disciple and Henry Kronk.
Description: Lanham : Rowman & Littlefield Publishers, 2023. | Includes bibliographical references and index.
Identifiers: LCCN 2022050703 (print) | LCCN 2022050704 (ebook) | ISBN 9781538174876 (cloth) | ISBN 9781538174883 (ebook) | ISBN 9798881807559 (paper)
Subjects: LCSH: DJ Disciple. | Disc Jockeys--New York (State)--New York--Biography. | House music--New York (State)--New York--History and criticism. | LCGFT: Autobiographies.
Classification: LCC ML429.D545 A3 2023 (print) | LCC ML429.D545 (ebook) | DDC 782.42164/1554 [B]--dc23/eng/20221108
LC record available at https://lccn.loc.gov/2022050703
LC ebook record available at https://lccn.loc.gov/2022050704

For product safety related questions contact productsafety@bloomsbury.com.

CONTENTS

Acknowledgments	vii
Foreword	ix
Introduction	1
The Houses	9
The Airwaves	33
The Clubs	55
The Underground	91
Exile	111
Rebirth	147
On and On	185
Endnotes	205
List of Interviews	211
Selected Bibliography	213
Index	215
About the Authors	219

ACKNOWLEDGMENTS

Special thanks from DJ Disciple:

To my collaborator, Henry Kronk. I owe you all the thanks in the world. It was amazing what we did together. I am so happy to share this with you. To everyone in the book, I thank you for your contributions.

To Carlos Alvez (who did the amazing photo designs). To my kids: Julia Banks and Jacob Daniels. To my family: Sherman Banks, Stanley Banks, Larry Banks, Deanna Greene, Pastor Mark VC Taylor, Rev. Joan-El Thompson, Darlene Page, Tyesha Tyrell, Sabrina Vazquez, Joyce Cox, Caryn Nurse, Keith Alexander, Deborah Stewart, Zakiya Bailey, Yusef Pickstock, Ihsan Pickstock, Rick Barnett, Reggie Dorsey, Jimmy Dorsey, Julius Dorsey, Amber Daniels, and Asia Tyrell.

To the Farragut Mothers: Risse Washington, Carol Terry, Carrie Bell (the first director of Farragut's Children's Montessori Daycare Center), Mary Andrews, Doris Brickhouse, Gladys Macbeth, Nell Wright, Thelma E. Tucker, Francina Goodman, Margie Johnson, Joyce McDonald, Mrs. White, Geraldine Wright, Mrs. Newsome, Amanda Ruth Stewart, and to every mother that was a trailblazer in the community to me.

To all my Farragut, Fort Greene, Bed-Stuy, Brownsville, and Flatbush family, Scooter Love (RIP), Danetta Ham, Darlene Regan, Vivian Anderson, Chiaki Yamada, Jo Sailly, Sally Macawthen, Sally Payne, Cinzia Fadda, Karen Session (RIP), Lucy McLaren, Karen Julien, Sol from Toronto, Kioka Jones, the Hardcore Crew, 514 Productions in Montreal, Jose Manso, Linda G., Oren Rosenberg, and Mike "Agent X" Clarke from Detroit. To Martel Toler and Nabiel Musleh from San Francisco. To the bosses: Antonios Zannikos, George Stertsios, Nicholas Sarantinos, Chris Minadakis, and George Liapis. Jim Hill, William Wright, Al Wilkin, JP Firman, Kim Benjamin, Matthew Kletter, Becky Nunez, Fred Milan, Eric Blackwell. Nikki Traxx, DJ Bruce, DJ Mad Marv, Anthony Leardo, Olivia Novik, Jacqueline Helpern, Darren

Ressler, Tamara Silberman, Samantha Warren, Guido Osorio (who made the "Caught Up" remix an anthem) and Brian Tappert and the Traxsource family.

Kraze (from Project X Records), Derrick Carter, DJ Behrouz, the Galaxy Radio Family, Steve Baker from the Greenbelt Festival, Ramon Wells, Chris Torella. Tonia Von Pear. Junior Vazquez, Peter, Tyrone, and Shams from Toronto, DJ Myka, Guida De Palma, DJ Gogos, Baggi Begovic, Prok & Fitch, Raquel R Sanchez, Jeffery Sugarman (thank you for being there for me), Fred Milan, Veronica Evans, Beste Miray Doğan, Darren Ressler, Christina Z White, Lenny Fontana, Albert Wilkins, Bruce C Grilikhes, The New Jersey Public Library, The New York Public Library, DJ Charisma Funk, DJ Lance, Rev Joan-El Thompson, Ed Dewey Brown, Kirsten Giardi, Cynthia Rose, Tony Touch, Ivette (Voodoo Rays' sister), Marcia Carr, Junior Sojal Fortune (RIP), Clemy Riley (RIP), Booker T., Deli G, Klea Clyne, Raquel Sanchez, Glyne Brathwaite, Jennifer Cusa (UAI Institute), Alvaro Lopez, Dawn Michelle Betancourt, DJ MK, Deacon Robert Lyons, Deacon Jimmy Aldrich, Tony Tune, Danny Buddha Morales, Cheryl Goodman, Tonya Wynne, Deborah Stewart, Anthony Leardo, Boo Williams, Glenn Underground, Kia Fikentscher, Derek Lance Simpson, Gary Crum, Francis, John, and Nicole Reddick, Paradise Exquisine AKA Spike and the twins, Ed Dewey Brown, The Real Shakar, DJ Pope, Frankie Paradise, Andre Collins, DJ Cloud 9, Deacon Jeffery Flowers, Michelle Hunter, Felicia Thomas, Sharon Taylor, Kim Lightfoot, DJ Cloud 9, Shino Blackk, Manski Jones, Gregory Knight, Robbi Walcott, Doug Gomez, Demarkus Lewis, Mijangos, Steve "Miggedy" Maestro, Beatweezy, Coflo, Harry "Choo Choo" Romero, Lord G, Bruce Tatum, Principal Stephanie Carroll (PS 307), Joe Claussell, Sister Evans, The Church Of The Open Door, DJ Suki, DJ Philla, Lil Ray, Andre Collins, C-Boogie, Muscle Cars, Sting International, Carlos Sanchez (RIP), Loli and the Mera Lounge Family, the Martha's Country Bakery Family, and to the Greater Refuge Temple Family. Last but not least I give all glory, all power, and all honor to my Lord and Savior Jesus Christ. To God be the glory.

Special thanks from Henry Kronk:

To my collaborator DJ Disciple: I can't thank you enough for trusting me with this undertaking. It has been an incredible honor . . . and a wild ride. Thank you also to my parents Kate and Eric, who gave me life. Thank you to my sisters and first critics in life, Sophie and Anna. And most of all, thank you Maria. I bask in your sunshine.

FOREWORD

Brooklyn-born and -bred, DJ Disciple has been on the New York City scene since the 1980s. I first heard about Disciple when he had his radio show *The Best Kept Secret* on WNYE FM. He always played upcoming and unreleased tracks, as well as the hottest house music. Always with a unique way of mixing, he lured you into his journey of sounds and had you running around trying to get those tracks at stores only to find out they were not released yet.

He knew how to pick just the right tracks that would later on become big club jams, a true tastemaker in his own right, and he also broke many new artists in the house genre. He used to come to the Sound Factory Bar and hang out at our Underground Network Parties (with Promoters Barbara Tucker, Don Welch, and me, the resident DJ). He even had occasional guest spots in the Funk Hut (the downstairs room at the Underground Network Parties) and raised that roof off the sucka.

He gained many followers who went to all his DJ gigs to hear what he would play next, especially at his infamous Tuesday nights at Sapphire Lounge, which was a go-to for us all. The New York City underground dance culture was always present, rockin' the dance floor. Whether at The Choice (the old Loft, which Richard Vasquez ran at the time) or Zanzibar, his guest spots were always well attended by his disciples. Soon after, DJ Disciple started venturing overseas, and it was there where he developed an even larger audience and began collaborations with Basement Jaxx and Mousse T., to name a few.

He is one of New York City's premiere DJs and a true native New Yorker at heart. Proud of his accomplishments and wanting to take it a step further, he has written a book on his take of the music industry from yesterday until today, giving you his insight on the world of electronic dance music. DJ Disciple, a DJ's DJ, never forgetting his roots but keeping to the future!!

—Louie Vega (Masters at Work, Elements of Life)

INTRODUCTION

It was ten miles from The Empire in Middlesbrough to the warehouse outside of town. But DJ Disciple had just a few minutes before his set.

The roads were deserted. It was 11:00 PM on December 31, 1999. Most of the North Yorkshire locals were in one of two places: at home, wondering if the world's computer systems and societies were about to self-destruct, or partying in one of the hundreds of theaters, community halls, industrial spaces, and pubs that transformed into dance clubs across northern England.

A light snow started to fall. Disciple had played The Empire with his fellow DJ and radio co-host Tony Walker earlier in the evening. They had formed the same bill the year before at the converted Victorian theater for a live set that aired on MTV. For that night in 1998, they had packed the three-level venue, so the promoters had it easy this time around. When word got out that Walker and Disciple would be headlining for Y2K, advance tickets sold out faster than they could be printed, and hopeful house heads gathered outside of the venue hours before the doors opened.

Disciple arrived at the gig with two aces up his sleeve: copies of "You Don't Know Me" by the up-and-coming Armand Van Helden and Frankie Knuckles' remix of Allison Limerick's "Where Love Lives." Both had driven The Empire crowd wild.

Now, Disciple had left Walker at the theater to head to an unknown location event. Word had circulated in the local house community. To get there, you had to show up to one spot where the promoters would shuttle partiers to the warehouse in question. The local fire marshal did not get the invite.

Disciple was riding on the kind of energy that only comes when you get paid overtime to do the thing you love. New Year's Eve meant double bubble—otherwise known as double pay—and Y2K pushed those DJ fees even higher. Disciple could use the extra funds to compose new beats, cut new tracks in the studio, and eat three meals a day in the process for months to come.

Middlesbrough became a glow on the horizon. The snow was coming down harder. They passed a club-goer decked out in full party attire with his thumb out. There was no time to stop. They were driving too fast, and besides, there was no room in the car to spare with the other passengers and Disciple's crates of records.

Less than a mile down the road, the driver failed to make a hard left. The car shot off the curb, rolled over and over down the embankment, and settled upside down in the ditch. Somehow, everyone was fine. Disciple jumped out of the car, gathered his records, and headed up to the road.

When the next car came along, Disciple didn't stick out his thumb. He waved like he was escaping a hostage situation. The car screeched to a halt. It was full of more clubbers who, after seeing the crashed car and understanding who they were dealing with, immediately jumped out and helped Disciple pack his records in the trunk. Everyone squeezed in, and he promised them that everyone would get in free if they got to the gig in time.

The warehouse was just three minutes down the road. They pulled up to the side loading dock and ran through to where the sound system was set up. The crowd at capacity was making the floor bounce. At the turntables, the resident DJ looked around, wondering if he needed to extend his two-hour set. When he saw Disciple, he nodded and got on the mic.

"Ladies and gentlemen, DJ Disciple is in the house."

Disciple prepared his records and got ready to make the hand-off. With the resident's last track spinning, Disciple carefully placed his wax on the vacant plate. He brought the levels up, and the crowd heard the words of Simion, the villain from *Dexter's Laboratory*: "What is my problem with man you ask? No, I ask you what was man's problem with *me*?"

The beat, sampled from Jaydee's "Plastic Dreams," dropped. Synths crept in. Duane Harden sang, "You don't even know me." The clock ticked down. A new millennium began.

———

Across the Atlantic, outside of Disciple's apartment in the Farragut Houses, in Brooklyn, the New York Police Department presence was heavy. Jennifer Lopez had appeared before a grand jury in Manhattan Supreme Court earlier that day to testify that Sean "Puffy" Combs didn't have a firearm on him when shooting broke out in the Carter Hotel in Midtown the Monday before.

INTRODUCTION

Firearm exchanges in Manhattan clubs were not uncommon occurrences. On the Brooklyn, Bronx, and Harlem streets, they were commonplace. An off-duty police officer was shot in the Bronx the day prior. The trial of the officers who murdered Amadou Diallo a few blocks over from the incident almost a year before was set for January 31 of the new year.

Around the Farragut Houses, and through many sections of Brooklyn, Queens, Manhattan, and the Bronx, this violence was a daily reality. Disciple's father said a prayer to thank God that his sons had careers that took them away from the streets they had grown up in.

Farragut was a world away from that Yorkshire warehouse in England. Disciple's UK agent, JP, always told him that he had to save up so he could move his family out of the projects.

But the Farragut Houses made Disciple the DJ he was. He first encountered mobile DJs throwing park jams in the yards between buildings. His neighbors included house and hip hop royalty, recording artists, and Grammy winners. He loved his community. He prayed in his community. He made music in his community. And when his tour ended in January 2000, he boarded a plane and flew home.

This is the story of David Banks, also known as DJ Disciple, a man who dedicated his life to house music. And throughout his forty-year-and-counting career, he saw most of it go down.

The traditional narrative of house music locates its origins in Chicago, at a club called The Warehouse where Frankie Knuckles was the resident DJ. Knuckles mixed together disco deep cuts, Philadelphia soul, R&B, some emerging hip hop, and European electro. These selections often prioritized a four-on-the-floor beat, along with deeper bass lines. Beginning in the early 1980s, Knuckles began to use a reel-to-reel player to create mixes that he would play at the club. With these mixes, he spliced sections of tracks together to extend rhythm breaks and maintain powerful bass lines. Later, he bought a Roland TR-909 drum machine to add further rhythmic elements to his sound.

The Warehouse drew a mostly gay Black and Latino crowd. But the vibe of the party and the musical innovations made by the DJs there began to draw a wider audience. The scene began to intermingle with folks coming from hardcore and post punk, though these integrations were not always so seamless.

From the beginning, house music DJs had a mandate to keep clubbers dancing far past when audiences of other genres would be asleep. The scene drew dancers whose skill level went unmatched in other crowds. In Chicago, a style of dancing known as jacking came to rise—hence early house tracks like Chip E's "Time to Jack" and "Jack Your Body" by Steve "Silk" Hurley. Lofting and footwork styles of dance also rose to prominence, though these were more closely tied to New York dancers.

On the radio, WBMX's group known as Hot Mix 5 began to play mix shows and early recorded house-style music. This DJ crew—composed of Farley "Funkin" Keith (who later played as Farley "Jackmaster" Funk), Mickey "Mixin" Oliver, Ralphi "Rockin" Rosario, Kenny "Jammin" Jason, and Scott "Smokin" Silz—was originally compiled as the resident DJs of the station's Saturday night program *Saturday Night Live Aint No Jive*. But their popularity led the station to program them for a Friday mix show, along with other spots throughout the week. Their popularity helped make WBMX the most popular station in Chicago, and their mixes were recorded and distributed throughout the United States.

While house music sounds are often associated with specific clubs and scenes, radio always casts the widest net. In nearby Belleville, Michigan, a town thirty miles outside of Detroit, three high school kids—Juan Atkins, Derrick May, and Kevin Saunderson—began to produce a form of music that would come to be known as techno. Their influences came mostly from what they heard on the radio, especially a late-night program called *The Midnight Funk Association* on Detroit's WGPR hosted by DJ Charles "The Electrifying Mojo" Johnson. The three later traveled to Chicago to check out the house music scene. It was Derrick May who sold Frankie Knuckles his TR-909.

Knuckles left The Warehouse in 1983 to open his own club, The Power Plant. The Warehouse was then rebranded as the Muzic Box, and the owners hired Ron Hardy as their new resident DJ. Hardy would become equally influential in the Chicago scene by bringing a charging energy to his mixes. Through the mid-1980s, producers like Farley "Jackmaster" Funk, Steve "Silk" Hurley, Marshall Jefferson, and Jesse Saunders cemented Chicago house as a music genre.

In many cases, Chicago house records barely made a splash where they were produced, but they had huge impacts elsewhere in the world. Tracks like "Love Can't Turn Around" by Farley "Jackmaster" Funk and "Jack Your Body" by Steve "Silk" Hurley barely sold in Chicago, but they charted in the United Kingdom. English audiences took these records and ran with them.

The UK acid house movement adopted the genre and became its primary culture bearer when popularity faded in the United States. Audiences elsewhere in Europe and East Asia also developed strong tastes for house, and many Chicago DJs would go on to make the bulk of their income from international touring and record sales.

There is no question that all of this is fact. But this book tells a different story. Although Frankie Knuckles made his mark in Chicago, he was born in the Bronx. He and his friend Larry Levan first learned how to DJ under the direction of Nicky Siano, who opened a club called The Gallery in SoHo in the early 1970s, which took its blueprint from David Mancuso's venue The Loft. Levan would go on to become the resident DJ at the Paradise Garage and originate his own sub-genre of dance music (known as garage). The legendary venue hosted a sound system, designed by audio engineer Richard Long, that many venues would attempt to copy. Before the Garage, Long had worked with clubs around New York, along with mobile DJs to perfect speaker cabinet designs, wiring systems, and devices that could control volumes at different frequencies. These developments helped lay important foundations for both house and hip hop. This was the world that Frankie Knuckles had come from.

While Chicago artists were making waves in the Midwest, an adjacent and interconnected generation of DJs and producers in New York were also developing the style. Besides Levan and Siano, Tony Humphries, Danny Krivit, Kenny Carpenter, Francois K, Timmy Regisford, D Train, Sinnamon, the Peech Boys (fronted by Levan), and many others led the charge in the early 1980s that helped put house music on the map. They were soon followed by David Morales, Little Louie Vega, Kenny Dope Gonzalez, Jellybean Benitez, Todd Terry, Roger Sanchez, Junior Vasquez, David Camacho, Bobby Konders, and DJ Disciple.

This group was also matched and mirrored by generations of New York hip hop DJs like Scott La Rock (BPD), DJ Maseo (De La Soul), Terminator X (Public Enemy), Moe Love (Ultramagnetic MCs), Clark Kent, Kid Capri, DJ Red Alert, Jam Master Jay (Run-DMC), DJ Jazzy Joyce, Chuck Chillout, Jazzy Jeff, Sammy B (Jungle Brothers), and, before them, Kool DJ Herc, Afrika Bambaataa, Marly Marl, Grand Wizzard Theodore, and Grandmaster Flash. But Flash was hardly New York's first Grandmaster. Before them all came the mobile DJs who made it all possible. Grandmaster Flowers, Maboya, Plummer, the Disco Twins, Hollywood, and countless others paved the way for hip hop and house music to take off. Many of their names have been forgotten.

Another factor of New York's early house scene has been lost. The venues where these DJs played, in many cases, brought together a representative mix of New York's diverse demographics onto the same dance floor. From the 1970s into the early 1990s, these DJs blended R&B, disco, gospel, electronic, funk, Black, white, straight, queer, American, African, European, Latin American, Asian, poor, rich, upper, downer, sober, secular, and faithful culture together into one sublime mixture of a musical experience.

This book covers the rise, fall, and rebirth of New York house music as seen through the eyes of DJ Disciple. It also follows the journey he made—along with many of his fellow DJs—to the United Kingdom, Europe, and hundreds of other regions around the world as house music began to be exported in the 1990s. This narrative begins with a look at the mobile DJ movement that provided the foundation for both house and hip hop. It also investigates Brooklyn and New York public housing in the second half of the twentieth century, the cultural influences therein, and their faith-based communities.

The story then moves to DJ Disciple's time at Baruch College and his entry into radio. His enrollment corresponded with the arrival of early recorded Chicago house music, like Larry Heard's "Mystery of Love" and Adonis' "No Way Back." Early and underground Chicago house records made their way through clubs, but they were almost unknown on the radio. Disciple launched a radio program on Baruch's college station, WBMB 590 AM, in 1985. He then landed a spot on the FM dial at WNYE 91.5 FM with the show *New York's Best Kept Secret*, where he made a name for himself by playing unreleased house records. While radio reached the widest audience, it was clubs that made the magic happen with massive sound systems, light shows, and DJs that took these records and transformed them into something new each night. Disciple first heard house music played at venues like The Palladium, Tunnel, and Studio 54. Within a few years, he was playing them himself.

These represented more mainstream venues. As Disciple got deeper into the scene, he discovered and played at mobile parties like Wild Pitch that moved from space to space around the city. Around the same time, clubs drew the ire of city officials. For safety reasons at first, and then under Mayor Rudolph Giuliani's quality-of-life initiatives, city regulators closed down huge swaths of New York nightlife. House DJs found themselves with fewer and fewer venues to play.

But while that occurred, house music appetites overseas grew stronger and stronger. Disciple and many others went to tour the United Kingdom, Europe, East Asia, and elsewhere for months out of the year, where they played for larger audiences and made more income than they had ever managed to in New York. The genre did eventually return to the city, but under different circumstances. Bottle service took off in the late 1990s and 2000s. Though it catered to a very different audience, it kept DJs employed and allowed them a platform to showcase their craft. Then, a few years later, electronic dance music came to the fore, and festivals became another important outlet.

In the past few years, house music has come back in a big way. Major mainstream recording artists like Beyoncé and Drake have drawn heavily on the genre in recent albums. Many hip hop, R&B, and pop artists tour with DJs. Artists like Disciple have seen the music come full circle.

This story is told through his point of view. But to tell it, the authors engaged in significant research over a period of four years. That involved reading everything they could on what had been written on house music, sifting through old newspaper clippings, going through archived websites, and looking through hundreds of old party flyers. They also conducted more than sixty interviews with a range of characters involved. Some interview subjects are well-known DJs, like Todd Terry, Bobby Konders, and Kenny Carpenter. Others were (or still are) promoters, dancers, producers, agents, or managers. Others were just part of the scene.

DJ Disciple says,

Not everyone understands house music, and not everyone understands me. Birthed from the genre of disco, I discovered house from a friend at Baruch College in 1986. The signature record, "Move Your Body" by Marshall Jefferson, resonated with my generation as we invaded nightclubs with the mantra "Gotta Have House Music." Radio ate up house music at first, but then spat it out when its relative hip hop became commodified and commercialized.

House DJs and producers have faced challenges over the years. Until recently, few major labels recognized our accomplishments. In the 1990s, local governments began to crack down on the nightlife scenes that welcomed us. When house music went further underground with raves, the American government stamped that out too. When the internet and file sharing came along, our industry watched our revenue streams go up in smoke overnight.

Still, house music refused to die. It makes you feel your heart beat in your chest. It makes you lose the need to speak and, instead, tells you to get up and dance. It makes us forget our differences. Some have tried to regulate the music. Others have tried to criminalize it. But every time, house music breaks free.

House music today can be heard across the internet, on TV commercials, and even in movies. Yet it continues to fight for its existence as music becomes more disposable.

My community, the Farragut Houses in Brooklyn, New York, has a similar story to tell. When I was growing up, the bus took me into white New York City schools in the morning. My brothers got chased home every afternoon. At first, Farragut was a refuge for me. It was where I found God and learned about my faith. It was a progressive neighborhood full of interesting, intelligent, and influential neighbors.

But as I got older, that changed. Farragut got hit hard by the crack epidemic, AIDS, broken windows policing, and gentrification. Management crises and budget issues have landed New York City Public Housing billions of dollars behind in repairs and regular maintenance.

I gained international success as DJ Disciple, but I risked losing my faith in the process. The oversaturation of house music today is threatening the genre. But it's also finally getting recognition from mainstream artists. The forces of gentrification make living in Farragut a constant battle. And the COVID-19 pandemic had the whole world wondering when they'll be able to dance in public again. Somehow, it's all connected. This is my story.

THE HOUSES

Long ago before David Banks, the future DJ Disciple, was born—before hip hop and house coalesced into their own genres, before "Rapper's Delight" hit the top forty and the Paradise Garage opened its doors—mobile DJs played the music that made the dancers dance.

Through Brooklyn, Queens, Harlem, and the Bronx—in parks, on beaches, and in vacant lots—crews hoisted metric tons of subwoofers, mids, tweeters, turntables, and crates and crates of records. They ran extension cords from streetlights, through shop doors, out apartment windows. And they brought these spaces to life.

DJs like Maboya, Plummer, Pete DJ Jones, Hollywood, Lovebug Starski, the Disco Twins, and countless others were among the first to deconstruct recorded music, mix records, and MC over it all. But before them, there was Grandmaster Flowers.

When Jonathan Cameron Flowers was growing up in the Farragut Houses in Brooklyn, he started doing things with sound that no one had ever done before. Flowers was one of the first DJs to mix two records together in sequence. He laid familiar melodies over new rhythms. He discovered records that few had ever heard. And above all else, he knew how to rock a crowd.

DJ Debonair, a lifelong resident of the Farragut Houses, learned the craft from him.

"Flowers became so popular," Debonair said. "He was known for his mixing. He was known for his sound. Back in the day, you couldn't get away with just two, three, or four or five speakers. Guys had *multiple* speakers. If you had a big sound, it would be known as superpowers. So you had your DJs, and then you had your DJs with superpowers. And Flowers had superpowers."

But compiling a system that could bring a loud, high-quality sound to an outdoor setting was just half the battle. You also had to be able to play. Big Bob came up in Bushwick and connected with Flowers in the early 1970s.

"Me and my man Rodney Heath, we was into playing," Big Bob said. "Rodney would play the records, and I would MC and dance. On Sundays, we would always go to church. One day, Rodney comes to me and says, 'Yo Big Bob, we got to go to Riis Beach and check out this guy called Flowers.' We was in high school. This was '72, '73. So one Sunday, we didn't go to church. We rode the bus all the way out to the beach. We got down by the courts. Flowers had four stacks set up down there. And he was *banging*. I thought me and Rodney had a nice set. But Flowers sounded *nice*. And his mix was so clean. He would go from A to Z, and you never even knew he left A."

When Big Bob graduated high school, he started running full time with Flowers. He would help him carry his speakers and records. And Flowers taught him his craft. There were two components to Flowers' genius: his sound system and his mix. He would tell his crew that plenty of DJs knew how to play records, but the most important thing is knowing how to set up and wire your sound. Through the late 1960s and 1970s, he hooked up with audio engineers to push his sound further and further. Foremost among these was Richard Long, who would go on to design world-famous systems. He helped Flowers find the speakers that would make his sound pop, and the two would collaborate on the proper wiring and placement of his stacks. The two devised means to efficiently wire multiple speakers without compromising power. They also began to experiment with speaker cabinet design.

But perhaps Flowers and Long's most important collaboration involved technology that would aid the mixing of records and change music forever. In those days, most DJs played records one at a time. Many began to hook up two turntables to their systems so that, as the first record began to wind down, they could play the next one without needing to stop the music to switch out the vinyl. But Flowers took this to the next level and began to play two records together, with the beat of one matching that of the other. Most records don't play at the same speed. So to do this, he would mark the labels of his records with a code. For the slowest ones he played, he wrote "SS," which stood for "slow slow." Slightly faster ones would be marked with a single S for slow. That continued up to "FF" for "fast fast," the fastest he would play.

Besides playing these records together, Flowers and Richard Long came up with a system to isolate ranges of frequencies. In those days through to today, sound systems contain a device—known as a crossover—that sends certain frequencies to the correct speaker. Bass frequencies go to the subwoofers, mids go to the mids, and highs go to the tweeters. But Long and Flowers came up with a means to actively control this process. The first crossover the two came up with isolated just the bass and the highs.

"Richard Long is the first one that made Flowers a bass and a high crossover," Big Bob said. "He had the table where he cut holes for the turntables. You know those round knob light switches you use to dim lights in your house? He had two of those hooked up to that crossover, one for bass and one for mids. Flowers had it like that—under the table—so you couldn't see what he was doing."

Today, crossovers (or their digital versions) are a crucial part of a DJ's process. DJs form their craft, in large part, around their ability to isolate the bass lines of one record and overlay the vocals or melody (in the high or mid ranges) of another, stacking two songs on top of each other and creating a new sonic experience. This musical innovation also provided the foundational bedrock for hip hop and house beats. But in the early 1970s, that kind of mixing was unheard of. Grandmaster Flowers helped develop this technique. And it brought crowds flocking to hear his sound.

"DJs used to kind of create these clubs off of the sound that these guys had," Debonair said. "They used to set up on the park along the Eastern Parkway in Brooklyn and battle. It was battle of the DJs and their sound. Thousands of people would go out there just like it was a football game. Or we would go out to Riis Beach. There was no residents there or anything like that. All the time, you would have like ten DJs set up there. And they would just battle to see who had the loudest sound and who's rocking the jams, you know?"

"Flowers—believe it or not—he had a big name, and he had a big name for a long time, but he didn't always have the loudest sound. Some other guys had bigger sounds. But Flowers could rock better than the other guys. This one guy came out named Maboya. Man, he had the fishes dancing. He had the fishes dancing in the water, his sound was so loud. But Flowers could rock better than anyone. A lot of people came up DJing under his tutelage, myself included. He was so legendary that the DJ world named him Grandmaster—he didn't call himself that. Back in the day, promoters and fans gave titles to DJs. Flowers earned his name."

Flowers played at weddings, birthdays, and social gatherings, but also in bars and clubs. Most venues' systems couldn't match Flowers' system, so he and his crew always brought their own superpowers.

"Flowers' name was so big," Debonair continued. "Back then, they didn't put pictures on flyers. That came later. They just had names. Flowers was so big that I had to be Flowers several different times. He overbooked himself. He booked two or three parties a night and sent another DJ to play them. That's when I first put together my own system. Because he didn't have a set to give me. He would give me half the pay. Back in the 1970s, $600 was a lot of money. I saw promoters go to Flowers and say, 'You don't have to come play. If you let me put your name on the flyer, I'll give you $600.' That's how popular this guy was."

Flowers also started playing while the ink was still drying on the Civil Rights Act of 1964. In New York, some segregation laws remained on the books into the twenty-first century. While they might not have always been enforced, social norms kept dance crowds in many venues segregated through the 1970s. But Flowers bucked that trend. "Flowers played for everybody," Big Bob said. "Every promoter wanted to book him, Black or white. They knew that, if his name was on the flyer, 300 people they didn't know were going to show up."

Many folks locate the birth of hip hop and house music with DJs like Kool Herc, Afrika Bambaataa, and Grandmaster Flash. But Flash was hardly New York's first Grandmaster. Generations of DJs came before and laid important groundwork for them to build upon.

FARRAGUT

Flowers came up in the Farragut Houses in Brooklyn. David Banks, the future DJ Disciple, along with his parents and four brothers, lived in the apartment directly below him. David has lived in that same apartment for all his life. The buildings sit east of Brooklyn Heights, west of Fort Greene, and just south of the area that has become known as Down Under the Manhattan Bridge Overpass (Dumbo). Construction of the housing project was completed in 1951. At the time, it cost $15,087,000 (in 1951 dollars) to build. Rent was first set at $8.82 per room per month.[1]

When Farragut first went up, it towered over the surrounding area. But over the following years, the massive engineering projects of New York's post-war boom slowly enclosed it. You can still see the fossils of this era preserved between the cafes and the multimillion-dollar high rises present today. Lofts, now converted into living spaces, were bustling industrial buildings. Factories, piers, and warehouses in the area were operated by longshoremen and factory laborers working long shifts around the clock. After families started moving into Farragut, the region saw the construction of the Brooklyn-Queens Expressway and the confluence of the Brooklyn and Manhattan Bridges.

Before all that, this corner of New York oiled and serviced the main economic motor in the area: the Brooklyn Navy Yard. World War II drew over seventy-five thousand men and women to the Yard during its peak. It produced ships like the USS *Missouri*—upon which Japanese envoys signed agreements of surrender in Tokyo Bay—and gave rise to hundreds of now-forgotten bars, tattoo parlors, restaurants, and brothels.

As the *Brooklyn Eagle* reported on March 25, 1951, when the first twenty families moved in to Farragut, the "State-aided project . . . replaces 16.6 acres of slums which, for many decades, blighted the area between the Brooklyn Navy Yard and the Manhattan Bridge."[2]

David's father, William, grew up in Manhattan, but his family moved to Brooklyn when he was a teenager. William's mom, Luella, threw rent parties to get by. She entertained guests by playing her piano. She also taught William to play. As a young man in the 1930s, he sat in on jams at clubs across Brooklyn and Manhattan. One time, he shared the stage with an up-and-coming Miles Davis. When World War II rolled around, he was drafted and sent to serve in the Pacific theater.

Private Banks saw action. Before a year had passed, the truck he was riding in hit a landmine and he was thrown from the vehicle. He served most of his time in Papua New Guinea, and he later recalled how some of his brothers-in-arms would pay locals an American quarter in exchange for the head of a Japanese soldier. He returned home four years later, honorably discharged and shell-shocked.

William Banks did not have the benefit of today's mental health services and treatments. He quickly and quietly made the transition from soldier to civilian and took up a position as an accountant. He dealt with his problems on his own.

William was resilient and hard-working. In the 1950s, Black men earned an average of $0.59 for every dollar a white man took in,[3] but William proved the exception to this rule. During the Civil Rights era, when leaders in the Black community advocated for Black Power and equality, William kept a stiff upper lip. When most of his community punched a clock in the factory, he went to work every day wearing a suit, holding a briefcase, and walking with a swagger.

Back stateside, he met a young woman named Julia Pearsall at The Savoy Ballroom, a jazz club in Harlem. Growing up, Julia had a turbulent childhood. Her grandfather was a minister at a church in Hopewell, Virginia. When Julia's mother, Lois Pearsall, got pregnant with her at the age of fourteen, she was thrown out of the house. Julia rarely knew a steady home. She was raised alternatively by Lois' eight siblings. They tossed her to and fro among them at their convenience.

When Julia and William started dating, Lois did not take kindly to him. William was older, straight out of combat, and, in her opinion, too dark-skinned. Lois subscribed to certain ideas about dark-skinned men. She thought Julia should be with a lighter man so that she could be more easily accepted by society. Lois was not comfortable with her own shade, and she used lightening products to appear less dark.

Julia was also young—just fourteen years of age—and Lois did not want her daughter to follow in her footsteps. Julia attended PS 3 in Brooklyn and later went to the Central High School of Needle Trades located on 225 West 24th Street in Manhattan, where she specialized in sewing. In his free time after work, William helped Julia with her homework. In spite of—or maybe because of—Lois' pushback, their romance continued to grow. Julia graduated in June of 1949 and, within a year, she married William, or Bill as she loved to call him.

Sherman Banks entered the world shortly after, and William needed to find a place to settle. He read that the New York City Housing Authority was accepting families, and he heard that they gave special treatment to veterans who served in the war. So the Banks family applied. They were accepted into Farragut, and they relocated to Brooklyn. Soon, they had more children—Stanley, then Larry, and then Leighton. On September 2, 1965, David, the fifth and final Banks son, was born.

NEIGHBORS AND THE NEIGHBORHOOD

The Farragut Houses accepted many GIs and their families after they first went up. But any martial spirit that might have once existed was gone by the 1960s. A highly musical, politically active, and creative neighborhood took its place.

"Farragut was an experiment," Larry Banks said. "That's how it was looked upon. It was a mixture, a combination of different types of people. You had your upwardly mobile people. You had some people from the South. Some were from Harlem. It was a combination of a particular group of people that were coming together to do something progressive and positive for themselves."

Farragut families could sign their kids up for cotillion as easily as they could sports, music, or other organized activities. The Banks family had no shortage of interesting and influential neighbors. In addition to Grandmaster Flowers, several were DJs and musicians.

Strafe Standard, also known as Steve Standard, lived at 177 Sands Street. He DJed on Farragut concrete in the 1970s. He made a name for himself as a composer, producer, studio musician, and arranger, but he was best known for his signature masterpiece "Set It Off," which was popular in the underground club scene for decades. The track is one of the most widely sampled recordings of all time. It has been used by artists such as Jennifer Lopez, Fat Joe & Big Pun, 50 Cent, Monica, Queen Latifah, Lil Jon, Tupac, Newcleus, Kid Capri, Fabolous, and Dead Prez.

Strafe was responsible for helping another Farragut resident, Kenny Carpenter, develop his skills as a DJ.

"I was always fascinated by the turntables with the mixer," Carpenter said. "During the 1970s, they called that the coffin, you know, the box with the turntables, the mixer, and whatever else inside. Anyway, Steve—they call him Strafe, but his real name is Steve—he's the only person that I knew in Farragut who was a DJ, a mobile DJ. There wasn't no club DJ then. You had to bring the sound with you. And your records. It was a lot of work.

"Steve used to do a party twice a month. I was living in 177 [Sands Street] on the first floor. One time, Steve was coming back from one of his gigs, and I was watching through the peephole in the door. He was bringing some stuff in the hallway and unloading from the truck. There was this other guy who lived in our building. As Steve was going to get something from the truck, this guy ran up and stole a crate of his 45s."

Since the advent of digital music, it has been easy to forget just how valuable records used to be. Not only were they purchased at substantial costs, but many, especially the hard-to-find and highly treasured non-commercial vinyl, had been printed in a limited run. Once that rare record was stolen, there's a good chance that it would be gone forever, and no amount of money could bring it back.

"Steve was so upset when he came back," Carpenter continued. "I felt bad for the brother. You know, I was collecting records too. So I went and knocked on his door, and I was like, 'Yo, I know who took your records, but don't mention my name, right?' So he got his records back, and he was so thankful. He said, 'Come on upstairs and hang out.' So I went up to his place and he had the whole setup up there. So I said, 'Damn, you know I never tried to play before, do you mind if I just see if I could mix? You know, I never seen this before do you think I could try?' And he said, 'Go ahead. Go ahead. Try it out.' So I started to play a little and I realized I could do it."

Carpenter would go on to become one of New York's most well-known DJs through the 1980s and beyond. He held a residency at Studio 54 and Bonds International Casino, among many other gigs.

Another Farragut neighbor, Rusty Taylor, has played bass for the artist Shannon for years. Shannon put four number one tracks on Billboard's US Dance chart, the first of which was "Let the Music Play" in October 1983.

The track was widely influential because it was one of the first to feature a Roland TR-808 drum machine mixed with a bass line from a Roland TB-303 synth and an unadjusted filter. The combination became popular in later years. Along with some other influences, it would lend its signature sound to acid house.

Rusty also worked with other artists throughout the 1970s like Jon Lucien. He grew into one of Farragut's biggest promoters. His events brought together some of the best DJs in the area, including DJ Debonair and KC the Prince of Soul, the first MC of the disco era.

Shah D and Charlie Victor also played impromptu park jams with their mobile sound systems. David Banks got more exposure to their music as a kid than to others. It was different than the disco he heard from Flowers and Debonair, harder, faster, and more cut up. Soon, it wasn't just one DJ playing for the neighborhood. Multiple jocks would come out into common spaces. These entertainers pulled out all the stops to put together the loudest systems possible to captivate their crowds, compete with each other, and represent their buildings.

OLD SCHOOL

David was an introvert growing up. He hardly spoke in his adolescent years, and the family grew concerned about his social skills. It wasn't rare for him to pass entire family gatherings without saying a word. He lived with a lot of anger and frustration as a kid. Most of these emotions were expressed through violence at school.

The *Brown v. Board of Education* decision arrived in 1954. Growing up, the Banks family knew all too well just how long it took for reality to catch up with the law. New York Public Schools weren't going to integrate themselves. Segregation in many Brooklyn districts actually increased during the second half of the 1950s.[4] At the same time, Julia Banks knew that if she was going to get her sons the best education possible, it was going to be at a white school. Her kids joined a generation that broke down the barriers previously imposed in American public education. School is difficult for any kid, but David and his brothers fought the segregation mentality in the classroom on a daily basis.

"My mother wanted me to get the best education I could," David Banks said. "That meant crossing unseen, but very real boundaries, for the privilege of a better education. Once the school day was over, everyone returned to their own neck of the concrete woods. Racially motivated attacks were not uncommon, especially in the 'graveyard path' near FDR High School."

"We were sent out to a white junior high school and a white high school," said Stanley, David's older brother. "We caught hell out there. We would be chased out of the community every day. One time, I was pushed onto the subway tracks with an oncoming train."

David struggled to walk the line between self-defense and acceptable classroom conduct. In second grade, he knocked a kid's tooth out. In third, he slapped his teacher and got suspended. In fourth grade, he was held back. Mr. Madden, David's teacher, sent a firm note home with him that read: "I sincerely hope David's efforts will increase—instantly."

Julia was constantly in and out of PS 105 to see Principal Flannagan. When David's teachers told his parents that they were considering special education for him, Julia took matters into her own hands. A few old-school parenting methods that involved the cane put David on the straight and narrow.

Things also changed when David entered Mrs. Eisenberg's class the next year. The two shared a connection, and Mrs. Eisenberg managed to inspire her student. That year, David's report card had nothing but As and Bs.

Not all was bad for the Banks brothers in American public education. Both Larry and Stanley learned music at FDR High School. This put them and the Banks family on a new path. Their teacher was Lawrence Bergstein. Besides teaching music, he also worked as a promoter and bandleader in the city. He regularly booked shows in Manhattan clubs and rubbed elbows with influential people in the New York music scene.

"Lawrence Charles Bergstein taught me on the violin, the viola, the cello, and the bass," Stanley said. "I stepped into a gold mine. When we were going to junior high school and then later in high school, this cat would come in and curse the kids out. He would say, 'You're playing garbage! This sounds like garbage! You're never gonna be anything. Last night, I had to play for the Supremes. I contracted the horns for the Temptations!'

"He was doing all this while we were in junior high school. It was hard to believe. One day, he told my mother, 'Look, I like your son. Get him a black jacket. I want to take him out to some of my jobs.' That's what he did at night. And during the day, he taught us."

Music was infused throughout David's and his brothers' childhood. Every Sunday, their father's one day off per week, Mr. Banks did one of two things: held court at a nearby bar or got his kids to listen to music. The living room hi-fi was like a shrine in their household. It wasn't uncommon for William to periodically bring home a new instrument for his kids. He encouraged them all to try their hands at something new, listen to new records, and play music with one another.

"I have to say," said Stanley Banks, "the music that my parents played when they turned on the radio on Sunday, that's deep within us. So the talent we got now, that came from the music that they were playing. I don't think they had a plan to make us musicians. When they were playing the music, they were just playing the music. But it was a big influence on us.

"David became a DJ. Why? I'd have to say it's the music that he heard around the house. We'd be all in the room listening to music when we were young. David would be down on his hands and his knees on the bed, with a pacifier in his mouth, looking at the record player. He's looking at the record player, and the record's going round and round, right? His head, his whole body, start going round and round with the record. That's what David did. That's how intrigued he was."

David's brother Larry introduced him to his second great love: comic books. The two couldn't get enough of the work of Jack Kirby, who illustrated series like *The Fantastic Four*, *Captain America*, and *The Avengers*. Back in the day, comic books were practically a currency. David traded his comics with his early friends Tracy Custis, Allen Tucker, and Vinson Washington. When his mother tuned in to his interest, taking away his comic books became her supreme form of punishment.

David was constantly behind the eight ball growing up. He dressed nerdy. In a world where sneakers were the main status marker, David rocked Pro-Keds when everyone wore Converse. When David switched to Converse, Puma became popular. Dances like The Freak, The Patty Duke, and The Spank were debunked when David got on the dance floor. People started looking forward to catching his awkward moves at park jams.

Other friends like Sean Cuff, Tyrone Robinson, and Russell Francis teased David about his getup and style. He didn't care. David marched to his own beat, he put no stock in what his friends thought about him, and he had enough skin to take their jokes. Their verbal sparring sessions lasted for hours.

Even though David didn't fit in at school, he found his place in Farragut. At school, diversity led quickly to violence and division. But not in Farragut. This community embraced difference.

Farragut and other housing projects were supposed to replace the "slums" that "blighted the area." But that element didn't stay away for long. On May 2, 1961, *The New York Times* reported on gang violence between the Albany Chaplains of the Albany Houses and the Corsair Lords, based in Kingsborough Houses in the nearby Bedford-Stuyvesant neighborhood. *Times* reporter Alfred Clark described the area in charged language as "Brooklyn's Little Harlem."[5] Organized crime was starting to intensify around and within New York's housing projects. Crews from Farragut began to spar with counterparts from Fort Greene, Bed-Stuy, Red Hook, and Marcy.

Then the Brooklyn Navy Yard closed in 1965, eliminating a primary source of revenue for the community. As David grew up, Farragut became increasingly dangerous.

David and his brother Larry found a safe haven in the nearby Dr. White Community Center. It was headed by Catholic nuns—Sister Catherine McCarthy, Sister Joan Soto, Sister Margaret Peeples, and Sister Francis Mary. The center offered Farragut kids a safe space after school and during the summer where they could create, learn, and hang out. It also held numerous Farragut community events. There, Larry earned a reputation for winning contests by impersonating James Brown's dance moves. After his song "I'm Black and I'm Proud" was released in 1968, kids often tried to mimic the James Brown split . . . and usually ripped their pants in the process. But Larry always pulled it off.

Dr. White was also a communal space for making music. Larry formed his own band and was allowed to practice and put on concerts there. As the Banks family grew older, both Larry and Stanley began to focus more on the bass. Julia decided to send David down another path, and she encouraged him to try out the drums. She put David in the Riverside Drum Corps, where David became the cymbals player for the Streamliners, the junior squad. He learned from the drummer in Larry's band, James Doyle.

Julia told James to be hard on him, and he became David's first source of discipline outside the family. Playing for the Riversiders outfit also gave David his first opportunity to travel—the group participated in competitions out of state. The team was coed, and it consisted of 130 members. They offered instruction in horn, drum, and color guard. Julia attended every local march

David played. Despite the support, the drums didn't come easily to David. Still, he stuck with them, even after Doyle left the group.

Schoolteachers also lived in Farragut, and they often worked at Dr. White. Debbie Isom and Nadine Brown were some of the first to see David's potential. Both lived in 111 Bridge Street. In 1981, Isom debuted David's acting skills in a play she wrote named *Farragut*. She included David in plays for the following three summers. Nadine Brown, on the other hand, helped David land his first job as a staff aide at Dr. White.

Back then, it was common for kids to get robbed on payday. David got wise to that when he was heading home with his third check. Two kids jumped him in the stairway of his building and ran off with his earnings. When he brought his next check home, the same kids approached. But this time, David was ready to fight. The kids, also from Farragut, backed down. Seeing them pass down the street after, they simply acknowledged him with a sign of respect.

"That's the way it was growing up," David said. "Respect had to be earned. If you allowed anyone to push you over, you'd earn a reputation for being soft. Anyone could take advantage of you. When I was in junior high, it was cool to be rebellious, not go to school, and indulge in behavior that would embarrass my family. But my brother Stanley saw that, and he decided I needed discipline. His resolution was to take me to a karate school on Bergen Street in downtown Brooklyn. My Sensei was George Cofield. He was the founder of Tong Dojo and one of the first Black people to introduce karate to America.

"Master George was also a Hall of Fame of World Karate award winner. He taught in the Shotokan style. In each class, he made sure to confer the Shotokan philosophy, which states that karate is not merely for self-defense. Karate is an art requiring sharp mental conditioning and the ability to think quickly in a controlled, disciplined manner. By studying karate, you are challenged to overcome your deepest fears, your limitations, and to become a more responsive, feeling person. The pursuit of these kinds of goals reduces the tension and frustration that make you want to fight."

Karate was a release for David, and soon he discovered that music could also help him channel his feelings in a healthy way.

FAITH INVADES BROOKLYN

As David emerged into his teenage years, forces were astir in Brooklyn. As of the 1950 census, the borough held over 2.7 million people, 92.2 percent of whom were white. By 1970, the population had declined to 2.6 million (while the rest of the United States experienced the baby boom) and, suddenly 25 percent of the city was Black. By 1980, it was 56 percent white, 32 percent Black, and 17.5 percent Hispanic (many census respondents identified as two or more races).[6] These demographic trends mixed and remixed cultural and religious traditions.

Though the Banks apartment was entirely secular, David fell in love with contemporary gospel music. He would play records by Walter Edwin and Tramaine Hawkins on repeat. His hero was drummer Joel Smith. David would head to the record store and read the liner notes. If he saw Joel Smith's name on the jacket, he'd take it to the register without a second thought.

Following his love of Gospel, David had his first spiritual experience.

"My brother Leighton was in a local choir called Voices of Eternity," David said. "He was also heavily involved with St. Ann's Catholic Church located two blocks away on York Street. Leighton had amazing people skills, and easily recruited vocalists to join the choir. Eventually Larry, after seeing what Leighton was doing, came around to going to church himself. He was playing the keyboards at the Church of the Open Door, and since it was on our block, I decided to come by one Sunday morning. I remember Reverend Kieller, the church's pastor, preaching a moving sermon that had me hooked. He made me want to be a better person and find a different group of friends. Reverend Kieller was backed by the Walter Johnson Choir. There was no drummer at the church, and I felt confident that I could fill that void. So in 1982, I joined, and took the right hand of fellowship. It was while I was at FDR High School studying under Professor Howard Weiner's music class that I met Leon Atkinson. He was a drummer too, and we shared a spiritual connection, with both of us wanting to be closer to God in our beliefs."

David, his brothers Larry and Leighton, and his friend Leon were hardly the only kids exploring their faith. During this period, a series of alternative religious movements flooded Brooklyn. A lot of the Farragut community was joining the Five-Percent Nation, also known as the Nation of Gods and Earths. It was founded in Harlem in 1964 by Clarence 13X, a former student of Malcolm X. He and others left the Nation of Islam following an ideological dispute with Elijah Muhammad. Five Percenters believe that the Black man was the original human on earth and, as such, is God personified. In their view, 10 percent of the world has access to the religious truth and they keep 85 percent of the world under their subservience through that knowledge. The remaining 5 percent, the Five Percenters, are dedicated to spreading truth, enlightenment, and freedom.

The Five-Percent Nation was a huge influence on early hip hop. Terms like "dropping science" and cipher circles are straight from the Nation of Gods and Earths. Artists like Big Daddy Kane, Jay-Z, World's Famous Supreme Team, Nas, AZ, Common, Brand Nubian, Poor Righteous Teachers, Rakim, and the Wu-Tang Clan were all influenced by the movement.

"This religion was spreading all over Farragut and Fort Greene," David said. "You felt challenged by your friends by just saying you believe in God. This caused a wedge between parents in the neighborhood and their kids. The older generation would often say that Christianity is the white man's religion. In our church we would say that isn't true. Scholars argue that the Garden of Eden refers to a region in Africa, by the Nile, in the Kingdom of Cush, the second region mentioned in the Bible. The first recorded belief in one God was found in Egypt."

This revival and split between kids and their parents played out in the Banks family, too. Julia wasn't having any religion under her roof.

"The Church of the Open Door was on the same block that we lived on. But, growing up, my mother forbade us to go there," Larry said. "According to what she thought, people gossip in church. You have a gossip scene, you know what I mean? And she didn't want anybody to get into her business. Never."

"Allen Tucker, my comic book trading partner, and his sister Bobby were involved in a prayer movement," David said. "I felt I was a part of something by going to prayer and church outings with them. Other friends like Robert Ewart, Timothy Lennon, Joanne Wynn, Karen Cole, Anthony Cole, Nadine Brown, and her siblings Vernell and Gregory were all together when we got to 177 Sands Street to have an hour of prayer and bible study. Ronald at the time was deep into it. Bobby's friend Vonda Cortijo was the first woman I heard speak in tongues and it scared me half to death. She was really talking to God and her expressions had a hold on me. I was determined to have that same experience."

David's interest brought him into contact with more and more developing religious practices.

"I didn't witness church shouting until I went to a revival with C. R. Johnson from the Brooklyn Tabernacle at Madison Square Garden," he said. "Although the group came together for prayer, I felt that there was a difference in Bible teachings that separated the group. Nadine, Vernell, Timmy, Joanne, and Ronald had been attending the Greater Refuge Temple in Harlem, where Bishop Bonner preached. Robert, Bobby, Allen, and I liked to go to other churches but we stuck with Reverend Kieller at the Open Door. The whole group of us locked in a constant gravitational pull to radio. His parents were strict. Born and raised in the Abraham Lincoln Houses at Park and East 132nd Street in Harlem, he grew up surrounded by park jams, mobile DJs, and the communities that would go on to originate hip hop and house music. But he wasn't allowed to participate. When his friends went out to the parties at St. Nicholas Park, across the Madison Avenue Bridge in the Bronx, or later to clubs like the Latin Quarter, he was stuck at home.

Still, he had gnawing hunger for music of all genres, especially hip hop. He sated this hunger by listening to radio stations like WBLS, Kiss FM, and 92 KTU. Late at night, he kept the dial locked on programs hosted by DJ Red Alert, Chuck Chillout, and Hank Love and the DNA.

There was also good music to be found on television. Davis seldom failed to miss *Video Music Box* and *New York Hot Tracks* on WABC. On Saturdays, he'd catch the performances broadcast on *Saturday Night Live*, *SCTV*, and *Don Kirshner's Rock Concert*.

At Intermediate School 166 Roberto Clemente, he was schooled in the arts of multimedia, producing radio plays, commercials, and thirty-five-millimeter film. The school also brought on local DJs to play during free periods. The school had punk rock day, and it was there that he was introduced to new wave acts like Devo, the B-52s, and Talking Heads. With gusto, he consumed rock, disco, R&B, soul, reggae, every album in his older sister's record collection, and every mixtape his friends brought back from jams and parties.

But most important of all, he had a front row seat to what would become hip hop history. The Crash Crew—an early and highly influential hip hop group—were also based in the Lincoln Houses. Like other groups at the time, they assembled their own sound system. And before long, like many mobile DJs before them, their sound reached superpower status.

"They built their own sound system," Davis said. "They called it the Mace Monster. You could hear their parties from blocks away. You could be six blocks away and you would hear that they had a jam going on somewhere."

He was friendly and familiar with the group's members, especially Disco Dave. The two studied and trained in karate at the same gym. In 1980, Dave and his brother Mix Master Mike formed an independent label called Mike and Dave Records. Their first release was the Crash Crew's LP *High Powered Rap*, and they would go on to support the early careers of The Boogie Boys, Biz Markie, Doug E. Fresh, and Rob Base. Mike and Dave left the Crash Crew after the group signed with Sugar Hill Records, but they maintained good relations.

believed in dressing sanctified. No street gear—the women always wore skirts and, when they were in church, they wore prayer caps. We wanted to live in a culture of holiness. Still, some of the friends I had who had joined the Five-Percent Nation also embraced the drug culture when it hit the streets."

COCAINE, CRACK, AND US FEDERAL LAW

The poverty rate in New York had been dropping since the Great Depression. But in the late 1970s, it started climbing again. And as poverty rose, so too did drug consumption. Up in Harlem, heroin was booming. New York Special Prosecutor Sterling Johnson in 1978 declared that Harlem was "the drug-trafficking center of the nation."[7] But Brooklyn was about to get its own reputation.

Though widely used in the 1970s and 1980s, heroin exacted a heavy toll. For other more casual users, mostly white professionals who had money to spend, cocaine was growing more popular. The retail price for a gram of cocaine in 1982 ranged between $100 to $120, making it prohibitively expensive for most.[8]

But in the late 1970s and early 1980s, cocaine production started outstripping consumption. The larger supply and unchanged demand caused the price to drop in some cities by as much as 80 percent. The value of dealers' investment disappeared seemingly overnight. So some began mixing their product with baking soda and water and boiling it down into small, smokable rocks that "cracked" in the pan. By doing so, dealers were able sell smaller amounts of product at the already-inflated price points and recoup some of their deflated profits. In the early 1980s, crack became available in cities like Detroit, Philadelphia, and New York for as little as $2.50 a hit.[9]

Meanwhile, Ronald Reagan was elected in 1980 and, shortly after, declared war on drugs. But he didn't declare war on all drugs. During the NBA draft in 1986, the Boston Celtics selected the All-American University of Maryland basketball star Len Bias for the second overall pick. Just two days later, he died from an overdose of cocaine. After another week, Cleveland Browns safety Don Rogers, who had been Defensive Rookie of the Year the previous season, also passed from a cocaine overdose. The media widely—and mistakenly—reported that both had died from smoking crack.

Within weeks, Congress passed the Anti-Drug Abuse Act, which mandated a minimum five-year prison sentence for trafficking or possessing just five grams of crack. The bill also included a mandatory minimum sentence for trafficking cocaine. But the amount of product that would land you this sentence stood in stark contrast to crack: five hundred grams. This measure led to what scholars now call the one-hundred-to-one sentencing disparity.[10]

In plain terms, it put poor, often Black and Latino crack users and dealers in jail, while wealthier cocaine dealers and users, many of whom were white, received a comparative slap on the wrist if they were caught.

The rest of America followed along watching the nightly news. Suddenly, Nancy Reagan was going on raids with the Los Angeles SWAT team and their battering ram. If it bled, it led. Over and over again, the media shone their spotlight on Black communities where crime had been committed.

David had been teaching first, second, and third graders in afterschool programs at Dr. White when he was promoted to work as an administrator. He was put in charge of hiring and managing high school kids as teachers for summer camps. Some potential hires had already opted into a different line of work.

"For welfare babies who had no structure at home, the drug trade was a way out," David said. "Kids my age were seeing hustlers as role models. There was a crack house in every Farragut building. Young men and women would sell out their community, crew up, and go to Albee Square Mall in downtown Brooklyn, flashing the latest jewelry and street gear on Dekalb Avenue. The dookie gold chain became a symbol of the hood status. The Mall was the mecca for hip hop fashion where gangsters would congregate. Dealers had appeal, plenty of cash, and women."

David and the Banks family watched their vibrant neighborhood succumb to the crack-cocaine epidemic before their eyes.

"Crack created a housing project pregnancy boom, destroyed the working class, shattered families, and had people from rival buildings killing each other," David said. "Dealers from Farragut were getting wholesale dope from Harlem dealers. You'd see lines of people waiting to get a fix in front of Farragut buildings in the early morning. Legends who were once great fell from grace. Members from the Church of the Open Door, and Larry's Walter Johnson Choir also fell victim to crack. The drug affected everyone."

"It was detrimental to the community," Larry Banks said. "You had kids, 14 or 15 years old, out there prostituting themselves. It was so crazy. It got to a level that was disgusting."

"You can't sugarcoat it," Stanley Banks said. "It was some rough times, but the most important thing is there was still some love. Everybody got together and some successful people came out of it, because of the toughness of it."

Drugs also began to infiltrate the mobile DJ movement. Sales would go down during jams. The New York Police Department put an end to jams at

Riis Beach after a gang fight got out of hand. Others began to use. Grandmaster Flowers was one of them. Through the 1980s, his DJing declined steadily. Addiction led him to sell his records and most of his equipment.

THE GREATER REFUGE TEMPLE

Through the gathering violence and conflict, David and his friends did their best to keep their heads above water. Like his brothers, he walked a path that would lead him to a career in music. He got the shock of his life as a young teenager when he met Gerald Hayward, a heavily influential R&B and gospel drummer who at the time played at the Institutional Church of God in Christ. He was blown away. Talking with high school friend and fellow drummer Leon Atkinson later, they agreed that Hayward was the greatest gospel drummer in Brooklyn.

David and Leon would hang out on Saturday nights, play gospel records, go see other acts, and compare notes. Leon was a better drummer and was involved in The Whole Truth Church, which was part of the Church of Our Lord Christ denomination, another religious community at the time.

With Leon wrapped up in the Church of Our Lord Jesus Christ, other friends heading up to the Greater Refuge Temple in Harlem, and others joining the Five Percenters, David struggled to find a spiritual home. While Reverend Kieller at the Open Door had changed his life, his church didn't play host to a music scene in the way others did. David quickly rose through the ranks of the Walter Johnson Choir, going from tenor to prayer chaplain to president. At the same time, he began spending more and more time at the Greater Refuge Temple in Harlem, where Reverend Bonner also preached a compelling sermon. As much as David learned moral discipline from karate, his spiritual discipline came from the Greater Refuge Temple in the form of prayer, an emphasis on the Gospel of Jesus Christ, a concern with justice, and possession of the Holy Spirit.

"Leon and I had a tight bond in those doctrine beliefs," David said. "My mother was too confused to know what was going on. Bonner preached that, more than anywhere else, you need to pray in your house like you pray in church, and more often. I took that and ran with it, shouting at the top of my voice, speaking in tongues, and freaking out my entire family. My father used to walk in the room like, 'What are you doing boy?' I was seeking a spiritual experience and rebirth."

Toward the end of high school, David joined Greater Refuge Temple officially and immediately entered their Cathedral Choir. Six months later, he became their percussionist. Within a year, he was drumming for every choir in the church.

Greater Refuge Temple was known widely for its zeal of worship and for its music. For some of its members, the former took a back seat to the latter. According to DJ, promoter, and club owner Richard Vasquez, many (including him) traced a direct line from church to dance music and club culture.

"I played the organ at Greater Refuge Temple for a couple minutes," Vasquez said. "I became friends with the musicians there at that time. It's an unusual church. But the music is great. The music is great and has always been great. When I was 17, 18, I used to listen to their radio broadcasts. It's a Pentecostal sect. Speaking in tongues and dancing in the spirit is very, very important in the church. Even though I disagreed with a lot of their doctrinal stuff, I liked the music."

But the music they were playing at Greater Refuge Temple was different from many other traditions.

"Church nurtures musicians," Vasquez said. "It offers children from a very early age the ability to develop their musical talents. A lot of Pentecostal and Baptist congregations developed a style of music out of the spiritual that picked up elements of Little Richard, Elvis Presley, Motown, and others. It has a very strong rhythmic background. The piano, which is a percussion instrument, is played *as* a percussion instrument. The bassline is very, very prominent in these churches. They want people to dance in the spirit. Brooklyn is filled with churches like this. Most of them are storefront, but some of them actually grow to be megachurches and have talented choir directors, musical directors, and also good preaching."

The musical scene at Greater Refuge Temple came to dominate David's life. Soon, he found himself traveling to and from Harlem four days a week to practice and play with various groups and choirs.

The recordings and sermons of Refuge Temple were televised throughout the tri-state area. The house of worship seated thousands of people in its massive sanctuary. On Sundays, David knew that one Julia Banks would be tuning in from Farragut. While she questioned David's path, she was still proud to see her son on television playing to a crowd. It helped her form a better understanding of the person he was becoming. Just a few years ago, he'd been playing the cymbals in the Streamliners.

As David entered his final years in high school, he took a job at Godfather's Pizza and set to thinking about college and a future career. He knew he liked music, but his parents often reminded him that was hardly a stable choice. In his senior year, he applied to Baruch College in the City University of New York system. Following pressure from his father, he decided to study accounting. There was just one problem.

"I was horrible at math, so I knew I wasn't going to last long there," David said. "Angela Anselmo, my guidance counselor, tried her best to get me on the right track, but to no avail. I was a slacker when it came to my studies and had no direction concerning my college degree."

Even though David didn't feel inspired by accounting, his passion for music burned stronger than ever. The accounting program might have been a dead end for David. But as a young man obsessed with music, Baruch College was the perfect fit. It had a diverse student body, an active social and musical scene, and most importantly of all, a radio station.

THE BANKS BROTHERS

David was about to begin walking a path that would turn him into a DJ. But before he did, his brothers provided him with important blueprints for careers both in and out of the music industry. Sherman, David's oldest brother, became an organizer and civil rights leader. He worked in the construction industry and fought for fair hiring practices and equal wages for Black workers. These efforts brought him in and out of jail. Around the block, he was also known for his peacekeeping practices. Sherman was fiercely protective of his brothers, and he used any weapon in his arsenal to ensure their safety. You didn't mess with the Banks brothers under Sherman's watch.

At FDR High School, Stanley Banks began following his band teacher, Lawrence Charles Bergstein, out to play shows at night. He went on to perform for two years with the New York City High School Orchestra and Chorus. They played at the David Geffen Hall in Lincoln Center in 1968 and 1969. Strafe Standard's father, who the Banks brothers knew as Mr. Steve, also taught Stanley bass at the Dr. White Community Center and helped him transition from acoustic to electric.

His efforts weren't made purely in the name of education. He soon formed a band called Mr. Steve and The Young Ones that included sixteen-year-old

Stanley on the bass, along with his son Steve, and Rodney Newell. It was Stanley's first time playing in nightclubs and lounges throughout Brooklyn. Bars were a hotbed for entertainment and frequently hosted live acts. After three years of local gigging, he was discovered by blues harmonica player and vocalist Billy Clarke and started playing in his band. Much like his father before him, Stanley often sat in with bigger acts and musicians on their way through town. This helped him get his first traveling gig playing with Eddie "Cleanhead" Vinson in Cincinnati in 1971.

Stanley eventually struck up a friendship with Stevie Wonder's percussion player, Daniel Ben Zebulon. The two often jammed together. One night, he called Stanley to sit in on a session at Cafe Wha?, a nightclub owned by Richie Havens at the time. It was there that Stanley met tenor saxophonist Pee Wee Ellis, who also worked as musical director for James Brown. He wrote some of Brown's biggest hits like "Cold Sweat" and "Say It Out Loud – I'm Black and I'm Proud."

Ellis was in search of a bass player to join another artist, Esther Phillips. After hearing him play, he wanted to know if Stanley would be interested. He was. Within a few weeks, he joined Phillips' band, which included drummers Chris Parker and Yogi Horton. After just a few more weeks with Phillips, Ellis promoted Stanley to the role of musical director. He was just twenty-one years old. The gig brought him out to California.

In 1973, Esther Phillips lived in a high-rise at 8440 Sunset Boulevard in Los Angeles, California, right across from the Comedy Store. Stanley answered the door one day to find Richard Pryor outside. The comedian was in his prime, and Stanley stood there for a stretch, at a loss for words. Pryor didn't have time for that. "Are you gonna let me in nigga?" he asked. He and Esther were good friends. Living in Los Angeles helped Stanley land better and better gigs. Everyone who respected Esther respected him.

But Los Angeles wasn't all positive. One night while standing around at a boutique, officers drove by flashing their lights at Stanley, supposedly because he had his hand on the door. They questioned him thoroughly. At one point, Stanley raised his hands and asked "What's all this about?" That was all the excuse the police needed. They knocked Stanley to the ground, beat him with their nightsticks, and threw him in jail for four days. The judge threw the case out in trial because the cops never showed up.

In 1975, Stanley's relationship with Esther Phillips began to fray. She went to New York to record and didn't take Stanley along. She recorded *What A Difference A Day Makes* during those sessions, which became a hit album.

Stanley later joined Phillips for a residency in Boston at Paul's Mall. At the time, George Benson was playing at another venue close by called the Jazz Workshop. Ronnie Foster, George Benson's keyboardist, walked into Paul's Mall one day after sound check and introduced himself to Stanley. The two jammed and hit it off. Eight months later, Benson's bass player quit and Ronnie invited Stanley to fill in. He was only supposed to be with the band for two weeks.

One thing led to another. Stanley moved back to New York to live in Farragut. In 1976, he started sitting in on recording sessions for what would become Benson's album *Breezin'*. One night when the family was sitting down to spaghetti dinner, "This Masquerade," the single from the album, came on WRVR. It was the first, but hardly the last time one of the Banks brothers could be heard over the airwaves.

Breezin' would go on to get certified triple-platinum and reach number one on the Billboard album charts that year. The musical pedigree of Farragut grew even larger, and, in the Banks family, Stanley was a huge source of pride.

David never forgot when his mother took him to the movie theater to see *The Greatest*. The film featured Muhammad Ali along with numerous tracks by George Benson with Stanley on bass. All of a sudden, twelve-year-old David's brother's music was accompanying one of the most polarizing and impactful boxing legends in history on screen. It left a huge impact on him.

George Benson took home a couple Grammys with Stanley on bass. David's brother would go on to play with artists like Chaka Khan, Aretha Franklin, Freddie Hubbard, Al Jarreau, David Sanborn, Etta James, Stanley Turrentine, and Manhattan Transfer, just to name a few.

Larry Banks, meanwhile, was making his own progress. He was writing original material for the Walter Johnson Choir at the Church of the Open Door. On bass, he both led his own projects and collaborated with artists like Vernon Reid and Arthur Rhames. They played in a band called Gabriel's Horn in 1983. Two years later, Reid and Greg Tate initiated the Black Rock Coalition. The non-profit organization still works to promote, record, distribute, develop, market, and fund the work of emerging Black artists. Reid would later go on to start the band Living Color. Larry also gigged separately with his own group, Subculture 9.

"I love rock and roll music," Larry said. "You know, the Allman Brothers, Steely Dan, the Eagles, the Doobie Brothers. I love all that. More than all of that, my biggest love is the Beatles. Forget about it. I remember Black dudes used to sit outside my project on a bench with their radios. If you played 'Hey Jude,' everybody would just sit around and say, 'Damn . . .' It was just unbelievable."

But this musical influence brought Larry in conflict with some club owners and promoters.

"I tell you, I swear to you, the best way I learned how to write music was by listening to the Beatles' songs," Larry continued. "The first time I heard 'Penny Lane,' the first time I heard 'Lucy in the Sky with Diamonds,' I thought, 'I've got to figure out how these guys come up with this music.' It's like they pulled it out of the air or something, you know? I think they were the masters of the art of music. But in the time period I grew up, it wasn't accepted for a Black person to play rock and roll. They didn't like that. They didn't want that. But that's what I did. And as a result, I didn't get that many gigs."

Still, Larry made a name for himself with Subculture 9 and Gabriel's Horn. Grooveline Records owner Jim McDermot convinced Larry to transition into R&B and cut a solo LP. His first record, *Lover Man*, was recorded at McDermot's studio in College Park, Maryland. While the album didn't go far, he was able to leverage it for a contract at Uptown Records, which was a subsidiary of MCA.

Working as a songwriter and producer, Larry composed Jeff Redd's single "Surrender" which came out on the album *A Quiet Storm*. While Larry was at Uptown, the label hired a young intern by the name of Sean Combs. Around the same time, Uptown signed a promising young backup singer by the name of Mary J. Blige. Larry was pegged to work with her to develop new music, including a cover of Chaka Khan's "Sweet Thing." Blige's management eventually stepped in, wishing to guide their artist in a different direction. Meanwhile, Larry decided to break his contract in order to pursue writing and producing gospel music at the Church of the Open Door full time.

"I was playing a little bit of piano. I was playing in college, and my girlfriend at the time, she was telling me that the church needed a piano player," Larry said. "I volunteered my service and I went over there. That was 40 years ago, and I've never left since then. What I liked about church was that I had the freedom to compose my own music. People would come to church, they would hear the music, and they would go out to the stores to try to buy it. I just told them, 'You have to come to church to hear it.'"

As a teenager, David took this all in. He knew he loved music. He knew his faith was important to him. And he knew he had to go to college. The rest lay hidden beyond the horizon.

1. Sherman, William, one-year-old David, Julia, Stanley, Larry, and Leighton Banks in 1966 *(author's collection)*. **2.** Leighton, Sherman, Stanley, and Larry Banks having rehearsal at the house *(author's collection)*. **3.** Stanley Banks *(author's collection)*. **4.** Larry Banks at the Church of the Open Door *(author's collection)*. **5.** Leighton Banks *(author's collection)*. **6.** David Banks and Leon Atkinson at F.D.R. graduation in 1984 *(author's collection)*. **7.** DJ Debonair with Michael Jones *(courtesy of DJ Debonair)*.

THE AIRWAVES

Here's a trivia question: What form of mass media communication was most widespread in the United States during the twentieth century? According to census data, daily newspaper circulation peaked at 62.8 million in 1985—not even close to the top spot. A lot of folks might point to television. After all, a majority of American households owned a television set by 1955. And by 1980, all but 2 percent of households had one. Still, not once during the 1900s did television beat out radio in terms of distribution. Beginning in 1970 on through to the new millennium, over 99 percent of American households owned a radio.[1] And while Americans might have turned to television for news, drama, and comedy, radio shows remained the lifeblood of American music.

Behind it all, radio DJs made the magic happen. They were among the most respected and valued members of the music community. Some spoke so beautifully, you could listen to them read a mechanic's manual. And they knew music better than almost anyone. This was a time when not everyone could go out to clubs. Not everyone could afford to buy a new record every week or every month. But just about everyone had access to radio. And radio DJs held the keys to the gate. They were the musical arbiters that often knew what you wanted to hear better than you did yourself.

Despite his dedication to drumming in church, Disciple heard the call of the radio studio. He got his feet wet in college radio. Then it was on to a station on the FM dial. Through it all, new genres of hip hop and house music bubbled to the surface, gathered steam, and eventually exploded into America's newest art forms.

KOOL D

"There's always that one person you meet that can change your life," David Banks said. "For me, that guy was Ralph Davis." Ralph Davis' upbringing was

"*High Powered Rap* was a totally independent record," Davis said. "They recorded and mixed that record by themselves. They promoted themselves, distributed, everything. They really understood the business side of things."

Davis enrolled in the computer intelligence program at Baruch College a year before David Banks arrived. He quickly found the college radio station, WBMB 590 AM, in one of the campus basements and got involved.

It was a scene. People would hang out, smoke weed, drink beers in the evenings, and play record after record after record. Ralph first paid his dues by engineering a show where the DJ exclusively played Bruce Springsteen.

"Once our show finished on the air, we'd just go out into the lounge area and hang out with everyone else," Davis said. "Everybody at WBMB—that was a tight-knit community. We were like a family. That was one of the reasons why I didn't join any of the fraternities. While I was at Baruch, some people came together to form a chapter of the Phi Beta Sigmas. I was offered the opportunity to become a founding member of that chapter, which was a real honor. I would have been part of the fraternity's history, of the college's history. But I said, 'Nah, WBMB is my fraternity.'"

After the onboarding process, he landed his own show. Following his main radio role model Hank Love and the DNA, he played fresh hip hop B sides and underground records. Observing the customs of the time, he called himself Kool D. His show was *The Sound Experience*.

"I was my own engineer starting out, so I also developed this other radio personality," Davis said. "When I was mixing and cuing the records, I called myself the Black Smurf. I had a black beanie and everything. I'd get on the mic and say, 'You're listening to *The Sound Experience* with DJ Kool D and the Black Smurf.' It was just me.

"We had a student newspaper, *The Ticker*. One day, someone came down to do a story on the station while my show was on. So they took my picture and interviewed me. A few days after that story came out in the paper, I was sitting in the student center, eating some food or something. Then, all of a sudden, this guy comes up and goes, 'Hey! You're Kool D, right? I saw you in the newspaper.' He had all this energy. I'm like, 'Yo, who's this strange dude rolling up in my face?'"

That strange dude was David Banks. David and Ralph had a lot in common. Both came up in New York City public housing. Both were in college at the behest of their parents. Both loved music. They both struggled financially and often put their money together just to get pizza for lunch on 23rd Street and Park Avenue. They started hanging out more and more at WBMB.

Kool D at Baruch College, 1985 *(courtesy of Ralph Davis)*.

At the station, David did everything he could to get involved. He began by writing for *The Ticker*. More often than not, his articles would include some review of contemporary gospel music. After a brief period, Ralph brought Disciple on to engineer his show.

Hip hop was barely known in the early 1980s, and radio shows tended toward pop and rock. *The Sound Experience* was a breath of fresh air for the WBMB programming. It became hugely popular. Crowds used to gather in the school cafeteria, which had two big speakers blaring 590 AM twenty-four/seven.

Soon, the show got another lift. Being a karate student of Disco Dave's, Ralph was offered the opportunity to work security at the parties they threw to promote their releases and push emerging hip hop. Besides the Crash Crew, they showcased artists like Grandmaster Flash & the Furious Five, the Treacherous Three, the Cold Crush Brothers, Master Don and the Def Committee, Kool DJ AJ, Doug E. Fresh, Biz Markie, Rob Base, and DJ E-Z Rock.

Running security at these events put Ralph in touch with some of the best emerging New York hip hop. He began to invite them to drop in on the show for interviews and performances. Through Ralph and *The Sound Experience*, these up-and-coming hip hop artists got access to new audiences. College radio stations provided an indispensable avenue for event promoters, too. Ralph landed interviews with groundbreaking hip hop artists of the day, like Stetsasonic, Audio 2, and the Ultra Magnetic MCs.

While the show gained stature, David got more comfortable behind the boards. The program director began giving him the chance to fill in on temporary DJ spots and spin some of his favorite music at the time. Then, after three months at the station, David pitched a gospel show to the programming director. WBMB bit.

DJ DISCIPLE IN THE MIX

With a foot in the door, the next step was selecting a DJ name. David was inspired by a message he heard often at the Greater Refuge Temple (which derives from 2 Corinthians): "Only what you do for Christ shall last." So in 1985, as a follower of Christ, DJ Disciple took to the airwaves for the first time.

The DJ Disciple Show aired from 10:00 AM to 12:00 PM on Thursday mornings. The Christian Community room was right across the hall from WBMB, and kids would gather to listen in.

From the get-go, David liked playing records live on air. He liked it a lot. He also quickly realized where his abilities stood in relation to other DJs. The practice of DJing essentially involves two general but completely different skills. The first is song selection. You need to understand every song you want to play, how it makes people feel, whether it brings the energy up or settles things down, and how it operates before or after other tracks.

The other skill is mixing. This can be as simple as cuing one record to follow another, or it can be as complicated as single-handedly picking out elements of numerous records to create an original song in real time. Having been raised in a hypermusical household and possessing a strong knowledge of contemporary gospel, Disciple had a nascent but natural ability with song selection. But with mixing, he was starting from scratch.

A lot of it came down to the hardware that was available. The studio at WBMB had two Technics SL 1200 MK2 turntables. These were the definitive turntables for DJs in the 1970s and 1980s. Since they were first introduced by Matsushita (which later became Panasonic) in 1972, they were manufactured all the way up to 2010, and then rebooted in 2016. The SL-1200 model was preceded by the SP-10, which was the first consumer turntable to feature a direct drive motor. This system reduced audio distortion common in belt-driven models (such as wow and flutter).[2] In addition to its sturdy construction and vibration-absorbing cabinet, the device also had one feature that had revolutionized DJing: a pitch control knob.

This feature changes the speed at which the record turns, thereby pitching the frequency higher or lower, and making the tempo faster or slower. Why would you need to change the speed at which a record turns? Back in the 1800s in the days of the gramophone, there was no standard speed at which records were supposed to turn. Listeners used a pitch control knob to speed up or slow down records until they found the key in which they were recorded. For non-musicians, this could make for a frustrating listening experience. So eventually the music industry settled—completely arbitrarily—on a standard playback speed of seventy-eight rotations per minute (RPM). As technology evolved and vinyl came into use, these standards were modified. The standard long play (LP) vinyl today turns at 33.3 RPM. Other common formats turn at forty-five RPM. In order to play each of these formats the way in which they were intended, your turntable needs to spin at each of these different speeds. As such, many mid-century turntables have individual settings to play records at 33.3, forty-five, and seventy-eight RPM.

On many turntables, the pitch control is limited to these three distinct settings. But as audiophile culture evolved in the twentieth century, engineers grew to understand that other factors could disrupt how a record turns. There could be mechanical issues with the drive that turns the platter on which the record sits. Any number of external forces can also disrupt the record spinning and cause the needle to skip. As a result, manufacturers began to also include a continuous pitch control slider or knob that could be used to fine-tune the record speed and quickly correct play when, for whatever reason, rotations became irregular.

It was also common in the post-war era to play the piano and other instruments alongside a record. However accurately tuned, instruments like pianos can go sharp or flat depending on factors like temperature and humidity. Turntables like the Garrard 301 included basic pitch control so that one could bring the record in tune with the piano.[3]

But if you can control the speed at which the record turns, you make a record play as fast or as slow as you like. In other words, by controlling RPM, you can also control a song's beats per minute. And if you have two records you want to mix together, but they have different tempos, you can match one to the other using the pitch control. This technique is known as beat-matching, and its invention is credited by some to the disco DJ Francis Grasso, who started playing at the New York Club Salvation II and then held a residency at Sanctuary through the late 1960s and early 1970s.[4] The Technics were not the first turntable to feature a pitch control function. Grasso and many others originally used Thorens TD 124s, which allowed you to speed or slow the song by as much as 3 percent.[5] The Technics, meanwhile, offered pitch control of ±8 percent—much more than the Thorens, Garrards, or other models. Coupled with their direct drive motor that would bring a record up to speed almost instantly (in 0.7 seconds), DJs began to prefer these models over competitors.

Mobile DJs like Grandmaster Flowers and DJ Kool Herc made a big leap forward by playing two records together at the same time and in sequence. But before the Technics came around, their mixing abilities were limited. They had to find records that naturally played at the same or near the same tempo. After the Technics came out, the doors were thrown wide open. Suddenly, you could mix together two records that played at noticeably different speeds.

Disciple was first taught the basics of mixing and beat-matching on Technics 1200s by WBMB sound engineer Richard LaMotte. "Richard was an excellent blender of music," Disciple said. "He gave me a two-month crash course on how to mix records on the station's Technics 1200s. He taught me to practice mixing the records from the pitch control on the right side of the turntable."

Then, there was song selection. Disciple had an excellent knowledge of gospel. But in other genres, his music education was lacking. As he grew more adept playing radio shows, he was given more opportunities to guest DJ for others when the host had to cancel. Filling in for drop-out spots at the station gave him broad exposure to other genres of music, like emerging hip hop, soul, funk, disco, and R&B. Gospel was Disciple's passion, but he didn't live on an island. Three or four times a week, he would get calls from WBMB to fill in for DJs who didn't show up. Disciple started to look forward to these random DJ spots. They allowed him to play new records and step outside of his niche.

Despite his busy schedule, he began to seek out DJ gigs outside the station. His search brought him to the Skate Key rink on Melrose and 161st in the Bronx and the Empire Roller Rink at Empire and Bedford in Brooklyn. At the Empire, resident DJ Big Bob (who used to work with Grandmaster Flowers) showed David a few more tricks of the trade, like how to mix with the crossover that isolated a song's frequencies and use other built-in effects. The Empire had a sound system designed by audio engineering wizard Richard Long. In the period since working with Grandmaster Flowers, Long had designed sound systems at the Warehouse in Chicago, the Paradise Garage, Club Zanzibar, and countless other legendary clubs. Playing the roller rinks, Disciple could experiment with more freedom and work more DJ techniques into his repertoire.

This was the first setting where he tried his hand beat-matching and mixing two different records together in sequence, like he had seen mobile DJs do on Farragut concrete since he was a kid. It was there that he came up with his first signature mix: laying the mids and treble of his favorite gospel tracks over hip hop breaks. Skaters began responding to David's unusual style. Some even returned to hear him spin. Pretty soon, church groups were showing up to hear DJ Disciple play.

While *The DJ Disciple Show* developed a loyal following, DJ Disciple wasn't technically challenged by it. To spin a good show was more about selecting the right records to set the mood. Still, new records coming out like *Let My People Go* by the Winans, *Love Alive III* by the Hawkins Family, *Chosen* by Vanessa Bell Armstrong, or *Continuation* by Phillip Bailey gave Disciple an edge that set him apart from other Christian programming on the airwaves at the time.

SHIFTING PRIORITIES

The rush of playing live and on-air put a few things in perspective for Disciple. Within months, it became very clear to him that he wouldn't be pursuing that accounting career. He struggled with math and figured he'd rather play music than push pencils for the time being. College for him soon became more about radio than any academic subject.

Hearing of this, Disciple's parents responded with mixed reactions. William Banks knew his son all too well, and he easily recognized that he wouldn't be pushing his kid into a job that he hated. Instead, he sat back, curious to see what he would do next.

"My dad was a proud employee for thirty years at Underwriters Salvage Company, working as an accountant and bookkeeper," DJ Disciple said. "One quality he had that I've embraced is his ability to serve. He taught me humility when we spoke, and he never had to preach it to me for me to get it. He'd tell me to help the next man out, empower yourself, and have an open mind. He also stayed out late drinking. He wasn't the kind of dad who took me to baseball games or movies.

"With mom, you had to be flexible because she was very domineering, strong, and controlling. I never bought into it. My mom was adamant that the DJ thing would not work. My dad, not so much. He already knew that the very thing he wanted for me, to be an accountant, was not going to happen, so he had little to say. He just watched to see how things played out. I continued to search for something, anything, in music that I could hold on to and grow in."

But while Disciple got the tentative go-ahead from his father to pursue DJing, he frequently met with opposition within himself.

"As engaged as I was in all the musical genres I was experiencing at the school, I called myself DJ Disciple originally as a reminder of the theme that 'Only what you do for Christ shall last,'" Disciple said. "My wanting to be a DJ and playing rap music went against the grain and doctrine of what the church was preaching. The church considered anything outside of gospel music worldly, and not of God. I kept the name DJ Disciple and used it as a strong reminder not to get too puffed up in my craft, but to remain humble in my devotion."

Disciple's faith led him to a pure life. He didn't drink. He didn't do drugs. He was still a virgin, although that might have had something to do with his nerd status. He also took his father's advice to help others while learning how to be self-reliant. But that commitment to faith, values, and practices was about to be challenged by a new temptation.

HOUSE MUSIC

Just as DJ Disciple was learning his craft, he met another Baruch friend, Jerome Anderson. He was even more tapped into New York music, he dabbled as a DJ and an MC, and he had records that blew Disciple's mind.

They sounded like disco or R&B . . . but different. They were cut up. They tossed out lyric verses in exchange for extended rhythm breaks. And in these breaks, they used equalizer and mix effects to transform the song into something completely different. Instead of a live band, some of the music was made with drum machines, keyboards, samplers, and, especially, new electronic instruments from the Roland Corporation that were just arriving in American stores. The TB 303 bass synth, the Juno-106 synthesizer, and the TR 808 and TR 909 drum machines not only produced unique sounds; they were affordable for a growing number of aspiring musicians. Jerome told Disciple about a legendary club in Chicago called the Warehouse, where they combined it all with disco, R&B, and soul records. What came out of the speakers came to be known as "house" music.

Anderson, who DJed as DJ Jazzy Jerome, and then later as DJ Jaz, grew up in the Riverbend Co-operative in Harlem. He had the benefit of two older brothers who were tapped into New York music and were willing to educate their younger sibling.

"One day, my brother Jeff came home with some 8-track tapes," Jaz said. "One of them was by a DJ named Lovebug Starsky and another was by Grandmaster Flash. That made me want to get into hip hop, rapping, and DJing. But I couldn't DJ that well at first. So that made me a rapper."

Jaz and four others formed a group called the Famous Five and started playing park jams, parties, and community centers. At one point, the newly established Cutting Records offered them a deal, but they didn't go for it. "We didn't understand the dynamics," Jaz said. "We didn't like the contract. Then the guys moved on and I started going to a lot of parties."

He also started learning how to mix from the group's former DJ, DJ Magician. Jaz's breakthrough moment came at a high school talent show. "I got the crowd really amped up and crazy," Jaz said. "My principal told me I could have caused the riot."

Jaz started DJing his own parties and would also play during the legendary basketball games at Rucker Park. ("I learned there that vinyl and the sun do not get along," Jaz said.) He also started collecting records. Around the same time, his brother James started bringing him out to clubs downtown where he heard even more house music.

Following different influences, Ralph Davis also converted to the ways of house music.

"This one college party, they were playing this house music," Davis said. "I didn't realize it was called house music at the time. I just referred to it as club music, which I really wasn't into. I go to this guy at the record player and I'm like, 'Man, the only thing playing here is club music. We want to hear some hip hop.' This guy was like, '*Hip hop?* Man, if you want to dance with these females here, brother, you got to learn how to get down with this house music.'

"But then I started to realize that the house beats I was hearing were often better than what was going on with hip hop. In a lot of cases, they were more creative, more driving. I started being like, 'Man, what is this? Who's that?' And that's how I met DJ Jazzy Jerome."

When Jaz linked up with David and Ralph D, he was listening to all the house he could find. At the time, that came in the form of Tony Humphries' show on Kiss FM and, more and more, records out of Chicago by artists like Larry Heard, Adonis, Marshall Jefferson, and, a few years later, Frankie Knuckles. (Knuckles didn't begin producing singles until 1986 and didn't release his first LP until 1991.)

It might seem strange that, at one time, hip hop and house could share an audience base. But in these early days of both genres, the difference between house music and hip hop was subtle. Both were formed from the chopped up, looped, and remixed breaks that could be heard in disco, soul, and R&B. Both placed a heavy emphasis on rhythm and dance. Both drew from the mobile DJ movement. Early hip hop innovators like DJ Kool Herc, Grandmaster Flash, and Afrika Bambaataa all started out as DJs. Meanwhile, vocal practices like MCing, rapping, or "toasting" in Caribbean cultures had been around for centuries. These traditions trace their roots back to West African griot storytelling traditions. But it wasn't until mobile DJs' deconstruction and remixing breakthroughs of the 1970s and 1980s that these vocal traditions found the musical foundation that would form the latest innovation in American music.

As DJ Disciple experienced more and more of early house and hip hop culture, he initially rejected the scene. These secular worlds were too much for this young DJ who sought to walk a path of grace. On weekend nights, Disciple was more interested in hanging out with a couple friends to listen to late-night radio shows and talk about comic books. He'd been playing the drums for all the choirs at Refuge Temple for the last two years, learning and adopting contemporary styles of the gospel music with keyboardist Julian Varner and bassist Warren Clark. That was the world he had committed to.

But at the same time, he couldn't tear himself away from the music he heard Jaz play. Besides Frankie Knuckles, Jaz exposed Disciple to other acts like the Peech Boys (fronted by Larry Levan, about whom Disciple was soon to learn much more), D-Train, and Sinnamon. He also started inviting Disciple out to his parties where he DJed. And Jaz started telling him about the clubs—like The Limelight, The Roxy, the Palladium, Area, Nell's, Danceteria, Studio 54, and, most notorious of all, the Paradise Garage—where the DJs and the sound systems that, by comparison, made the music played on the radio sound like a chorus of kazoos.

Slowly but surely, he started asking him more questions about his experiences. Disciple was drawn to house music, in part, because it mostly did not promote violence, the belittling of women, drugs, or illicit sex, at least not overtly. That was a plus in his book. But while the messages didn't fall down partisan lines, the culture around early 1980s dance music was definitely what Revered Bonner would consider worldly. "Being a disciple means exercising discipline. It means putting your beliefs before your actions," Disciple said. "At its core, music taps into something beyond race or culture. It can also put forward a message. It can be used for good or evil."

THE SOUND EXPERIENCE CREW

When DJ Jaz threw an early party in the Baruch Student Center in 1986, curiosity got the better of Disciple. He showed up to hear Jaz's sound and check out his setup. At the party that evening, Jaz spun countless songs Disciple had never heard before.

"It must have been a taste of what would go down at the Paradise Garage," Disciple said. "Jaz played 'Jack Your Body' by Steve 'Silk' Hurley along with other Chicago records that would make the whole student center go off on a tangent. Jaz loved seeing the dance floor react. It was exhilarating to him—sharing the music that he loved and making people have a good time. It gave him a sense of self-indulgence. DJing for Jaz was all about the enjoyment of seeing other people feeling what you're doing and controlling the moods of people you're playing to. What was attractive to me was the ability to express yourself without using words."

These tracks were some of the first proper house records Disciple heard on a big sound system, and that brought yet another dimension to the mix. Between emerging hip hop in 1986 and what would soon be the end of an era in dance music, Disciple, Kool D, Jaz, Rockin Rich LaMotte, and many others were trying to figure out how to fit in. Soon after Jaz's party, these Baruch DJs decided the time had come to form their own crew.

"Following Kool D's show, we were called The Sound Experience Crew," Disciple said. "We started enlisting other people to join the station, and had our first party together at the student lounge. It was the first time I played for a live audience. Still in touch with rap, I'd gotten a promo recording of Run-DMC's 'My Adidas,' and I played it at the start of my set. It had the biggest response. Run was huge. People got hyped up! (Or so I thought.)

"I thought I was doing something special. Then Jaz got on the decks. He was like, 'Hey, you did great, Disciple. But watch this.' Then Jaz dropped a record that would live with me a long time: Marshall Jefferson's 'Move Your Body,' otherwise known as the House Music National Anthem. The room went crazy. It was something I'd never seen before."

With the Sound Experience Crew formed, Disciple, Kool D, and Jaz got to work. They took every opportunity they could to throw a party. And they began to escalate their program. Ralph knew Ced Gee of the Ultra Magnetic MCs from the Mike and Dave parties where he ran security, and he brought them down to the station for an interview for *The Sound Experience* radio show.

They were promoting their new single, "Ego Trippin,'" at the time. The group was comprised of Kool Keith, Ced Gee, TR Love, and Moe Love. Ced Gee had grown up with DJ Scott La Rock of Boogie Down Productions. Although uncredited, he produced most of Boogie Down Productions' *Criminal Minded* and also contributed to Eric and Rakim's *Paid in Full*. Ced was cousins with Moe and TR. Mrs. Love co-signed on a loan so the group could pick up an Emu SP-12, a hybrid sampler and drum machine. You can hear the device and the artistic influence listening to the album and the MCs work at the time.[6] KRS-One was also friends with MCs, and everyone used to get together to make music before any record label got involved.[7]

"After our interview, we gave them a tour of the radio station and took them up to the student center," Ralph Davis said. "Ced Gee goes, 'Man, you know what? This place is nice.' They were checking out all the females. And they were like, 'We want to come back here and do a party.' I said, 'Man, that would be cool. But, you know we don't have any money right? We can't pay you.' They said, 'We don't care about that.' We said, 'Well, we're throwing a party this Friday. If you come, we'll put you on for a set.' They said, 'Fine.' I didn't think they would show up.

"We were playing at the 23rd Street Baruch building in the downstairs," Davis continued. "This other crew had the upstairs. They had status. They had better equipment than us. They even had matching uniforms. We didn't have anybody down for our party. Everyone was upstairs. But then, sure enough, the Ultra Magnetic MCs arrived. Jerome was playing and we kicked him off. We were like 'Yo Ultra Magnetic MCs are on.'

"They started playing 'Ego Trippin,' which was a hit at the time. People started finding out upstairs and everyone came down. Everyone was like, 'It's actually the Ultra Magnetic MCs!' The place was packed. Moe Love had the party rocking. Then they finished up their set, Jerome got back on to play some house records. That right there put the Sound Experience Crew on the map. I'll never forget that."

It turned out that Moe Love lived near Disciple over in Fort Greene. A few days after the party, he had him over to show him the SP-12 up close, along with his process of sampling, cutting, and scratching.

Nineteen eighty-seven proved a watershed year for New York music. The legendary club known as the Paradise Garage closed, and three hip hop albums came out that would transform the course of the city and music history. Public Enemy's *Yo! Bum Rush the Show*, Boogie Down Productions' *Criminal Minded*, and Eric and Rakim's *Paid in Full* are considered by many to be the holy trinity of 1980s New York hip hop.[8]

Today, this era is remembered for artists incorporating political messages into hip hop. All of a sudden, rappers weren't just navel-gazing or rhyming about their birthdays—they were using their platform to spread awareness about issues like the poverty, the drug trade, crime and violence, religion, the economy, and racism. Much of it was a response to Ronald Reagan's presidency. Hip hop provided a means to register dissent.

But this narrative, which holds up front men like KRS-One and Chuck D spitting "message rap," hides the innovations made by the DJs in these groups. Eric B., with some help from Ced Gee and the MC's Emu SP-12, was among the first to spin "chopped" samples of pre-recorded TV and radio, which is exemplified by their single "Paid in Full." DJs Scott La Rock (Boogie Down Productions) and Terminator X (Public Enemy) also helped cement the New York sound in a time when hip hop was known for its non-commercial identity and regional flavors.

The next year, 1988, would also prove groundbreaking for house music. Chicago producer Larry Heard—who was recording as Mr. Fingers in the mid-1980s—brought together vocalists Robert Owens and Ron Wilson to form Fingers Inc. Their debut album, *Another Side*, is considered the first full-length house LP. As Pitchfork's Andy Beta writes, the album "suggests that at its inception, 'house' was not a simple square but instead polygonal."[9]

Disciple first heard the record at a bikini party Jaz threw up in the Riverbend Co-op. It made him seriously recalculate any resistance he had maintained to the house music genre.

"It was an anonymous a capella laid to the groove of Fingers Inc.'s 'Mystery of Love' that got me open," Disciple said. "DJ Jazzy Jerome blended the two together before I heard Robert Owens' sultry unique vocals making me trainspot [when one DJ looks at what the other DJ is playing]. These were the first two records that would lead me to vinyl whoreism.

"It was all Larry Heard's fault. I was happy just being a gospel DJ, content with mixing Commission records over Run-DMC beats. But if Larry Heard pushed me to the edge it was Adonis that made me take the house music plunge with his atmospheric 'No Way Back.' The way my friends Louisa Harris, Kassim Hinds, Lian, Roche, and Sean moved to the house music Jaz was playing that night was like nothing I'd ever seen before. Gliding up and down the floor, getting up close and personal and meshing bodies closely together like dirty dancing in a futuristic vision. Then 'Baby Wants to Ride' by Jamie Principle mixed up political, social, sexual, and spiritual messages to one dirty, grinding, gritty groove. Some dancers were 'jacking.' Others were 'lofters.' It was the first time I saw a blend of dance styles look so exciting. Like hip hop, there was no solid definition to how you dance to house music. It was an unrestricted expression."

Hip hop and house were moving fast in the late 1980s. The era saw both genres go from their underground foundational phases to commercial viability.

"On one end, you had the emergence of Eric B. and Rakim, Boogie Down Productions, Public Enemy, DJ Jazzy Jeff and The Fresh Prince, and Big Daddy Kane," Disciple said. "On the other side, you had Todd Terry, Inner City, Fingers Inc., Xavier Gold, and Steve 'Silk' Hurley making the kind of music that broke barriers. They transcended race, sexual orientation, and made a global impact."

Looking back on this era, house legend Todd Terry has a different take.

"When I first did house music I thought it was a joke," Terry said. "I didn't take it seriously. I was just doing it because my friend said it was cool. I wasn't getting any rap record deals. So I said you know what? I'll just do a couple of these beats and see how it goes. That's when I got my first record deal. I always liked to fuse James Brown into a house beat. It's funky to me and I think that it has more longevity to it than just a plain kick and snare."

After Jaz tipped Disciple over the edge, he found he had fewer inhibitions about the worldly places these new genres of music got play. Then, right around the same time, Manhattan club The Palladium brought in a new resident DJ: Roman Ricardo. He spun on Wednesday nights, which were eighteen-and-over. (The drinking age in New York changed to twenty-one in 1985.) One night, when Jaz headed out to catch his set, Disciple joined him. Ricardo immediately entranced him with his technique.

"It was amazing to witness Roman Ricardo rocking the party," Disciple said. "I'd study him from 10:00 PM until the last record at 4:00 AM. He had an amazing talent of blending hip hop and house together with such ease. I was eager to duplicate what he'd done. That first night, I watched him playing the music, some of which the crowd didn't know, and I realized something important: the people come first. Without the crowd, nothing else matters. People dance to feel good, and music is the ultimate language. Ricardo was breaking down barriers by playing a multidimensional house set. He proved even then that house was diverse. That quality and his ability to bring people together converted me. The 18-and-over parties on Wednesday nights appealed to college kids but people from Farragut and Fort Greene would also go. Ricardo knew how to find the mixture of people and culture. Playing at WBMB and for our Sound Experience Crew events was no longer enough for me. Ricardo made it no secret that he'd often shop at Downtown Records so for a while I shopped exclusively at that store too."

Ricardo started DJing professionally in 1976. By the early 1980s, he was playing late-night spots all around the city. He often spun at the Roxy (which later became the 1018) and started promoting as well. Throughout the decade, he helped break acts like LL Cool J and the Beastie Boys, along with Chicago house artists like Darryl Pandy. He also played a hand in the development of Toddy Terry, who used to bring the DJ copies of his early work.

"Acetates were something I always wanted to do because I used to bring Roman reel-to-reels," Terry said. "They were hard to make and hard to EQ the right way. The easier way to do it was to have acetates. I used to go to Eurodisc or Prime Cuts with Steve Balkan. I used to make 5–6 acetates. Even if it was something I was just testing, I would do it so Roman could play it in the clubs. A lot of heads were like, 'Bring me acetates; I'm definitely going to rock it.' I was getting tested, me hearing it on the dance floor; it lets me know I can do this or that better before the record comes out."

The acetate copies Todd Terry made for Ricardo—along with his other producing work—helped lay the foundation for the New York hard house movement. The genre wasn't smooth like other sub-genres. It was rugged and broken up, with a bone-rattling beat—a stark contrast from other more polished productions.

NEW GENRES, NEW DRAMAS

In the late 1980s, New York club music was shifting toward new tracks coming out of Chicago and Detroit. In the late 1980s, New York club music was shifting toward new tracks out of Chicago and Detroit. Acid house was emerging on the scene. Driven by late 1980s tracks like Tyree's "Acid Crash" and "Acid Thunder,"

Blake Baxter's "Sexuality," "Oochy Koochy" by Baby Ford, Reese and Santonio's "Rock to the Beat," "Give It to Me" by Bam Bam, "French Kiss" by Lil Louis, and "Voodoo Ray" by A Guy Named Gerald, house was growing and splintering into new sub-genres just a few years after its formation. Alongside this early acid house, more techno-style singles were also emerging like Joey Beltran's "Energy Flash," "Dexterous" by Nightmares on Wax, Inner City's "Good Life," and 808 State's "Pacific State."

Many hip hop acts and producers also began incorporating house into the mix. The era is best remembered for beef kicked up by Tyree Cooper, who claimed that his 1989 track "Turn Up the Bass" was "the first hip house record on vinyl." The British group the Beatmasters quickly pointed out that Tyree was three years late; their hip house record "Rock Da House" was cut in 1986.[10]

In reality, there were several crossover hip hop and house records that preceded "Turn Up the Bass." The period was a time of experimentation and collaboration. Liz Torres' work with Master C & J on tracks like "Can't Get Enough," "In The City," and "Mind Games" introduced hip hop fans to house beats. The Jungle Brothers came out with "I'll House You" in 1988, and Technotronic's "Pump Up the Jam," Doug Lazy's "Let It Roll," and "Grandpa's Party" by Monie Love were other important examples. Other artists like Queen Latifah not only made hit songs featuring house beats, but also supported the scene as well.

"To me, the origins of house and hip hop are intermeshed," said Ralph Davis. "All these DJs in Chicago . . . you know, the Black community, wherever we are, we pretty much go to the same spot. There was a period of time here in New York when we would argue about hip hop, house, hip house, what it all meant. Because after a while, groups like the Jungle Brothers, Special Ed, and J.V.C. Force started using house beats, and even putting out house tracks on their album."

This narrative also holds true, to some degree, for the United Kingdom. JP Firman would soon become DJ Disciple's UK agent and collaborator. But before that, he worked for record stores.

"When I first started out, I was buying records for collectors and record shops," Firman said. "I was a hip hop guy. But then, when house started coming out, I got into it, and then there was US house. Both were coming out of disco, using disco breaks. Both the soulful house and hip hop used similar beats."

These fusions worked to bring fans from different backgrounds together and, especially for the younger crowd that was less likely to have strong musical affiliations, made it easier for DJs to keep the crowd moving late into the night. Crossover tracks and records also created rifts among certain groups who thought their genre of choice was losing its soul. This tended to be true among the older club crowd, who preferred a mix of the non-commercial classic deep tracks in the style of the Paradise Garage DJ Larry Levan. "A lot of the strictly house people, they couldn't stand hip house," Ralph Davis said. "They thought it was an abomination. It was like sacrilegious to the genre. But it's intermeshed. It's all about the DJ. Look at Kenny Dope Gonzalez. He's a hip hop DJ. But he's also half of Masters at Work."

The mixing of genres occurred simultaneously with a new flow of heads between clubs, which were growing more adventurous in the music they allowed. Clubs at one time acted as silos where audiences and genres would develop in isolation. But that tradition started to erode.

"In those days, I played a lot at The World," DJ Todd Terry said. "That's where me and DJ Ulysses used to play funk, soul, reggae, house music, we had to play a little bit of everything. I also started to play the Palladium and 1018. In each of those venues, from hip hop to freestyle to house, those transitions got bigger. The merging was really powerful."

WNYE 91.5 FM and *New York's Best Kept Secret*

In 1984, a hip hop show known as *Video Music Box* debuted on local station 25 WNYC-TV. Hosted by Ralph McDaniels and Lionel Martin, the show featured rap music videos with interludes of on-location, man-on-the-street interview segments.

The show happened to broadcast from the studios in Brooklyn Technical High School, which was also home to WNYE 91.5 FM and walking distance from the Farragut Houses. In the spring of 1988, Disciple met with Program Director Terrence O'Driscoll. He showed Disciple around the station and let him know that if he wanted his own show, he'd need to pay his dues with a six-month internship. It was a huge opportunity, and Disciple immediately accepted the offer.

Before four months had passed, Disciple was offered his own show. But WNYE was not interested in any religious programming, so playing gospel records was out. Instead, Disciple's show would be two hours of house music. The only other house programming on the FM dial at the time was the legendary Marley Marl's noon mix on WBLS, Tony Humphries on 98.7 Kiss FM, and a few others late at night. If you stayed up, you could hear people like Tony Tune and DJ Paradise who also had a show on WNYE on Friday. Disciple knew there was both room and appetite for one more.

New York's Best Kept Secret—The DJ Disciple Show debuted on WNYE 91.5 FM on Tuesday, September 15, 1988, at 3:00 PM. The show had a mandate to push cutting-edge music throughout its two-hour block. Disciple broadcast live from Brooklyn Technical High School. Compared to WBMB, the studio had a similar setup, but featured better microphones, bigger studio monitors, and knobs instead of levers for the master volume. Dale Burley, the studio engineer, monitored the show with his assistant Marvin Memminger.

Getting your own spot on the FM dial was a huge deal in the 1980s and 1990s. Disciple had attracted a very niche, local following spinning at WBMB, at the skating rinks, and with the Sound Experience Crew. But now he was speaking to, and playing for, all of New York and the greater tri-state area. The Banks family was beginning to come around to the fact that David might not end up as an accountant or a teacher.

"Music was the one interest my mom shared with me when I was growing up," Disciple said. "When she found out I got my own show, she couldn't wait to tell the whole family and the neighborhood. Things were starting to come full circle. At the same time, she started experiencing the effects of rheumatoid arthritis."

Throughout the 1980s, Julia Banks' mobility slowly declined as her rheumatoid arthritis worsened. She eventually relied on a wheelchair to get around.

"Mom was a tortured soul," Disciple said. "She dealt with dysfunction with her and dad, and things got worse when Leighton and Sherman left home. I was trying to find myself. I had to break away. Still, mommy got into house music before my brothers. Larry and Stanley hated it. In house, I found my independence. My dad had a thing where he didn't want anyone to touch the equipment in the living room, but he let my mom blast it when I was on the air. In this way, I got to bond with my mom through this music."

FRESH PROMOS

Disciple poured his energy into *New York's Best Kept Secret*. On air, he tried to push the envelope as far as it could go, incorporating wildly different musical styles into his sets. Disciple's growing house head network loved this quality and encouraged Disciple to see how far he could take his two-hour spot.

In 1989 *Best Kept Secret* moved to the WNYE Channel 25 location at 112 Tillary Street, and Disciple earned an extra hour of air time. He started bringing on DJs for live interviews. His first ever was Frankie Knuckles.

"He came into the studio to promote his collaboration with Satoshi Tomiie, which featured Robert Owens, on the single 'Tears,'" Disciple said. "After the interview, he told me, 'Disciple, you're good, but you got a ways to go.' That shook me. I thought we had hit it off. But in retrospect, I realize that it was good advice, and coming from THE Godfather of house music, no less."

Almost overnight, the *Best Kept Secret* listenership grew to between thirty thousand and forty thousand, depending on the week. Disciple was not solely responsible for this success. Every show needs a personality, and Disciple had help from India Lawson, who is still in the music business under the name ND. She, Mark Mann, Darrell "Doc" Lee, Scott Thomas, Felicia Thomas, and Cheryl Harvin were Disciple's first fans that tuned in every week and came out to every one of his shows. Devin Harris, Justin Hyppolite Jr., and Arthur Jay from Baruch also came out on a regular basis.

These friends both provided crucial feedback to Disciple and also occasionally came on air as well. This group *knew* house music, and Disciple often relied on them for their know-how. Another friend, Diamond, came after India to take calls from listeners and gave the show a wider appeal. She was the kind of club kid who hung out at Albee Square Mall in downtown Brooklyn, not Washington Square Park.

Following the growth of the show, something unexpected happened. Disciple started to receive music in the mail from record labels. One day, he decided to take it on himself to visit a label that had some of the hottest tracks coming out of the city—Strictly Rhythm.

At their Park Avenue office, Disciple met Gladys Pizarro. Not only did she gladly hand Disciple some new records, but she got him material that had yet to be released. A lightbulb went off in Disciple's head. He realized that this access to unreleased music might not be uniquely available at Strictly Rhythm. He would be able to potentially hit up every label in the city and arrange a similar deal.

That vision was quickly realized. Many labels established an open-door policy with him, and it was not uncommon for him to visit at least five a day. Nelson Roman, an A&R rep at Big Beat, introduced Disciple to Jay Williams' socially conscious "Sweat." One day, after a visit to Nu Groove, Disciple came away with Bobby Konders' "The Poem," which sampled poet Mutabaruka's "Dis Poem."

Each week, Disciple began to visit the offices of dozens of record labels. But as time went on, he found that the music coming out of Strictly Rhythm, Nu Groove, Big Beat, and Downtown Records (the label, not the record store) more often than not would make it onto the show. That programming helped *New York's Best Kept Secret* earn its name and resulted in a huge fan base for Disciple. He began to earn city-wide acclaim.

Disciple played records that came straight from the studio. Some artists eager for exposure would record fresh cuts on a DAT or cassette and put them right in Disciple's pocket. As an artist, this was a powerful way to circumvent the channels that be and get the dance heads moving to their underground beat. There is no better musical barometer than the DJ-enraptured dance floor to determine the power of a song. Looking to prove their merit, many artists did what they could to get Disciple their music. In turn, Disciple had a huge well of musical talent to draw from.

As *New York's Best Kept Secret* kept expanding, however, the uncharted waters into which Disciple was venturing were not always friendly. Sometimes spinning unreleased tracks got him in hot water with a label. David Morales once called him out for playing the Robert Owens single "I'll Be Your Friend," which Morales had produced. It had yet to be released, and Morales was worried his work was getting leaked and bootlegged.

He managed to make peace with Morales on that recording, but Disciple was still operating outside of what some considered to be acceptable customs. Still, this access to new music was also his ticket to success. *Best Kept Secret* became so well known that Disciple was asked to do a show for Bay FM in Japan. In the days before internet streaming, cassette recordings of the show were sold in London at Camden Market.

"Disciple was crazy about getting what's new," said DJ Todd Terry. "He didn't care where he had to go. I lived in Brighton Beach. He would come from New Jersey to Brighton Beach, and then from there he would go to the Bronx. He would stay up all night and make sure he got the new record to play on his radio show. He was serious about getting the best records. The first ten tracks he played on his show wouldn't even come out for the next two or three months. He knew how to talk over everything so that no one could really bootleg it.

"Still, that got him blacklisted. Some label owners and executives hated him. One in particular would say, 'Make sure Disciple don't get nothing.' I'm like, 'What? I'm giving Disciple this dub tomorrow.' She was like, 'Why's he always got to have the records first before everybody?'

"'Cause he's DJ Disciple and if he plays it then it fuses the kids together. He's the one connected to the whole Jersey thing where the kids go, 'That's the jam. That's what I want to hear in the club.' Now you're one up on your sales because he's giving it hype before it even comes out. That's what turned into promo records, or exclusives, where you'd promo your records before they came out. He's playing on the radio and his show gets to England. How did that happen?"

1. Larry Banks and the Walter Johnson Choir from the Church of the Open Door, 1981 (courtesy of the Church of the Open Door). **2.** DJ Disciple at WBMB 590 playing gospel music (courtesy of Rich LaMotte), **3.** Disco Dave, Jomo Simmonds, and Ralph Davis, 1986 (courtesy of Jomo Simmonds). **4.** Artists Shannon and Rusty Taylor (courtesy of Rusty Taylor). **5.** Mike and Dave party crowd, 1985 (courtesy of Jomo Simmonds).

THE CLUBS

In 1977, Bianca Jagger mounted a horse and rode it through Studio 54. When the Paradise Garage opened in the same year, it featured one of the most sophisticated sound systems on earth. Tunnel had a half-pipe, a ball pit, and a full-service bar in the co-ed bathroom. Millions of people—if not more—passed through New York clubs in the 1960s, 1970s, 1980s, and 1990s. Many remember these days through rose-colored glasses. Nostalgia for late nights and early mornings spent at the Paradise Garage, Studio 54, Danceteria, the Palladium, Area, the Limelight, the Roxy, Tunnel, or the hundreds of other venues that provided the foundations of Gotham nightlife is inescapable. The era saw innovations in music, rhythm, and dance; an amplified spirit of cultural inclusion that brought together diverse communities; and, through it all, the fruits of the high-fidelity golden age in which emerging stereo technology brought sound to unrealized heights.

In many cases, however, these memories are just that: mental images and stories in which the details grow blurrier and more distorted with every retelling. By contrast, empirical data is in short supply. What remains today gives us fleeting glimpses. There is one thing we can know for certain: New York had a *lot* of clubs. Following the Happy Land fire in 1990, a city task force went out to investigate the city's club venues. They found 1,391 institutions that were operating *illegally*.[1] We can only guess how many venues there were in total.

Most of the city's establishments had a capacity that ranged from a few hundred to a few thousand. The Paradise Garage had an official capacity of fourteen hundred. The Palladium could fit twenty-one hundred. Studio 54 maxed out at one thousand. Over seventeen million people lived in the tristate area in 1970. How many of these folks went out clubbing on a regular basis? What about the roughly ten million tourists who came to New York every year? How many clubs could this population support? It's hard to grapple with these scales.

But questions aside, we can be sure of another factor: during this time, New York was dangerous. Beginning in 1960, following years of stability, crime surged in the five boroughs. Murders more than quadrupled from 482 in 1960 to 2,245 in 1990. Muggings, break-ins, rapes, and assaults also shot up. This crime wave follows an overall trend that occurred in much of the Western world—but it was most pronounced in American cities, and especially so in New York.[2]

At the same time, a series of economic recessions occurred in the 1970s and 1980s. Between 1970 and 1980, New York's population shrank by over eight hundred thousand, largely due to people moving to the suburbs. In the neighborhoods left behind, it became common for people to burn or destroy their property in order to collect insurance claims. In the year 1970, 72,961 abandoned cars were towed out of the city.[3] The same occurred, to some extent, with buildings. Mayor John Lindsay (in office from 1966 to 1973) reshuffled and reduced the Fire Department of New York in an effort to cut costs. As a result, the number of fires burnt buildings throughout Brooklyn, and especially the Bronx, to the ground. In the 1970s, there were 289 census tracts in the Bronx. Forty-four lost more than 50 percent of their buildings. Seven of them lost 97 percent. Conventional wisdom states that these fires were set mostly by building owners to reclaim insurance money. But author Joe Flood problematizes that account. Only 7 percent, Flood reports, of building fires at their peak were due to arson. The remainder can be explained through city mismanagement.[4] In the aftermath, many New York neighborhoods resembled a war zone.

Many clubs were dangerous too. As Sal Abbatiello, who owned the Bronx venue Disco Fever (which was open from 1977 to 1985), told Frank Broughton and Bill Brewster, "It was violent, but the whole neighborhood was violent, you know? I had three murders in the club in ten years, but if you compare that to the neighborhood . . . they had one every week!"[5] In contrast, many clubbers remember certain nightclubs as being safe. Venues like The Loft and the Paradise Garage provided safe spaces in a very literal sense. Most others were safer than your average alleyway, but still far more dangerous than suburban communities at the time.

Another factor affected clubs in ways that are hard to measure. HIV/AIDS was first recognized as a new disease by the Centers for Disease Control in 1981. We know today that the virus developed long before that time. It had been present in the United States in the 1960s and likely earlier.[6] Through the 1980s and 1990s, cases surged, deaths mounted, and fear gripped the country. In responding, federal, state, and city governments dragged their feet. The first funding to study HIV came from the Gay Men's Health Crisis organization. Many clubs and parties played a key role in fundraising and education as well.

Journalist Steve Weinstein, writing for *Vice*, remembers how going out served as a crucial function to simply track who was still alive and who had passed.

> [M]y own clubbing experience involved mainstream rooms like Palladium and Tunnel, to weekdays at the Chapel, the gay back section of Limelight, gay nights like Bump at Club USA; holiday special events from the Saint at Large; and summer weekends at Fire Island's Pavilion. Club culture inevitably affected and was affected by the epidemic. Often, I was relieved to see people at the Saint at Large parties; I had assumed they had died in the interim.[7]

Considering the effect the virus had on the city, it's incredible that an inclusive spirit remained in New York clubland through the early years of house and hip hop. Yet that is what most sources interviewed for this book remember. Just as many clubs and parties brought white-collar Midtown and Wall Street professionals onto the same dance floor as blue-collar partyers from public housing, gay and straight folks mixed freely, and people of all races could be found at the same club. Of course, there were gay clubs and events as well. But in many cases, these were the most sought-after parties, and straight folk lined up to get in all the same. New York nightlife experienced a renaissance that lasted from the late 1970s into the early 1990s. But a series of factors brought about its end. With it went the popularity of house music and employment opportunities for DJs.

NEW YORK CLUBLAND OF THE LATE 1980s

The *Saturday Night Fever* disco club days of the 1970s wound down in the early 1980s, while early hip hop and house grew in popularity. The years of 1985 to 1988 marked a period of death and rebirth in the New York club scene. In 1985, the long-time music venue The Palladium went through a conversion. Originally designed as a movie theater, the East 14th Street space also had incredible acoustics and a state-of-the-art sound system. Popular rock acts would play the venue in the middle of stadium tours for the vibrations they could bounce off the walls, often to record a live album. Acts on The Palladium live album honor roll include the Rolling Stones, Bruce Springsteen, the Grateful Dead, and Iron Maiden. In 1985, it got a makeover from renowned Japanese architect Arata Isozaki. He left the 1927 glitzy interior intact while adding a structure of his own design. As Paul Golderberg, writing for the *New York Times*, put it in 1985:

> The new structure is a great grid of horizontal and vertical pieces mounting up for several stories, with a proscenium-like arch leaping across their middle. Within it is the main dance floor; behind it, most of the original mezzanine and balcony remain, permitting visitors to climb up and look down on the activity within the Isozaki structure.[8]

Artist Keith Haring also provided a massive mural on one wall. When the party started going, one could find ravers on the dance floor, in the wings, and even on top of the concrete encasements that housed the speakers.

Tunnel, which would soon become another dance mecca, was opened a year later in 1986. It was an old railroad freight terminal located on 12th Avenue in Chelsea and had a huge, cavernous space inside. There were smaller rooms located on several levels along with dance cages hanging from the ceiling. The Palladium and Tunnel became institutions in New York clubland. But their reputation and impact paled in comparison to the Paradise Garage.

The Garage was opened by Michael Brody in 1977 at 84 King Street in SoHo. Throughout the 1980s, it became *the* definitive dance club in Manhattan, if not the universe. Inspired by David Mancuso's The Loft, the Garage didn't serve alcohol and wasn't open to the general public. To get in, you had to be a card-carrying member or know somebody who was. The vibe inside was all-accepting and, above all, safe. The primary mode of social interaction was dancing on the sprung dance floor—music played too loud for conversation over a custom sound system designed by Richard Long. The DJ booth sat in the center and commanded attention. It closed in 1987 and, when it did, it opened a vacuum that many other venues and promoters rushed to fill. The dance music developed there went on to form its own sub-genre (garage), although the term has taken on numerous different meanings over the years.

"When I discovered the Paradise Garage, I found that it did not have the nightclub vibe that you would find in dance parties," said DJ and club owner Richard Vasquez. "It was more like a church. I just really felt at home. I was meeting people not because of 'what you can do for me or what I can do for you' but because we have the same vibe and we have the same intense interest in music. I found myself there almost every weekend from late Saturday night until early Sunday morning. A lot of the kids at the Garage—they would put their Sunday clothes in the lockers. They had lockers where you could keep things. They'd put their Sunday clothes in the lockers and then you'd see them stop dancing around 8:00 AM. They would go shower—there was even a place to shower. And then they would be singing in their choir by 10:00 or 11:00."

Besides the revolutionary setup, the Garage was also home to the greatest DJ on earth. If turntables spinning records (hooked up to a custom Richard Long sound system) form an instrument, Larry Levan stretched that instrument's range, timbre, and expressiveness galaxies beyond what was formerly possible.

Levan grew up in Brooklyn. He first hooked up with dance culture through gay clubs and the drag scene. He knew foundational New York queens Duchess and Paris in the late 1960s and, at age fourteen and fifteen, would help them bead their outfits. He later fell in with a group that was connected to the Fashion Institute of Technology, and, for much of his early life, fashion was his primary creative outlet. Levan met Frankie Knuckles through the drag community as well, and the two became good friends. Many of the venues that hosted the scene at the time played music from jukeboxes. At first, it was about community, drag, and dance. But that changed when the two began to frequent music-oriented clubs, like The Loft, through the late 1960s and 1970s.[9]

At the Loft, the two friends met Nicky Siano. It's difficult to understate the importance of this connection for dance music history. The three were all within a year of each other—and still teenagers—and none knew how to DJ. But Siano knew without question that he wanted to learn. In 1971, he was hired for his first DJing gig at a club called the Round Table.

Siano knew music. And behind the turntables, he was a natural. With almost none of the technology DJs would come to lean on in future years, he developed his own ability to match beats and mix by playing the record he planned to queue softly through a speaker near the DJ booth. By 1972, Siano and his brother Joe put together enough capital to open their own venue. The Gallery, as it was known, would be the first place that Levan and Knuckles tried their hands at DJing.[10] The two developed their skills throughout the 1970s and branched out to other venues, like the Continental Baths.

Over the course of the 1970s, all three friends grew to be foundational, pioneering DJs. Knuckles' friend Robert Williams coaxed him to move to Chicago, where he planned to open a club called the Warehouse. By 1982, Knuckles had bought his first drum machine from Detroit techno pioneer Derrick May, started making his own reel-to-reel mixes, and the rest is house music history. Back in New York, Levan developed into an audiophile with a refined musical palate. He sought to make a record sound as good as possible. He avoided mixing techniques that would bend sound away from how it was intended to be heard. But the Garage system also had a reel-to-reel player. Like Knuckles and many other early house DJs, Levan made his own mixes using basic cut-and-paste editing that he would play at night. He also liked to feed his sound through a DeltaLab digital delay, along with other flanger, chorus, phaser, and echo processors.[11] Still, he liked to play records in their entirety, and he only used live mixing techniques on a limited basis.

Levan was also an aggressive tastemaker. Others have debated what agenda went into his selections, but no one disputes the fact that, if Larry played an unknown record, it was going to sell. If the crowd didn't like it at first, Levan would play it again and again. As Tim Lawrence writes in *Life and Death on the New York Dancefloor, 1980–1983*:

> He knew how to work a record so that the crowd would beg for it. Larry would break records, whereas DJs would just play them. The Garage DJ would also select a record several times during the night so that it would be imprinted on the memory of his crowd, and the next day you would walk by record stores asking for it. People started going to the Garage not to hear the music that was happening, but to hear the music that Larry was making happen.[12]

Levan also had a relationship with WBLS DJ Frankie Crocker, who was himself known for making or breaking records on the radio. The work of Levan and Crocker, besides their countless contributions to New York music, helped establish the DJ as someone who presided over the market potential of a record.

Accompanying his older brother, Jerome Anderson also got a taste of Levan's style. "I actually did not like the music that Larry Levan was playing at first," Jaz said. "I didn't know any of the songs. But when more house music started coming out, I decided to give the Garage another try. So I went back and, that night, Larry was playing this song 'Move Your Body' by Marshall Jefferson. That became really popular, it crossed over into the R&B clubs.

"I had been hanging out with one of the guys from the record store, and I saw him in the subway station selling copies of that record. I bought one right then and there. I get home around 5:00 or 6:00 in the morning and I'm in my room and I'm playing this record over and over and over and over again. Then I went back to the record store and I bought another copy."

Levan was moody, both controlling and complacent, and obsessed with music. As former Garage DJ David DePino told *Red Bull Music*:

The way I clean and vacuum my house, Larry shined the mirror ball and made sure the floors were waxed. Everything had to be perfect. If he saw the mirror ball wasn't as shiny as it should have been, he would get out the ladder and people would sit. They would sit on the floor and wait for him to finish, because they knew he was getting into the party. Sometimes he would go up after shining the mirror ball, and then he blacked out the room and pumped up the sound. They would scream and applaud him. They knew the party was getting ready to start.[13]

Farragut native DJ Debonair believes the true secret to Levan's success was the Richard Long sound system on which he played. "The first time I went to the Paradise Garage," Debonair said, "that's when I heard the greatest sound system I've ever encountered. Richard Long was a genius. I still have one of his pieces. It's a crossover network. I'll never sell it. To this day, when I set up, I tell my crew, 'Make sure you keep your eye on that piece.'

"Levan's magic was this: he was playing on the greatest sound system in the world. He could have played 'Mary Had a Little Lamb,' and it would have sounded *good* on that Garage sound system. That was Larry's power. He knew how to control that sound system. He knew everything about it. He could tell if one of the tweeters had blown."

Levan's obsession with sound represents the culmination of a growing trend of audiophile culture that rose among New York clubs and clubbers in the 1960s and 1970s. A lot of it had to do with David Mancuso. He moved to New York in 1965 and reveled in the city's kaleidoscopic cultural scenes. "Don't forget, you had the civil rights movement going on, you had gay liberation going on," he told *Red Bull Music*. "You had all these movements going on. All this music that was coming from all different directions, it was all over the place. As long as you had a neutral place where people could come and just enjoy themselves, there was such incredibly good music."[14]

Mancuso was also an amateur audiophile. His sonic ethos pushed him to seek to replicate exactly how a record was intended to sound. He made a huge step forward in this lifelong search when he heard a friend play records through Klipschorn speakers. The next chance he got, he invested in a set of his own. That investment was significant, and he began to throw rent parties through the late 1960s to compensate. At these parties, he prioritized personal safety, a non-commercial environment, and a crystal-clear sonic experience. His events picked up steam, and, on Valentine's Day 1970, he threw his first Love Saves the Day party. And so The Loft—the venue he established in his apartment—was born. The invite-only, alcohol-free, high-quality audio nature of Mancuso's events provided an important blueprint for the Garage and numerous other clubs in the years to come.[15]

When compiling and improving his sound system at The Loft, Mancuso consulted with audio engineering legend Alex Rosner. He would send his apprentice, a man by the name of Richard Long, out to repair systems and be on call when he wasn't available. Characteristic of The Loft and Mancuso's audio philosophy, Rosner prioritized clarity of sound. But Long had a different outlook. While Rosner and Mancuso wired together arrays of tweeters that would ensure a record's high frequencies came through in crystal fidelity, Long favored the bass. Through the 1970s, he moved from experimenting with mobile DJ setups to devising and installing club sound systems. He would design bass horns with openings that stretched ten feet or more in width. One of Long's designs, a bass horn, is still known by some audiophiles today as the "Levan."[16] Many who remember Long's systems emphasize the tactile nature of the experience. As one clubber put it, "Richard's sound system used to make love to me."[17]

Very little is known about the life of Richard Long. Even those who were friendly with him personally can recall few details. Through the 1960s, he had a day job, moonlighted for Rosner, and developed his systems, until he struck out on his own. When Michael Brody opened the Garage, he turned to Richard Long and Associates to design the sound. "When I turned the system up you could feel your heart skip a beat," Garage DJ Joey Llanos told *Red Bull Music*. "That's how powerful it was."[18]

ENTER DJ DISCIPLE

Throughout 1985 and 1986, DJ Jaz could be found at the Garage, Tunnel, the Palladium, and elsewhere on any night of the week when his favorite DJs took to the booth. As DJ Disciple fell in love with DJing, he naturally grew more curious about the folks who were pushing the cutting edge of the craft. It was only a matter of time before he began going out to clubs himself on a regular basis.

He also launched his own house music record collection. He started following Jerome when he went record shopping. They'd regularly travel the same route between record stores. It started at Downtown Records at 23rd and 6th. From there, they went to Vinylmania in the Village and wrapped up at

Disc-O-Rama on West 4th. Washington Square Park would be full of college kids and artists. Dance heads would hang out there through the evening and then go to their favorite clubs.

"After seeing those stores, the vinyl junkie in me kicked in," Disciple said. "Comic books went to the back burner, but not completely. John Byrne and George Perez were doing their best illustrations and I had to keep up to date. Reading comics was my first escape as a kid. With house music, I had the same feeling. The music put a smile on my face, gave me another way to find happiness, and introduced me to a whole new world of people."

As a DJ, Disciple's skills started coming together. He soon graduated from the skating rinks and landed what was supposed to be his first gig at Brown's Guest House, an afterhours venue, in the summer of 1988. Located at Myrtle and Waverly in Brooklyn, it was the kind of place where open drug use was allowed and encouraged. It was also the kind of place where nobody wanted to listen to house music.

"It was rap, R&B, or old-school classics," Disciple said. "I clashed with the promoter, who was high on drugs when I arrived and stalled when it was time to pay me." Disciple never took the booth that night. Gang members walked through the door before he was set to begin. A rival gang was hanging out inside. Shots were fired. Disciple packed up his records and went home early with empty pockets.

He knew that if he was going to get serious about becoming a house DJ, he'd have to make it at the serious dance clubs. Manhattan venues were far more open and accepting, in part, because of their support from the LGBTQ+ community.

"After late-hour shifts on Thursday nights at Baruch College, I started venturing out to hear Johnny Dynell at the Tunnel," Disciple said. "He and Roman Ricardo became my favorite DJs. Dynell had a strong LGBTQ and clubber fan base. The crowd was far more welcoming, and I never got any drama at the door. Everyone came for the music. Dynell was mind-blowing. It was the first time I heard records like 'Let's Go' by Fast Eddie. Willy Ninja and his crew would be in the center of the dance floor voguing. The style of dance was just beginning to move Downtown out of Harlem.

"At the Palladium, the DJ booth looked down at the crowd. But the DJ booth at the Tunnel is right in the middle of the dance floor and more accessible. You can go up to the DJ and talk to him. Dynell was a humble and nice guy, and always generous with his time. Rafael Soler, aka 'Ralphie,' pulled records for me at Downtown, and when I'd mention that I saw Johnny Dynell the night before, it would be like he read my mind. He would pull out every song Dynell played or what was in his musical range. This cultural exchange on wax made a big impact on how I formed my style."

Besides the music itself, New York dance culture also had its own fashion.

"People were dressing in ways that identified with the music," Disciple remembers. "Rap had its own look: Kangol hats, Cazal glasses, sheepskin coats, Gucci, Louis Vuitton, Lee Jeans, and Adidas sneakers. The house clubber had a different identity. Men would get a faded mohawk and sometimes dye it. The apparel consisted of ripped jeans, spandex, baggy pants (for the serious dancer), Patton boots, Velour suits, Doc Martens, Benetton, biker shorts, combat boots, and Fila sneakers."

Disciple was telling his parents at this point that he'd go back to teaching when all this DJ stuff quieted down. It wasn't accounting like his father wanted, but it was still respectable and fell much more in line with the person Disciple had become. He also had some experience with the Dr. White Community Center.

"I felt there needed to be more Black males representing in education," Disciple said. "My parents agreed, and I continued to enroll in Baruch's courses. But the parties took on a life and study of their own. Harnessing my voice by doing countless hours of radio and parties coupled by the techniques of mixing I learned from Rockin' Rich LaMotte took a toll on my studies and ate into my church life too. I was constantly at a spiritual battle with my inner soul. I was studying my craft at a time when AIDS was rampant and crack was out of control. Black-on-Black crime was happening, teenage pregnancy was everywhere. I knew I was toeing a very thin line."

Although Disciple valued his education studies, his real passion was still in music. It was difficult to find a balance, but he wasn't willing to give up on his DJ career.

THE SIGMAS

When Disciple started playing shows at college campuses, he didn't realize how popular house music would be with the student crowd. Noting that response, he started looking for other opportunities.

"During the spring of 1988, I dropped in at WHCS, the Hunter College Radio station located on 68th Street," he said. "The program director was looking for new DJs to come in, so it was easy for me to land my own show. At 12:30 in the afternoon on a Thursday, I started playing. The station played constantly in the school cafeteria, and when the students heard, they reacted immediately. One of them, Steve Miller, came down to the station and asked Program Director Nikki Jones who was playing the house music. People in the cafeteria were partying."

The program director brought Steve into the studio and introduced him to Disciple. Steve, in turn, took Disciple back up to the cafeteria to show him what was going on. It was 1:00 PM, and everyone in the space was dancing. Steve brought Disciple over and introduced him to his friend and fellow Phi Beta Sigma brother Monty Collins.

"On the spot, they asked me to play one of their parties," Disciple said. "Monty told me, 'I think you'd be a great fit with what we're trying to do. We've got a party in September, and we want you to be down but we also want to know if you really know house music. September is a long way off, but we're willing to give you a try. To be down with us, you gotta play like Larry Levan.'"

That was a tall order. Since the venue closed earlier in 1987, Levan had migrated to Studio 54. While Disciple had heard constant talk of Levan over the years, he'd never seen him play in person.

"That summer Monty and Steve invited me to come down to the party at Studio 54," Disciple said. "Fraternities like Phi Beta Sigma often booked house music parties, promoted the culture, and exposed it to college students. Following the release of *School Daze* by Spike Lee, frat parties became the go-to events in the city. Down at Studio 54, Levan's set was more mature than the frat scene, and even more refined than the selections Ricardo or Johnny Dynell played. That night was also the first time I got any real attention from a woman. Caryn Nurse would be the first girl I'd dance with for the whole night. Like me, she sported a high fade—but hers was much more attractive. It suited her."

Despite the distraction, Disciple never failed to appreciate Levan's style or his command of the Studio 54 sound system, another Richard Long and Associates production.

"'You see how he's rocking?' Monty kept telling me," Disciple said. "'That's what we expect from you.' I fired back, 'Come down to the Baruch Student Center next week. You can check me out there.' At first, Monty's attitude was that anyone could sound good on the air, but the club was different. My last time playing for a Sound Experience Crew party was also my audition for Monty and Steve to see if I'd be a good fit. It was the first week back at school, and kids were already excited to party. Seeing the Baruch students letting loose was all the evidence Monty and Steve needed."

Disciple was keen to spin at Sigma parties, but he didn't have his own sound system. The Sound Experience Crew used Jaz's. Disciple heard that someone in Farragut might be able to help him out. DJ Debonair, who came up under Grandmaster Flowers, had superpowers of his own. Specifically, he built his sound with eight Cerwin Vega L36 speakers; eight EV tops; four Al Tech horns; four Bullets; two Crown amps in 2400s, 1800s, and 1200s; a QSC EQ; a Urei mixer; and, of course, two Technics SL 1200 turntables.

"The Debonair sound system exceeded the Sigmas' expectations at their party on 68th and Lexington in the East Lounge," Disciple said. "The party went from 9:00 PM to 2:00 AM. When Monty and Steve heard me play, they were all in. Not just for the one event they had planned, but for any in the future. The Sigmas had a stronghold on the college parties in the [City University of New York] system. My association with them would help me become a bigger DJ. Changes for the better were brewing. That party was the first time I was paid real money as a DJ. I also got to know incredible dancers like Brian 'Footwork' Green, Keith 'Boogie' Williams, and Frank Thomas."

For many dancers and promoters, college parties provided a staple crop of future partygoers and a stepping stone into the wider universe of New York clubland.

"The Hunter College parties brought college partygoers and club partygoers together," Frank Thomas said. "I saw for a lot of Hunter, City College, and [Borough of Manhattan Community College] students, these parties were the 'safer' doorways into the possible exploration of the non-hip hop club scene. Also the music being played by Disciple and other DJs made them receptive to the clubs that played the same genre of what would be coined house music.

"My own club footprint was different than the majority of my generation and peers. It likely started off the same, going to U.S.A. Skates, Empire Skating Rink, Skate Key, and block parties. But by a young age, I was already going to the Funhouse. My Park Slope crew were in the clubs already. I grew up with Chris—known as Father Chris in the club scene now—and his brothers. I was pretty much done with the Paradise Garage before my senior year of high school was over in 1985. By then I was already a Pied Piper of sorts. I would trek out to any place I thought I could get in by myself, scout it out, then gather the crew. So basically wherever I said was the 'spot'—that was automatically valid. I pollinated a lot of different parties with a lot of different crews of young folk who likely would never have interacted if not for me."

Disciple started playing more Hunter College parties, while keeping his radio spots at WHCS and WNYE. The members of The Sound Experience Crew, meanwhile, started going their own ways.

"The Sound Experience Crew continued to do events, but I was striking out on my own, and so were Jerome and Rich," Disciple said. "Rich started playing at the club Private Eyes, while Jaz was doing private parties on a regular basis. Ralph kept working for the radio station. In the meantime, I would spend more time in WHCS because there were more people there who loved house music. They were more connected to what was going on in the clubs."

Disciple began to weave together his various gigs and habits into a symbiotic house music ecosystem. He'd hang out at Hunter with Monty, Steve, and Caryn to get more intel on the music Levan played at the Paradise Garage and keep his ear to the ground for new house tracks. Out at clubs like the Palladium or the Tunnel, he'd pay careful attention to the records he heard. "The DJs were humble and would give me any information I needed," he said. "Clubs came to be places where I built up new friendships. Producers like Todd Terry were leading the charge for the New York house sound. Already experimenting with house tracks from Chicago and Detroit, I was equally interested in music that came from the United Kingdom and other imports from abroad."

Disciple would then use these records to curate cutting-edge programming on his shows on WNYE and WHCS. And in turn, he'd use his airtime to promote the Sigma parties where Steve and Monty kept asking him back.

In doing so, Disciple came to realize the magic of the New York music scene. It starts with the audience. Many people seek out music during most functions of everyday life. Whether it's doing the laundry, exercising, cooking, or just hanging out, most of us would prefer to have a record or the radio playing. But in New York in the 1970s and 1980s, the availability of music in everyday life was elevated. Impromptu park jams would draw crowds. People playing music on their boomboxes didn't just play the latest hits of the day. Music heads sought out the best records they could find. In turn, DJs, artists, and producers delivered. Using the music and technology that lay at hand, mobile DJs did their thing. At a time when the Bronx, Brooklyn, and Manhattan were at their most dangerous, run-down, and neglected, their residents came up with hip hop and house music. Local labels printed and distributed it. Audiophiles like David Mancuso and Michael Brody tapped the sound engineering genius of Alex Rosner and Richard Long to equip their clubs with the most sophisticated sound systems available. Venues from the heyday of New York clubbing provided DJs and artists the stage to perform. Audiences thronged to hear them. Through it all, radio stations connected hungry listeners to the best new music available. In turn, they promoted clubs and labels. New York music was a stool supported by three legs: artists and DJs (the producers), radio and labels (the distributors), and clubs (the party). Take any one away, and the whole system would topple.

With Disciple behind the decks, the reputation of Hunter parties started to grow. Attendance went from hundreds to a few thousand kids on a Friday night lining up to what Monty and Steve would call Slick & Smooth Productions parties. Frat brothers and sorority sisters from all over the city would mingle with Disciple's fan base and friends from Farragut. Soon the Sigmas needed a bigger venue to keep up with the growth of their parties. Monty and Steve, along with fellow Sigma Stan Dennis, came through on their promise to rent out Studio 54.

STUDIO 54

Similar to The Palladium, Studio 54 was a 1927 opera house which, by the late 1980s, needed a fresh coat of paint. The Midtown venue was designed by architect Eugene De Rosa and went through a series of owners between when it opened and 1943, when CBS bought it for use as a television and radio stage. Steve Rubell and Ian Schrager acquired the venue in 1976 and converted it into a nightclub.[19] It soon became one of the most popular spots in Midtown.

It was during this period that Bianca Jagger rode through her birthday party on horseback[20] and promoter Robert Isabell dumped an estimated four tons of glitter on the floor.[21] Schrager and Rubell later got picked up by the Internal Revenue Service on charges of tax evasion, and during the mid- to late 1980s, the venue went into a period of decline. This made it perfect (and more affordable) for a Slick & Smooth Productions party.

Disciple had never spun for a room that size. Monty helped him prepare.

"He told me to play house music, go into dancehall reggae to break things up, and then finish off with classics," Disciple remembers. "He told me to play only a few signature rap records. Rob Base's 'It Takes Two' and Big Daddy Kane's 'Raw' used to tear through Slick & Smooth parties when I played them. The college kids were also big on Paradise Garage classics like ESG's 'Standing in Line,' Carl Bean's 'I Was Born This Way,' and Booker T. & the MG's 'Melting Pot.'"

On the night of the party, Monty and Steve followed through on their end. They packed the venue to capacity and sent a line of partygoers down the block, waiting to get in. Disciple had done his homework. Now it was time to take the exam.

"That night, with Monty's help, I learned the approach to DJing that I would stick to throughout my career: I met the crowd where they were at, and guided them on a journey," Disciple said. "Thanks to Monty's suggestions, I knew which records would go over well, and which records would turn the dance floor inside out. From that day forward, I knew that I wouldn't always have a promoter like Monty with such specific record suggestions. But if I could figure out the audience and meet them halfway, we were gonna hit it off. With the venue packed to legal capacity, and people waiting to get in, I spun up in the mezzanine, looking down at the orchestra of the five hundred college kids dancing up a storm, doing the electric slide. Debonair was my escort that night and, needless to say, he was impressed."

As Debonair remembers, "That night with Disciple—he kept turning to ask us, 'Yo, how did I do? How did I do?' I said, 'Disciple! You don't see that crowd?! You rocked it!'"

The Slick & Smooth Productions party at Studio 54 was a success. Monty and Steve made a handsome profit. Thousands of kids had the experience they didn't even know they were looking for. And Disciple learned that one big party can lead to many others. Other fraternities and promoters started reaching out to book him, including Leonard Gabbidon (another Sigma) and Stan Dennis. Working for these two in the coming months, Disciple started backing up live acts. He closed shows for artists like Liz Torres, Jomanda, Main Source, Special Ed, and Brand Nubian. These shows culminated in the 1989 Syracuse Greekfest where Disciple followed Run-D.M.C.

"Kool D, DJ Jaz, and I were at Madison Square Garden to see Run-D.M.C. a few years before," Disciple said. "They had everyone in the Garden lift up their Adidas sneakers. Now, here I was, playing behind the legendary trio. I was starstruck. Leonard and Stan kept bringing me back to Syracuse and had me play events over at Jones Beach. More frat parties at St. John's University and City College followed."

"With our event, we wanted to promote the experience, hospitality, and acceptance—the key elements we saw at the Garage," Leonard Gabiddon said. "After the Garage closed, I made the point that you could get two or three great house acts for the same price as a hip hop group. And so, from 1988 to 1991, we brought lots of house acts in."

YOU'VE GOT TO STAY ON YOUR J-O-B

By 1990, at the age of twenty-five, DJ Disciple had compiled an impressive resume. He had his own radio show on the FM dial and DJed regularly around New York. He had access to some of the newest house tracks that continued to emerge from the studios around the city, and he also maintained a growing catalogue of certified Paradise Garage classics. But his income as a DJ wasn't paying the rent, and that was starting to take a toll.

"My father had a lot to do with me staying on my path," Disciple said. "Who knows how many times I wanted to give up this career and get a real job. Plenty of my friends who started out with me playing music had already moved on. The way I saw it, having a 'real job' is overrated. I don't speak of not having a job out of laziness or doing your passion in the workforce, it's just that most people where I come from work for a paycheck. They use their real abilities and skills to be complacent, to live adequately and sufficiently—not abundantly. My friends spend most of their lives in a job they don't like doing. If they spend ten hours a day working and eight hours a day sleeping, how can my friends really achieve their purpose? How can they accomplish what they were designed to do? My dad showed me that having a career in whatever your passion is, if correctly used, could produce a lifestyle of abundance."

This quality in William Banks contrasted with another father in Disciple's life. Though they shared so many qualities in common, Ralph Davis' dad had a different perspective on DJing.

"My parents were born in the 1920s in the South," Davis said. "They lived through just about every legalized period of segregation here in the United States. Growing up, they didn't have access to the education and employment that I did. That was a big part of their reasoning. My father was always the type of person who believed in unions. He was always telling me to get a union job. That way, your employers can't just fire you. They hire someone to go to arbitration to fight on your behalf. You get a decent paycheck, and when you retire, you get a pension. My father believed that, as a man, you had to have stability. You know, financial stability. You got to be able to provide for yourself and you definitely couldn't think about caring for family if you weren't financially stable.

"Dave was over at my apartment one time with my parents. And my dad told us, 'You're wasting your time with these records.' But it wasn't like that. It was more like, 'You're wasting your time with these damn records, boy.' He couldn't see the value in it. He came from a different background."

This influence, in part, led Ralph down a different path. One day, Disco Dave from Mike and Dave records handed him an application for the New York Police Department. "I took the exam, and they called me back," Davis said.

Resolving to turn your passion into your profession is never simple—or even possible. In the end, Kool D chose a path that would allow him to raise a family. Resigning himself to a future of insecurity, Disciple rolled the dice.

"People shape their lives around their jobs," Disciple said. "Your job dictates when you take a vacation, tells you what time of day you eat, tells you how many hours you need to work to get a raise, and how much time you need to put in before you can retire. Some jobs are designed to take you off your purpose and away from whatever vision you wish to attain. Jobs are constructed to make you lose sight of what you were born and created to do. It takes the energy and strength from you to do whatever you first had a desire to do. It's for this reason that most in my circle who started off in music never came back to music once they got a job. My father should know. It happened to him."

HOUSE IN PRINT

Through the 1980s and early 1990s, New York DJs had certainly drawn inspiration from artists throughout the rest of the United States, as well as from the United Kingdom and Europe. But New York house was still an insular scene. As time went on, that perspective began to shift. Windows to the rest of the world began to open up here and there. The industry and fan-facing magazines that started showing up in the city record stores and newsstands helped make this happen.

Two UK publications vied for the top spot in terms of authority. *Mixmag* printed its first edition back in 1983, but had taken some time to make its way across the Atlantic. *DJ Magazine* opened shop in 1991 and quickly caught on as a leading trade publication. Reading these, Disciple was amazed at the DJ profiles and club culture that existed around the world. Magazines presented a powerful medium for artists to gain promotion and exposure. The magazines also alerted fans to emerging scenes. To Disciple's surprise, they knew about him. He started seeing his name mentioned in playlists and event announcements. These magazines helped Disciple conduct research. In a few years, they would feature his profile.

NEW JERSEY

This expanded world of house music got Disciple thinking. He began to extend his reach outside of the five boroughs. While New York had become the North American capital for house music and clubbing, a new scene was developing across the Hudson.

Club Zanzibar had been in operation since 1979 at 430 Broad Street in Newark. And since 1982, their resident DJ had been the indomitable Tony Humphries. While Larry Levan was drawing crowds at the Garage, Humphries was doing the same at Zanzibar. Both were DJ pioneers, and both were responsible—almost single-handedly—for curating their own sub-genre. While Levan's mixes went on to generate American garage, Humphries played all the underground releases from Jersey he could find. The "Jersey sound" was more soulful than the tracks Levan favored and drew in more gospel vibes. It was occasionally more raw and less produced. The tracks that fueled it came from labels like Movin' Records, Ace Beat, Quark, and Easy Street, to name just a few.

One might think that New Jersey served as New York's B side, but these labels were known internationally. Their releases often eclipsed their New York counterparts. JP Firman, Disciple's future UK agent, started his first label as an outfit that licensed Movin' Records releases for UK distribution. One of their first releases was a Tony Humphries remix of "Don't Turn Your Love" by Park Avenue, a Movin' Records track.

New Jersey clubs were no less prestigious. Club Zanzibar itself was strikingly similar to the Garage. Both featured sound systems designed by Richard Long. Both encouraged an eclectic mix of music and patrons. Both brought together dance heads from all walks of life.

Disciple was eight years younger than Humphries, and his development as a DJ stood somewhere between following in his footsteps and progressing independently. The two share many things in common. Both were born in Brooklyn. Both their fathers were musicians. Both started DJing in college. Both incorporated contemporary gospel into their mixes. Both had house shows on the FM dial. (Humphries landed a program in 1982 on the newly formed WRKS 98.7 Kiss FM after a chance encounter with Shep Pettibone.)

Despite Humphries packing Zanzibar to capacity, the venue began to decline in the early 1990s. Meanwhile, an event promoter by the name of Latif Summer saw an opportunity to bring Disciple to New Jersey. He got in touch about a stint at Club 280, which was just a few blocks away from Zanzibar at 370 Orange Street. The venue was an old paper factory that had been converted to an event space by Nelson "Butchie" Nieves. When Disciple showed up, it still looked like a massive warehouse, but with a huge DJ booth and a state-of-the-art light show.

Originally named Hardcore, Club 280 hosted resident DJs such as Hippie Torrales and Duce Martinez. Hippie Torrales was a Jersey DJ pioneer. He initially opened a venue called Docks with Butchie Nieves and then went on to hold a residency at Abe's Disco, which later became Club Zanzibar. When Zanzibar opened, Hippie was their first resident DJ. While working at Zanzibar, he won the Billboard Disco Forum 8 Award for the best disc jockey in the state of New Jersey the same year Larry Levan won the award for New York. Both Dave Camacho and Naeem Johnson—two movers in the scene and important connections Disciple was soon to make—came from the school of Hippie Torrales. While Camacho took off in New York, Naeem found similar success working at WBLS from 1980 to 1984. He also held a residency at Zanzibar on Wednesday nights alternating with David Morales and on Fridays alternating with Larry Patterson. He and DJ and producer Timmy Regisford were also close, and Naeem was instrumental in breaking numerous Regisford hits, especially those produced by Boyd Jarvis in the early days before house music exploded. When Timmy Regisford left WBLS to work at MCA, Naeem took his place.

Another Club 280 resident, Duce Martinez, was responsible for shaping the b-boy scene in Newark and was in the outfit The Dynamic Rockers, who often joined Run-DMC and Whodini on the Fresh Tour. He had a knack for the soundboard and became an accomplished studio engineer for R&B artists like Aaron Hall and Lauryn Hill.

As Latif began bringing Disciple over on a regular basis, he got to know the whole scene. Soon, Disciple was hopping in a cab every Friday night with his box of records and heading through the Holland Tunnel.

"Sometimes it would be a nightmare knowing how to find the club," Disciple said. "Dancers like Marjory Smarth, Ejoe Wilson, Caleaf Sellers, David and Derrick Storey, Shannon 'Whichway' Sha, Tony McGregor, and Cardrian Massey would follow me from New York to catch my set. Baruch College buddies Art, Justin, and Devin regularly came as well while Mark, Doc, and Scott from Fort Greene would find their way out there too. Sometimes I would come crewed up with people from Farragut."

For these sets, Disciple hung his hat on tracks like Robert Owens' "I'll Be Your Friend," the song that that got him in hot water with David Morales. It became a major club hit. Kerri Chandler also had a string of hot tracks coming from his studio including "Deeper" by Susan Clark, "Drink On Me," by Teulé, various album cuts from Dee Dee Brave, and "Get It Off" by Chandler himself. After breaking "Follow Me" on the radio, Disciple also brought Aly-Us on for a live performance one night at 280. Word caught on, and Club 280 with Disciple behind the decks eventually got so big that, by 1991, their following eclipsed the crowd at Zanzibar.

Another DJ friend, Roger Sanchez, headed down to Miami to catch the Winter Music Conference in March of 1991. When he returned, he handed Disciple a promo copy of "Gypsy Woman" by Crystal Waters. "After playing it on the radio I got an immediate reaction," Disciple recalls. "That Friday I played it at Club 280 three times with the crowd immediately knowing the words to the song the third time around."

ZANZIBAR

Disciple made another important connection at this time. Barbarito Capote met him browsing vinyl at Downtown Records one day and the two hit it off. One night in New Jersey, Disciple left all of his unreleased material at his apartment in Brooklyn. Barbarito took Disciple's keys, went to his apartment in Farragut, got his material, and brought it back to him before his DJ set. Disciple knew from that moment on that he could trust Barbarito. Also known as DJ Dove, he became part of the WNYE *Best Kept Secret* team of Darlene, LaShay Baltazar, Althea McQueen, Marvelous Marvin Memminger, and Dale Burley.

Then came what seemed like a stroke of luck. Tony Humphries left Zanzibar for a residency in London at the Ministry of Sound, a club that was exploding in popularity across the Atlantic. Latif later that summer made the decision that, since the Club 280 party had grown so much, they could move the party to Zanzibar. Disciple was reluctant to do this, and it made the owner of Club 280 furious. Still, Latif was confident and pulled out all the stops for Disciple's first night. 98.7 Kiss FM promoted the event, and the news impressed people in the music industry, along with friends and neighbors from Farragut. But the hype was short-lived. After the initial party, the event began to struggle. "In a snap, the dancers who once followed me at Club 280 were nowhere to be seen at Zanzibar," Disciple said. "Timmy Regisford's 12-hour marathon experience at The Shelter in New York became the next hot thing for house heads."

Regisford, along with Freddy Sannon and Merlin Bobb, opened The Shelter in 1991 at 6 Hubert Street in the Meatpacking District. The neighborhood was a wasteland at the time, but the venue had a state-of-the-art sound system, and Regisford started drawing massive crowds with marathon twelve- to eighteen-hour sets. These were a phenomenon in their time.

Music scholar Glenn Berry, who was writing his master's thesis on the underground club scene in New York in the early 1990s, caught Disciple at Zanzibar. "I remember somebody stealing tapes from Disciple one night," Berry said. "I don't think Disciple failed at all [referring to the decline of the party at Zanzibar]. He stayed true to the house sound he loves. There's nothing wrong with that. The crowd wanted to hear dancehall, but Disciple played house instead—and that shows how authentic he was."

"There were still good options in New York," Disciple said, "and many clubbers felt they were wasting their time by going to Jersey. The older crowd that went to Zanzibar wanted to hear more of the musical legacy left behind by Humphries, while the new kids that came in wanted me to play dancehall and hip hop. I would play well, but in the crowd's opinion, I wasn't playing it right. My sound for that venue wasn't a good fit. Eventually I realized I'd rather they boo me than give me an early exit, but that still happened once too often.

"While I was trying to push my sound and music and create a new energy in the club, the club itself was the foundation that Tony Humphries built and no one else could compete. Latif and I got the boot after a two-month stretch. We had burned our bridges at 280 and, just like Crystal Waters' "Gypsy Woman,"

we were homeless in New Jersey clubland. I'd still be used for special occasions, but the residency was gone. It was a major blow to my ego but, at the same time, it was also a humbling experience.

"Being a DJ is an emotional rollercoaster at times. You hit bumps on the road. There are seasons when you feel just lousy, coming short on your goal for the night. DJing, it can test you. It can put you at your wit's end. You might love it, but it doesn't love you back. Zanzibar was my first major failure as a DJ. I managed to keep my feet in the storm and remembered the purpose I have in this life."

After Zanzibar, a valuable lesson became clear in Disciple's mind. Some DJs try to suss out what the crowd is feeling. Others try to stay true to their own musical identity and try to convert the crowd. Whichever philosophy you follow, some crowds will reject you no matter what you play. At the end of the day, the only way forward as a DJ is to make sure you're happy with the set you're putting together.

"Kevin Oliphant, also known as Kevin O, was the DJ that replaced Tony Humphries and was a fan of my radio show," Disciple said. "At 19, he'd be given his own night, while playing other venues in New Jersey. He believed that I was the victim of circumstances. We had mutual respect for each other, as Kevin O was well versed in knowing what worked for the Zanzibar audience he played for."

In comparison, Disciple's style was too different for the Jersey Sound, and Zanzibar became the first venue to which he could not adapt. Some people in the crowd, however, did love what Disciple was playing. One was Naeem Johnson. The two met at Zanzibar briefly and exchanged numbers. Disciple and Johnson helped grow each other's networks. After the fallout at Zanzibar, he helped book Disciple shows at other New Jersey clubs. In turn Disciple introduced Barbarito Capote a.k.a. DJ Dove to Naeem. Naeem knew of Dove through *Best Kept Secret*. Naeem also let Disciple know that he played not too far from Zanzibar at a club called The Mirage. He'd have Disciple as a guest DJ every now and then alongside Dove.

Disciple studied the way Naeem played in New Jersey and learned a good deal from him. Borne by the success of *Best Kept Secret* and his residency at 280, he managed to maintain a fan base in New Jersey. Zanzibar had not been a complete loss, but a lesson. Jazzy B, another person who loved Disciple's direction at Zanzibar, was notorious for doing college parties in New Jersey. He helped Disciple land gigs at Club 88, Peppermint Lounge, Soweto's/Blackbox, Club Sensations, and Scandals.

The New Jersey club community helped Disciple grow his talents. By 1992 he'd come back to play at Club 280, but things weren't the same. Still, the collaboration he gained working with Naeem Johnson and Jazzy B gave him hope. To reciprocate, Disciple had Jazzy play with him in New York. The duo worked with Monty and Steve on New York events to combine the New Jersey and New York audiences.

Naeem liked to spin tracks by artists such as Brothers of Peace, Kenny Bobien, Michael Watford, Daryl D'Bonneau, Cassioware, and just about anything that came out of Smack Productions. He infused the New York records he was getting with some of the Jersey music that the crowds knew. Naeem was a culture bearer. He became instrumental in his own right in keeping the Jersey sound alive after Humphries left for London.

THE UNDERGROUND NETWORK AT THE SAVAGE/SOUND FACTORY BAR

Back in New York, a new industry night led by Barbara Tucker and Don Welch was taking place at The Savage, a reputable R&B club. On Wednesdays, they had Louie Vega as resident and featured numerous guest DJs and dancers.

"I first met Louie Vega at Trax," Disciple said. "He knew about my radio show and would always have me come by to pick up the latest thing he was doing in the studio at Bass Hit. Todd Terry, Kenny Dope, and Roger Sanchez all worked out of this studio. Going in there, I felt like a modern-day musical crack addict, waiting for my latest fix of music they would give me."

During one of these nights in the spring of 1992, Disciple ran into Grandmaster Flowers for the first time since he started DJing. The DJ pioneer and Farragut neighbor had recently recovered from drug addiction. The two hadn't seen each other in years. They spent time catching up and filling each other in on the goings-on of each other's families. Disciple told him all that DJ Debonair, his former apprentice, had done for him. "I remember Flowers told me that, sometimes, there's no blueprint for you to become successful as a DJ," Disciple said. "You could have a strategy, but still fail or succeed in it. But if you get the right set of circumstances, and the right people who believe in you, there's nothing you can't do."

It was exactly the advice Disciple needed, and he asked Flowers to sit in for guest sets on *Best Kept Secret*. Flowers unfortunately never made it over to the WNYE studios. He passed away shortly after. Disciple dedicated a radio special in his honor.

The next year, the Underground Network relocated to Sound Factory Bar, which was located at 12 West 21st Street between 5th and 6th Avenues.

"Sound Factory Bar was my connection to the world," Disciple said. "Besides regulars like Louie Vega, Roger Sanchez, Kenny Dope, and Todd Terry, most of the people who ran independent labels in the city would show up as well. DJ Camacho would play downstairs sometimes and he would tell me who's who in the industry if I didn't know them already. There was no shortage of DJs, producers, and singers looking to network or collaborate."

Wednesday nights at the Sound Factory Bar came just in time. They were soon Disciple's main tie to New York house. Promoters were calling less and less. Everyone knew about *New York's Best Kept Secret*, and Disciple still showed progress, but his reputation as a DJ was beginning to slip. Every DJ career is about maintaining momentum, and Disciple was taking every chance he got to push the ball forward. But he also still had one card left to play. He had never worked in the studio. It was another way to spread music, forge connections, and stay relevant.

One Wednesday night, Disciple met Bobby Davis, owner and operator of the S.U.R.E. Record Pool. Bobby started Spinner Unlimited Recording Enterprises (S.U.R.E.) in May 1978 in order to provide the growing number of DJs with music that, at the time, was not available to them anywhere else. He eventually gave Disciple his first opportunity to record in a studio and also started sponsoring *Best Kept Secret*.

"Bobby gave me the opportunity to meet with Chris Mellor from *DJ Magazine* during the New Music Seminar," Disciple said. "I bonded closely with Bobby, and he told me that he had a studio in the Bronx. I was desperate to learn how to work in the studio and do my own music. Bobby allowed me to record with the belief that I would put out a record on his label, Muzik Pushers. I also met a young man who was enthused about the music he was hearing. His name was Todd Edwards. He would give me cassette tapes of music that he'd just finished to play on my radio show the next day. He'd later remember these times in an interview with Red Bull Academy."

"So I had a couple things out, and I always wanted to have my music played on this one radio station that DJ Disciple had," Edwards told interviewer Emma Warren. "I loved his show. I mean, DJ Disciple's show was amazing. It was college radio, and everyone tuned in to hear the newest tracks before they were out. That was the other thing, too, it's like, you have the internet, you can get stuff on SoundCloud. Back then, it was, to have a dubplate, or something before anyone else, that was amazing, 'Oh my God! What is that?' 'It's not out yet,' you know? 'It's Masters at Work,' or something. But I wanted my track played on his show."[22]

"Because of the reputation I built playing in clubs in New Jersey and the radio show in New York, Michael Cameron from Smack Productions called me up to come to the studio to get more unreleased music from him," Disciple said. "When I get to New Jersey to meet him, he introduced me to Eddie Perez and Paul Simpson. Simpson was a prominent producer for Adeva. She had a string of successful house and R&B hits in the late 1980s and early 1990s, including 'Warning,' 'I Thank You,' and 'Respect.'"

Perez, a keyboardist, and Disciple also befriended each other and agreed to work together in the studio. The deal was that Perez would lay down keys on Disciple's first EP out of Muzik Pushers. Disciple, in turn, would help Perez out with his other projects he was working on at Smack.

"Bobby Davis, Smack Productions, Bass Hit Studios, and Todd Edwards were my inspiration for producing music," Disciple said. "For the first three months, I drove Bobby's engineer Rolando Maldonado crazy in the studio. Remembering my time with Moe Love, I bought an E-mu SP-1200 and loaded it with drum sounds that Roger Sanchez gave me. Maldonado had to figure out how to integrate the drum machine with his Cubase digital audio workstation. We would spend hours programming around the drum machine. Once we did it, and with Eddie playing his Juno 9 keyboard, projects came out like magic.

"In the studio, you have to come up with ideas quickly, as the time would move fast. Changing your mind in any session would be considered a setback. I'd have constructive arguments with Eddie or Rolando about the sound or arrangement of the track being worked on. We had a trusting relationship because, musically, they understood me. We knew how to compromise. We bounced ideas off each other and found the right balance."

With the tracks cut, Disciple left things in the hands of Davis for the time being.

THE HAPPY LAND FIRE

By the early 1990s, the golden age of New York clubs was on its way out. In March 1990, Julio Gonzalez got into an argument with his girlfriend, Lydia Feliciano, at the Happy Land social club in the Bronx, where she was working the coat check. The club had previously been ordered closed by the city for numerous code violations, including lack of fire exits. Feliciano reportedly broke up with Gonzalez that night and he was thrown out of the club by a bouncer at 3:00 AM. He walked across the street, purchased a dollar's worth of gasoline at a nearby station, and, pouring it across the base of the staircase at the club's only entrance, lit the club on fire. Eighty-seven people died in the blaze. At the time, it was the largest mass murder in American history.[23]

Instead of strengthening safety laws, the city government under Mayor David Dinkins brought the hammer down on the clubs themselves and pushed them further underground. Former mayor Ed Koch had created a task force of ten teams (composed of police officers and building and fire inspectors) after a similar fire in the Bronx that claimed eight lives. Mayor Dinkins had initially reduced this task force to one team. But after Happy Land, he increased it to twenty. These teams found 1,391 New York clubs that were operating illegally, 209 of which were open on a weekly basis. The task force closed 505 establishments in all.[24]

"They used a lot of publicity to demonize clubs as being the worst possible thing that could be going on in New York," said DJ and club owner Richard Vasquez. "You know, 'Close them down.' It was front-page news, and it was a photo-op for Dinkins, who basically was not going to accomplish very much else. It just got so dangerous during the Dinkins administration. But [closing clubs] was an easy thing to do. That was an easy photo."

FUNERALS EVERY WEEK

Violent crime in New York reached its height in 1990. The 1980s had been a decade of struggle and resilience. But in the 1990s, New Yorkers had to reckon with the fallout. The same was true within the Banks family. For Julia Banks, listening to her sons' music on the radio and television wasn't enough—she just wanted to be able to walk to see her kids perform. Early in the new decade, she had a breakthrough. John R. Thomas, a deacon at the Church of the Open Door, convinced Disciple's mother to attend a Sunday service. Reverend Kieller had retired a few years before. Reverend Dr. Mark Taylor took his place. When Deacon Thomas prayed with Julia after on the phone, she felt the spirit. While she had constantly discouraged Disciple's faith as a teenager and young man, she accepted Jesus into her life. She was baptized on February 17, 1991, and began rehabilitating herself to walk again. All the same, rheumatoid arthritis began to take hold. Through the early 1990s, she began to struggle with mobility more and more. In 1994, she entered Brooklyn Hospital.

One Thursday while Disciple was live on air, his brother Larry came to the studio for the first time. The show was in its last half-hour.

"I was thinking, 'Finally, after I've had a show for six years, here's Larry coming to visit his brother in the studio for the first time,'" Disciple said. "Instead, he gave me the news. Mom was dead. I couldn't breathe, let alone DJ. Dove covered the last part of the show while Lashay consoled me and Larry outside."

The funeral took place a week later at the Church of the Open Door. Reverend Taylor brought the house down with his sermon. He then invited each Banks brother to reflect on their mother. Julia had devoted her life to her sons. As grown men, the Banks brothers had dispersed across the country. The funeral brought everyone back together and created a stronger bond between them.

"Stanley and Jaz came to the radio show after the funeral so that we could play my mother's favorite records," Disciple said. William Banks, meanwhile, got saved and baptized at the Church of the Open Door. He began regularly attending services as a member and started to reconnect with Larry, who had been thriving as the musical director. A longtime alcoholic and occasional cocaine user, he got completely clean when he turned fifty. He had good reason to do so.

Julia's passing made for a moment of calm in the storm that was sweeping through Farragut. Crime was just starting to come down from a historic high. Crack and violence were widely available. Legitimate employment opportunities were scarce. Too many of Disciple's friends felt the consequences.

"Walking around Farragut, it became a ritual when passing someone you knew to say, 'What's up?' and keep it moving," Disciple said. "No one wanted to stop, and most actually didn't want to know what was going on, because more often that not, it was bad. More and more of my friends were falling into one of three categories: addicted, jailed, or murdered. A couple got away injured or paralyzed, but in most instances, the drug trade became an expedited sentence for either prison or death. Crack and crime went hand in hand."

Pastor Taylor and the Banks family started witnessing multiple funerals on a weekly basis. Larry was playing them, and Pastor Taylor was delivering them. Gunplay was a nightly phenomenon in Farragut, and even residents minding their own business could get caught in the crossfire.

In response, some friends and neighbors went into law enforcement. Ralph Davis was one of them. He worked undercover and later earned his detective badge. Monty and Steve also joined the force. Many women in Farragut took to law enforcement as well.

Newly elected President Bill Clinton wasn't making the situation any better. In 1994, Congress passed the Violent Crime Control and Law Enforcement Act. The act bumped up funding for community police departments and banned certain military weapons. But most importantly, it made it so that anyone who committed three violent felonies would be sentenced to life in prison without parole. All states, in addition, had mandatory sentencing laws on the books before the crime bill. But it facilitated even harsher enforcement.[25] Leighton Banks nearly came to witness this measure firsthand.

"Leighton was the black sheep of the family," Disciple said. "He got into shenanigans early in life and left the home at a young age. Drug culture caught him, and when the crack epidemic exploded in the late eighties, he was heavily involved. He traveled first to Denver and then to Los Angeles where he was introduced to the Crips, the Bloods, and Skid Row. After a few years in that world, Leighton went to jail for armed robbery. He robbed a number of convenience stores, and the woman he was staying with turned him in. After doing three years in jail, he came home, gave up that lifestyle completely, and never looked back.

"Like David Faison, his grandfather, Leighton could talk his way out of any situation he got himself into. I went ten years without seeing him. At mom's funeral in Brooklyn, he came back a clean man. No longer addicted to the surroundings of people, places, and things, he became the first of my brothers to get married. His bride was Mary Esquivivas. I was extremely proud of Leighton for leaving the crack trade when he did."

BROKEN WINDOWS

The reunion of the Banks brothers provided Disciple comfort at a time when his career was foundering. As the 1990s marched on, it became clear that Happy Land was just the prelude. The salad days of New York nightlife began to draw to a close. While work had slowed in New Jersey for Disciple, it had all but dried up back in New York. He was hardly alone. A trend began during these years in which New York DJs struggled more and more to make a living with their craft. This would push DJs out of the city, across the United States and overseas. A few factors caused the house music well to run dry. For one, hip hop was growing more popular, and it became clear that it had an either/or relationship with house. "By 1991, people's taste buds for house music changed," Disciple said. "One record in particular, 'OPP' by Naughty By Nature, told me that hip hop was coming at us very hard. That song was the warning shot that let me know that young people in New York wouldn't be interested in house music like they had previously."

The predominance of hip hop came to be felt in small ways. Sean Puffy Combs started doing hip hop industry parties at the Red Zone, which had for years booked house DJs. Music communities began to shift. Techno came to the fore, but it grew in popularity predominantly with younger, white audiences. When it made its way to New York, it clashed with house, instead of amplifying it. When house emerged from Chicago a decade earlier, it was recorded and played mostly by Black artists. But it was also a genre based on fusion, integration, and remixing. From the beginning, it drew diverse audiences.

Now the pendulum began to swing in the other direction. Music scenes grew more divided and more distinct. Suddenly, kids weren't listening to house and hip hop; they were choosing one over the other. And more and more, the Black kids were going with hip hop, while the white kids chose house.

"Major record labels were dropping house music acts left and right," Disciple said. "CeCe Penniston, Frankie Knuckles, Adeva, Crystal Waters, and other artists managed a few hit records. Others fell off the map completely. The house music scene became more and more marginalized. In my opinion, gangsta rap signaled the end of house music for young Black kids. I went from being a DJ who everyone wanted to go out and see on a Friday night, to almost unknown."

House was also getting less radio play, and hip hop began to demonstrate a stronger market viability. DJ Jaz attributes this in part to the HIV/AIDS pandemic.

"I felt that when AIDS came out, that was the main reason why the hip hop generation was kind of skeptical about the gay community and house music," Jaz said. "There was some dormant homophobia. But when AIDS started happening, nobody knew how you caught it, and the hip hop crowd wanted to be separate completely and hang out in separate clubs."

Then came the 1993 New York mayoral election. It rang the death knell for clubs across the city. On November 2, Rudy Giuliani defeated David Dinkins by a slim margin with the promise to clean up the city and pursue a tougher tack on crime than his predecessor. These policies mostly brought about change in the boroughs that Giuliani lost. Large majorities of voters in Queens and Staten Island propelled the White Flatbush native to victory, while Dinkins won Brooklyn, Manhattan, and the Bronx.[26]

This was bad news for New York clubs. Mayor Dinkins had played his part in closing dancing establishments. Besides the actions taken after the Happy Land fire in 1990, he brought further pressure a year later when Sean Combs, along with rapper Heavy D, were promoting a rap show and charity basketball game at City College. They oversold the event, and City College failed to account for the flow of people into the building. A stampede on the way in left nine dead and twenty-eight injured. Dinkins had expanded the New York Police Department by nearly 25 percent during his term, integrated precincts, and directed over five thousand officers to police neighborhoods on foot in ten-person teams.[27] These actions helped end a thirty-year increase in metro crime.[28] After Dinkins' first year in office, crime had declined by 6 percent. All the same, his successor kicked these efforts into overdrive.

Once in office, Giuliani further added to the police force and set about implementing the Broken Windows Policing theory developed by sociologists James Wilson and George Kelling. Their theory states that tolerance of minor crimes generates a dangerous environment. In other words, a neighborhood covered by graffiti and full of broken windows feels less safe and, thereby, encourages unsafe behavior.

Kelling and Wilson lay out these ideas in their March 1982 *Atlantic* article "Broken Windows":

> A stable neighborhood of families who care for their homes, mind each other's children, and confidently frown on unwanted intruders can change, in a few years or even a few months, to an inhospitable and frightening jungle. A piece of property is abandoned, weeds grow up, a window is smashed. Adults stop scolding rowdy children; the children, emboldened, become more rowdy. Families move out, unattached adults move in. Teenagers gather in front of the corner store. The merchant asks them to move; they refuse. Fights occur. Litter accumulates. People start drinking in front of the grocery; in time, an inebriate slumps to the sidewalk and is allowed to sleep it off. Pedestrians are approached by panhandlers.

In answer, the authors suggest the model tested by the city of Newark, New Jersey, for a period in the 1970s. Newark's Safe and Clean Neighborhoods Program expanded foot patrol policing. Officers had a more personal, on-the-ground presence in neighborhoods, where they often maintained a set of informal rules along with local, state, and federal laws. The authors acknowledged that "foot patrol had not reduced crime rates. But residents of the foot patrolled neighborhoods seemed to feel more secure than persons in other areas, tended to believe that crime had been reduced, and seemed to take fewer steps to protect themselves from crime." They also concede that "many aspects of order maintenance in neighborhoods can probably best be handled in ways that involve the police minimally if at all." Still, they conclude with an effective metaphor, "Just as physicians now recognize the importance of fostering health rather than simply treating illness, so the police—and the rest of us—ought to recognize the importance of maintaining, intact, communities without broken windows."[29]

Common knowledge has it that Giuliani took this perspective to heart. But it would be more appropriate to describe his approach as "zero tolerance." He did away with several aspects of community policing and aggressively pursued all crime, from murder down to the smallest misdemeanor. As Giuliani summed up in a public forum a few months after his election, freedom does not mean that "people can do anything they want [or], be anything they can be. Freedom is about the willingness of every single human being to cede to lawful authority a great deal of discretion about what you do and how you do it."[30]

"I remember Giuliani came on TV," said DJ Keoki, who played The Limelight, Save the Robots, Tunnel, Palladium, and many other New York clubs and parties through the 1990s. "He was standing next to some tourists in front of the post office at 34th and 8th where I lived. There had been all these homeless people living there. But that day, they had cleared them all away. And Giuliani was on camera saying, 'Yes, New York City is great now.' Some other lady was saying, 'I don't know why they're saying what they are about New York, it's beautiful!' And they were standing right where homeless people had been living for years."

Part of this effort to clean up the city targeted New York nightlife. Giuliani set about systematically closing down clubs, ostensibly in an effort to make the city feel safer. To do this, he went beyond the building inspection task forces created by Koch and Dinkins and turned to New York's archaic Cabaret Laws. During Prohibition and the Harlem Renaissance in the 1920s, the city passed a racist measure to prohibit white and Black people dancing and socializing together in the same clubs. Under the law, clubs technically needed a cabaret license to operate a dance floor. It should surprise no one that, in the 1990s, few clubs made it through this costly and tenuous application. In 2016, a year before the law was revoked, the New York City Department of Consumer Affairs reported that only 118 cabaret licenses were on the books in a city that counted 25,100 licensed food service establishments.[31] Giuliani, however, used the cabaret laws to "improve quality of life" and "clean up" clubs.

"It's war, they say," began a 1996 *New York Times* article covering the Quality of (Night) Life Forum convened by club owners to launch what became the New York Nightclub Association. As journalist Elisabeth Bumiller writes:

> Don Hill, the owner of a nightclub on the edge of SoHo, is ready for combat because he had to pay a $100 fine after a city inspector caught 40 people dancing at his place last year. Larry Bloch, the owner of Wetlands, a nightclub in TriBeCa, is fighting mad because if a band puts up illegal posters advertising its appearance on his stage, he is the one

who is cited for violations, the result of a city law he says is reminiscent of a "Gestapo state."[32]

DJ Romain played the underground party Save the Robots and at clubs like Limelight and Club USA through the 1990s. "The after hours spots like Save the Robots weren't supposed to serve alcohol," Romain said. "They used to hide it underneath the floor. Every once and awhile we'd be run up on by the cops. We had a little flashlight up in the DJ booth. When they flashed it, that meant the cops are here, so I'd have to put on jazz or something chill. The cops would come down, search, whatever and they would leave.

"But all that changed with Giuliani. He sent out a club task force. It would be a group of seven or eight police that would literally go in and raid the spots. You know, come in, shut the music off, arrest some people. I almost got arrested a couple times. When the task force came in, that was serious. That was when they shut you down."

No example illustrates Giuliani's crusade against New York nightlife better than the multiple prosecutions brought against Peter Gatien. An eye-patched transplant from small-town Ontario, Canada, Gatien could credibly claim the title of New York Club King in the 1990s. His four enormous clubs—The Limelight, The Palladium, Tunnel, and Club USA (which closed in 1995)—drew thousands of clubbers on most nights of the week. This era, and these clubs, provided the setting for the rise of club kids. A loose community composed of people like Michael Alig, Amanda Lepore, Michael Tronn, Richie Rich, James St. James, Waltpaper, and dozens, if not hundreds, of others made a name for themselves producing experimental art, music, and fashion. Club dance floors served as canvases, stages, and platforms for their eccentric behavior.

DJ Keoki ran an acid house party with club kid Michael Alig at The World. They hooked up with Gatien and decided to move it to Limelight.

"We built it up," Keoki said. "Once it became solid, there was no stopping us. We had all kinds of people in there. I mean, every type of person you could imagine. We were pushing the envelope. From 10:00 PM to 6:00 AM, I played every Wednesday night for six years. In the middle of the night, we'd have the hot body contest. Then, after that, I would play the weirdest acid house, the trippiest techno, and that's when all the club kids would come out and take their acid or whatever.

"Imagine you're some preppy, out at night, drunk. You're going to leave, but then you see the hot body contest, some hot people stripping or whatever. Then that ends, and Clara the Carefree Chicken comes out and starts giving you her little prescriptions. And then I start playing the trippy music. And then the kids come out looking like aliens from outer space. You know, the dance floor was the best. It was the best dance floor in the world. It was amazing."

Through the early 1990s, reports filtered through various law enforcement channels that Peter Gatien venues had become hotspots for the sale and consumption of a number of drugs, most notably, ecstasy. On September 30, 1995, law enforcement raided The Limelight. Officers didn't find any ecstasy. Out of the thirty-five hundred clubbers in attendance that night, they found small quantities of cannabis on just three of them.[33] Nevertheless, the media in coming days and weeks began to describe the club as a "drug supermarket." Months after the raid, Gatien himself was arrested on charges that he conspired to sell drugs at his venues. Gatien's assets were frozen, and he had to rely on, among many others, his ex-wife and his kid's tutor (who staked his collection of books and records, his most substantial asset) to post bail.

The US prosectors' case against Gatien quickly fell apart. Two of their three primary witnesses were caught dealing drugs before the case went to trial. The third, Disco 2000 Wednesdays promoter Michael Alig, along with Robert "Freeze" Riggs, murdered fellow club kid Angel Melendez in March of 1996. DJ Keoki had known, dated, partied with, and worked with Alig for years.

"We were both messed up on drugs," said Keoki. "I was in LA when it happened, writing my *Ego-Trip* album. I had people protecting me. I had a good deal with Moonshine Music. So my management, the producers, the label, they were all protecting me from New York. I avoided that darkness.

"Michael and Angel got into a fight. And he killed him. The one thing that gets in peoples' minds is what he did afterward to get rid of the body. It's like a monster thing. Like, a crazy Jeffrey Dahmer thing."

After the murder, Alig and Riggs dismembered Melendez's body, wrapped his limbs in garbage bags, placed those in individual duffel bags, and dumped them in the Hudson River. They then wrapped Melendez's upper body in a plastic sheet, placed it in a cardboard box, rode with it in a taxi out to the Westside Highway, and threw that in the river too.

"In reality, Michael didn't know what to do," Keoki said. "There was an accident. He was messed up on drugs. He wasn't trying to kill anybody. When he got out of jail, I asked him, 'How could you cut off someone's leg?' You know, 'How did that get into your head?' He said, 'Well, I did seventeen bags of heroin. And then I turned into Foghorn Leghorn from the cartoon. And I just thought, 'OK, we're gonna cut the bone.'

"If I'd been there, maybe I would have been able to say, 'Look, there's a dead body. You need to call the cops now. It's done.' But he didn't do that. He just got more and more messed up and started thinking twisted things. People can't get over that. Michael was not a monster like that. He was actually very sweet. He was a kind-hearted soul. He just got caught up in this mess and there was no one to help him."

That news also came out before Alig was set to testify at Peter Gatien's trial. It made headlines around the world and caused the prosecutors going after Gatien to drop Alig as a witness. Though each of their original witnesses had been compromised, the US attorneys proceeded anyway. In his memoir, Peter Gatien treats Alig, a person who had agreed to help prosecutors send him to jail, with little charity.

"I originally signed Michael on because he'd attended Manhattan's Fashion Institute of Technology, and FIT served as a locus for the young, hip, and creative," Gatien writes. "FIT students salted the Limelight crowd with a bit of flamboyance and color. I liked Alig well enough, but most of the time he was like a gnat buzzing around my head, asking for favors, claiming my attention. He was born to push people's buttons, and he shared that characteristic with a lot of people on the club scene. . . .

"Not a single element of the crime took place anywhere near Limelight. But rumors swirled, as rumors will. That I employed Angel to supply my clubs with drugs (nope). That he was killed in Limelight's basement (of course not). That I ordered the hit (no, no, no). The stories were wild, and eventually the incident came to symbolize the druggy decadence that supposedly infested New York's nightlife at the time. . . .

"Yes, absolutely, there were drugs being consumed in my clubs. But there were drugs being consumed pretty much everywhere else in the known universe. Any claims—and there were many—that I employed "house dealers" to supply them to club-goers was fantasy, a macabre straight-world vision of what a downtown club was like. . . .

"Through the year and a half that I waited for my case to come to trial, I gradually realized that the government doesn't play fair. In my case, at least, the US Attorney's Office had embarked on a crusade to end my life. . . . The prosecutors were out for blood. I tried to think of reasons why this might be so. The only answer I could come up with was that Rudy Giuliani was invested in this legal assault, and that it wouldn't stop until it landed me behind bars."[34]

Gatien was acquitted of all charges in February 1998. But that wasn't the end of his trouble. Over the following years, New York regulators threw everything they had at the club owner and his venues. He would get shut down over and over again, sometimes for months at a time. "It was methodical," DJ Romain said. "Like 'We're hitting that. Now we're shutting down that. Now that.' Till all the big clubs were gone."

Charges of tax evasion finally stuck. Gatien claims to have kept scrupulous books. But tracking roughly fifty million dollars in all-cash receipts over five years would be onerous for any accountant. In the end, the State of New York found he hadn't paid tax on six hundred thousand dollars, just over 1 percent of his gross profits. Regulators used this excuse to deport Gatien back to Canada.

"Throughout the process, I had become reacquainted with a grim truth: if the government ever decides to take you down, you are definitely going down, because the government will find a way," Gatien writes. "Especially if you slip through the clutches of someone like Rudy Giuliani, you can rest assured he'll come back to get you. Giuliani wound up standing beside Donald Trump as the president's personal lawyer, pronouncing the immortal line, 'Truth isn't truth.'"[35]

In the end, Giuliani's vendetta to improve the quality of life in New York resulted in near-fatal damage to New York nightlife. From small venues to institutions like Tunnel and The Limelight, DJs, hip hop acts, and house artists found fewer and fewer opportunities to play. Clubbers and audiences, in turn, had to find other sources of diversion.

"Giuliani killed everything," DJ Keoki said. "He went after the gay scene. He went after the freaky clubs. He went after the drugs. A cigarette law came in where you couldn't smoke inside or the club would get fined $100 and you would get fined $100 yourself. He was the worst.

"You used to be able to go to a club and talk to anybody. You could hang out with a trans person, a prep, a freak. Anybody could be anybody. And everybody could have a good time. All that was taken away."

"I started likening NYC to the town in *Footloose*, where dancing was illegal!" writes author and longtime *Village Voice* columnist Michael Musto. "Eighties clubs like Area had been focused on art, performance, and dance, but now, sitting down and paying way too much for a drink was considered the height of expression."[36]

Giuliani fundamentally transformed New York City. The panhandlers were gone. The Times Square peep shows were gone. When his second term ended in 2001, New York's treasured clubs were gone too.

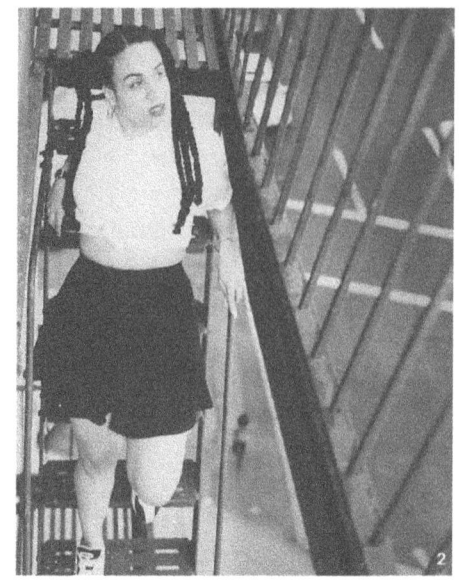

1. Hippie Torrales, New Jersey DJ legend *(courtesy of Donna Ward)*. **2.** Diamond Genung, DJ Disciple's 91.5 secretary poses on a Brooklyn stairwell, 1989 *(courtesy of Diamond Genung)*. **3.** The Mayor's Social Club Inspection Task Force *(courtesy of Louis 'Loose' Kee)*. **4.** Roman Ricardo at Tunnel, 1987 *(courtesy of Roman Ricardo)*. **5.** Leonard Gabbidon at the Syracuse Greek Fest, 1989 *(courtesy of Leonard Gabbidon)*.

THE UNDERGROUND

Before the Giuliani era, dance music thrived in 1980s New York clubland. As it grew, it decamped from fixed, brick-and-mortar locations. Party posters decorated storefronts, telephone poles, and message boards advertising ad hoc, unlicensed parties. These events went down in basements, in vacant apartments, and in spaces that would otherwise remain empty at night. House music first went underground because of the value proposition. You didn't need an expensive monthly lease at a venue to throw a party. You really only needed a spot to use for a few hours on a given night. Plus promoters, security, a sound system, and a DJ.

One party grew quickly in popularity through the mid- and late 1980s. Disciple first got in touch with this scene via a Manhattan club called The Space. He was investigating the party at the suggestion of his friend Sabrina, a certified house head who intimately knew the downtown scene. At the bar, Disciple met a man named David Camacho, also known as DJ Camacho. He had been spinning for over a decade out of his home base in New Jersey. His legendary Wild Pitch parties, which he threw with fellow promoter Greg Daye and others, were in full swing. Camacho had heard Disciple's radio show and told him he should come out to one of his events. It would be a relationship that would last decades.

Disciple kept an eye out for Wild Pitch party flyers and began attending religiously. These events bridged the gap between the older classics and the newer styles. While DJs often catered to the Paradise Garage crowd, they were also encouraged to break the mold and bring new flavors and mix techniques to the dance floor. Camacho himself exemplified this spirit. While he pushed New York's emerging house labels, he inflected his sets with signature 1970s deep cuts. He was inspired by his use of disco classics. In the mid-1980s, disco had been out for years. But with careful track selection, Camacho brought a unique injection of energy into his sets with these records. Besides these classics, Camacho picked out a mixture of music that Disciple was playing on the radio and blended in Garage classics. The two DJs started trading vinyl, and Disciple found himself pulling more disco into his repertoire. Camacho exposed Disciple to artists coming out of New Jersey, while Disciple gave him material from fellow producers in New York that he'd hardly heard of.

At Wild Pitch, Disciple watched and learned as he saw numerous DJs bring their own style and musical vibe to new depths. True, the party was initially a side show compared to established venues. But it and other underground parties soon became the best places to hear cutting-edge house music. They helped ensure that the genre survived in a city that was being split apart by AIDS, the crack cocaine epidemic, and a series of mayors that wanted to stamp out certain forms of nightlife altogether.

Ex–Garage members, college kids (including Disciple and his friends at Baruch) who were just coming online, and emerging DJs struggling to gain consistent work found their footing on the Wild Pitch dance floor. A party that moved around Manhattan through clubs and DIY spaces, Wild Pitch went down just about every Friday (and many Saturdays) from the mid-1980s well into the late 1990s. Not only did it bring together a diverse mix of New Yorkers unified by the common denominator of emerging dance music, but it also cemented a spirit of musical fusion and acceptance at a time when scenes and genres were splintering.

On a given night, you might catch Bobby Konders' dancehall mixes, fresh house from Nick Jones and Timmy Richardson, DJ Camacho's disco throwbacks, the gospel-inflected sets from DJ Disciple, or the legendary beats of Larry Levan, Tony Humphries, Louie Vega, David Morales, and Francois K. The party also hosted numerous live performances from house legends like Fingers Inc., Robert Owens, and Aly-Us.

Notorious New York dancers Voodoo Ray, Marjory Smarth, and Monique Brooks would work the door, then carry the party on to 10:00 AM the next day. Behind it all was promoter Greg Daye, whose commitment to New York dance music was unwavering.

It all started with a group of friends from Brooklyn cutting their teeth, throwing their own events. Patrick Lafontant, Trevor Biggs, Ernest Manigo, Mark Blagrove, and Greg Daye all went to school at South Shore High School in Canarsie. They'd cobble together a sound system, print some flyers, and get busy promoting. They'd co-opt a friend's house, a gymnasium, or if nothing else was available, Lafontant's basement.

Randy Anderson, who went on to work at Downstairs Records, came up in the scene. He used to play baseball against a young Tony Humphries.

"Pat's basement was amazing," Anderson said. "It was like the club Tunnel in Manhattan. It was dark, and you didn't know where it ended. It just kept going. But we set up the party so it would be like the Paradise Garage."

Promoting under the name Just Us, Lafontant would design the flyers and handle distribution, Biggs took care of the money, and Daye booked the DJs. Then, on the night of the party, it was all hands on deck. When there was a gap in DJ sets or someone dropped out, Lafontant would fill in behind the boards.

They started branching out in the early 1980s. Daye got a job working the door at Danceteria for Soul Boy Sundays, an outfit that included Rocco, Steven Lewis, and Collin and Courtney Williams. Here, Daye learned some invaluable lessons.

"They taught me about consistency," Daye said. "They would say how everyone can't get in, this party isn't for everyone. To this day, I'm still the same guy. No baseball caps and no pants hanging off your ass. They hated me at the front door. They hated, hated, hated me. 'You're a racist, da da da.' I'm like, 'So what? You're still not getting in.'"

The Just Us and Soul Boys team soon joined forces. At the time, Nick Jones was DJing at a club called Lovelight and working at the record shop Hi-Tech Music during the day. He got to know future collaborators like Daye, Bobby Konders, David Camacho, Timmy Richardson, and a stampede of other New York DJs because they would come in to buy records.

"Greg was one of my customers in the record store," said Nick Jones. "He would come buy records, laugh, have a good time, and then we'd go out to different clubs together. Then, David Camacho was DJing at a club called The Space. It was somewhere in the 20s on the west side. We wanted to bring him on. He gladly accepted and brought his crowd."

At first, this group was heavy on commitment but light on entrepreneurial savvy. They operated as promoters for their own party at various venues and learned the business by doing the business. Their relationship with venue owners often turned oppositional, and many needed just a hint of an excuse to find new promoters. In answer, the crew made sure they had the lights dimmed and the music going every weekend. "We didn't know how to market ourselves back then," Daye said. "We just made sure we were doing a party every Friday, otherwise these guys would throw us out. It was us against the owners. And the owners learned the hard way."

That hard work soon paid off. Before long, the parties drew an audience a few hundred strong on a given night. One weekend, a label known as Wild

Pitch sponsored the event. The name stuck. "After that, people just kept calling it the Wild Pitch parties," Lafontant said.

And then, in September 1987, the dance world turned upside down: the Paradise Garage closed. Suddenly, thousands of New York's most dedicated club kids, music fans, and dance heads had to find a new place to go. Nick Jones remembers it as the end of an era and the beginning of a new chapter. "The Garage was a second home for a lot of us," Jones said. "A lot of us learned at Larry's feet. But if I'm being honest, we knew [the Garage closing] would be an opportunity. There was about to be a bunch of people who needed to find a new home to go party at."

"When the Garage closed, we were right there," Daye said. "We didn't miss a beat."

In the aftermath, Wild Pitch gained new audiences, promoters, and DJs. Daye and his team cast a wide net. One new addition had a popular mix show on 107.5 FM WBLS. "They hollered at me and said, 'Come DJ,'" said Bobby Konders. "We became friends."

With the addition of DJ Timmy Richardson (TOT [The Other Timmy besides Regisford]), the core group was set. A classic night would feature some combination of Timmy Richardson, Bobby Konders, David Camacho, and Nick Jones, along with a wide range of guests that, as time went on, would feature New York's top DJs.

Wild Pitch parties went down in lofts, studios, and other DIY spaces around Manhattan. Occasionally the event would move to a club like Trax/Kilimanjaro, the Tunnel, The Loft, or The World.

But the party truly leveled up when the organizers made contact with a dance studio located at 626 Broadway just north of Houston. Almost always vacant on a Friday or Saturday night, the studio became the go-to Wild Pitch location. Besides an electrical and plumbing system that were up to code, the studio had two large rooms. Daye, Biggs, and Lafontant began experimenting. They started throwing together a second sound system and hosting two DJs playing different styles at the same time.

"All these clubs like Danceteria, they were all one room," Daye said. "We had too many great DJs. We needed two rooms. Patrick and Bobby's room alone would have 500 or 600 people. And we'd have 800 to 1,000 in the main room. We couldn't even open up without that capacity."

In terms of music, Larry Levan had set the bar at the Garage. Wild Pitch DJs set out to push it further. And Wild Pitch had one thing going for it that the Garage never had: Bobby Konders. "Back then, reggae wasn't implemented in the city yet," said promoter Trevor Biggs. "We kind of took that off with Bobby Konders."

"Bobby was another one of my customers who'd come in to buy records at Hi-Tech Music," Jones said. "He really brought in a different perspective with the reggae he was playing. We cultivated that."

"I was a DJ who played everything," Konders said. "I was very much into the house and the deep house of that era: Larry Heard, Marshall Jefferson, the stuff coming out of Jersey. . . . And then I got into the studio and started to produce some stuff and started drawing on reggae. I fused the two together."

Konders wasn't the only one innovating. Camacho, TOT, and Jones fostered an "anything goes" mentality that ensured that no Wild Pitch party would be like any other.

"Camacho was one of the greatest underrated DJs ever. *Ever*. He could mix records like you've never heard," Daye said. "Him and Nick. On the boards, mind you—just pitch up three and pitch down three. It wasn't like the [Technics] 1200s. You had very little wiggle room. I just wanted people I knew to produce their own night. Like, look at the crowd, see what's going on, and write them a script."

"Today, you have these lineups of DJs and they're all playing the same music," said Timmy Richardson. "It kind of doesn't make any sense. But we had three DJs with a purpose. The first guy was breaking the new music. The second guy was playing the reggae or something different. And the third one was coming in with the classics. I didn't know of anybody else that was doing that."

With the notable exception of the Paradise Garage, this marked a break from the status quo. Whether it was DJs, radio shows, or clubs, many at the time sought to cultivate a specific audience by playing a specific genre of music. As Bobby Konders remembers things, Wild Pitch had a different common denominator.

"The trendy clubs that were picking and choosing people, it was pretty much just one format of music," Konders said. "But Wild Pitch was an eccentric party. It drew a very music- and dancer-oriented crowd. Whatever the DJs brought to the table—the idea was to keep people dancing."

That spirit came straight from the Garage and got elevated at Wild Pitch.

"If you know what you're doing, you can get the crowd to dance to anything or like anything," Timmy Richardson said. "That goes back to Larry Levan who *made* you like records. We would have a goal every week of breaking two or three new songs. Sometimes that meant continuously playing them."

"That's the thing that Timmy, Camacho, and Nick would do," Daye said. "You don't have to play the record only once a night. They used to play a record ten times in a night. I remember once I wanted to kill Larry [Levan]. He was in there playing 'Karma Chameleon' like eight times in a row. Like enough Boy George, Larry."

But Wild Pitch didn't want to simply copy the Garage. The party was just as appealing to college students and kids who were too young to spend a night at 84 King Street. Promoters like Frank Thomas, who had a large undergraduate network, became indispensable.

"There were a lot of Garage heads who would not go anywhere else," said Nick Jones. "We wanted that audience. But we also realized, hey, let's bring in and cultivate some of these younger kids, these younger college students. So we start promoting heavy at colleges. We had a real mixture. It was about trying to take the younger people into what the Garage was and also present to them the new music of that day. Even what David Mancuso did at the Loft—we would mix that all together.

"It grew. The kids were hungry. The Garage was gone, and they couldn't get into some of the other clubs because they were too young. Each week, it grew and grew."

Kim Santoro, who often worked coat check at Wild Pitch, remembers an eclectic cast of characters walking through the door. "There would be all walks of life all under the same roof: homeboys, Bboys, doctors, lawyers, pornstars, mothers, queens, junkies, lords. They were all out for the music. In the dark, they'd just be shadows of movement," Santoro said.

"At 7:00 AM in the morning, the audience would still be dancing with the same energy, bringing out tambourines, pouring baby powder on the floor, and listening to great classics from the Paradise Garage," Disciple said. "Many musicians, DJs, music composers, and producers have had connections with Wild Pitch."

There was one factor that did separate this party from the standard set by the Garage. It was accessible. The Garage required membership for entry, in part, to protect its close-knit LGBTQ+ community at a time when being out was not feasible for many of its members. For partially the same reasons, David Mancuso's The Loft was invitation-only for much of its lifetime. Maybe it was the mobile nature of Wild Pitch. Maybe it was a sign of changing times. But open and closeted queer partygoers attended Wild Pitch in large numbers.

"We had a very mixed crowd—straight, gay, Black, white, Hispanic, it didn't matter," Biggs said. "It was about the music. You could hear that. At Wild Pitch, there were two types of music: good music and bad music. As long as you were moving the crowd, who cares? It didn't really matter. People felt safe there."

Outside Wild Pitch doors, the only thing you needed to show was a willingness to rise to the vibe. "Our door guys weren't looking at you to see if you had money to spend," Lafontant said. "They were like, 'Ok, you look like you're going to make the party even better, come on in.'"

There was another complicating factor: long lines outside of non-venue New York spaces were sure to raise the eyebrows of skeptical onlookers. "We had to get the crowd off the street as fast as possible," Biggs said. "Just in case."

There was one thing, however, that was strictly forbidden at Wild Pitch: overplayed music produced by corporate labels.

"People who went to the Choice and Wild Pitch parties didn't want to hear commercial music," Disciple said. "Dancers attending these parties used acrobatics, tap-dancing, gymnastics, Latin and African dance, all molded into one gyrating rainbow. If you didn't play what they wanted to hear, they would let you know."

"Similar to how we see some people in love with the speakers, or just there to drink and hang out, and that's what they speak about 'being free in the music, and loving themselves,'" said dancer Brian "Footwork" Green. "We have those that talk about loving to dance with the girls or boys and always speak about 'connecting/communicating.'

"We have those that love to have some instrument in their hands and play or sing with a song while dancing, and their conversation will be about what the music will do to them. Then we have those that love to make circles or circles form around them, and they are highlighted parts of the club night that all remember and talk about after the clubs. They speak of just 'getting down, getting at, and/or exchanging with' other dancers in the culture. All in the club are an important part of the club experience."

More than a few celebrities were spotted at Wild Pitch over the years. A short list of semi-regulars includes Jennifer Lopez, Rosie Perez, Wesley Snipes, Drena De Niro, and Heather Hunter.

"It wasn't a big deal," Timmy Richardson said. "Everybody just wanted to go inside the party and dance."

"I remember smoking with the Fab Five, John F. Kennedy Jr., and Brooke Shields at some high school gymnasium. It was a high school in the Village," Daye recalls.

"Mike Tyson came up to me to get a bottle of champagne," Biggs said. "I was like, 'I got you two already, that's enough.'"

"But for the most part, they would just blend in with the crowd," Lafontant said. "Back then, nobody really cared. Most people were just interested in hanging out and having a good time."

This attitude started at the door, which was supervised by some of New York's most legendary dancers, promoters, and personalities. Voodoo Ray, Marjory Smarth, Monique Brooks, Christopher Bell, David Cole, David Ian Xtravanganza, Frank Thomas, Ejoe Wilson, and many others who would achieve fame in the dance world once presided over the Wild Pitch entrance. Inside, they mixed emerging dance styles like jacking, popping, locking, breaking, lofting, house, and voguing. The scene of dancers and promoters often paralleled that of DJs.

"I saw [Voodoo] Ray and Josie [his sister] in the clubs sometimes with a few of his boys from uptown but we didn't speak," said Frank Thomas. "I was already known in the clubs by then, but I knew from my seven-day-a-week club hopping that Ray was out there at spots too. When Marjory and I started dating, it was she who actually introduced him to me and we just hit it off. I introduced him to all the various circles I was chilling with, and he became part of the collective. Marjory later brought Ejoe [Wilson] into the scene as well as most of the known 'house/teacher' dancers. I knew them from their beginning days solely because of Marjory. She gained quite a name for herself and then went on to create her own lane."

Just as for DJs, underground parties kept the scene alive for dancers. And it opened up other opportunities for them to make a living. Music video directors often recruited at Wild Pitch. And, just like DJs, New York dancers would soon become a major export for the rest of the world.

"Music videos were a new thing, and it was a way for people around the world to see dancers," said dancer Brian "Footwork" Green. "When it came to hip hop, house, new jack swing, and other music genre videos, the dancers were many and plenty. Marjory and Chris 'Shaik' Mathis were noted faces in various music videos in the 1980s and 1990s. They went back and forth with their styles from hip hop to house.

"Voodoo Ray's name really expanded when he joined Basil at Kilimanjaro. Then he and Ejoe went into teaching house dancing here and overseas before everyone else, if I recall correctly. Ejoe would become an iconic house dancer and teacher internationally. Ray introduced me to Rosie Perez over several nights and got me in a video she was choreographing. It wound up being in the Diana Ross 'Working Overtime' video in 1988. Voodoo was supposed to be in the video with me but was unable to make it, which would have been the first video he and I did together."

"There was just a lot of love," Daye said. "Especially between the DJs. At block parties, it used to be that DJs would black out the labels so nobody could see the name of the record they were playing, and all that nonsense. We were like, 'Get out of here. We're trying to make the party flow.'"

At Wild Pitch, like countless parties before and since, the night would be made by playing the perfect record at the perfect time. Greg Daye remembers how DJs would bring libraries of vinyl to draw from, just to have the right choice when the moment called for it.

"Camacho couldn't go anywhere without 15 crates of records," Daye said. "Every record we had in there was playable, but the real DJs knew the time to put the record on because they knew the crowd. After that, you've got them hooked, and you can play anything. After you play that one right record, you got 'em hooked."

Things came full circle when Larry Levan himself started showing up. For a time in the late 1980s, he became a semi-regular Wild Pitch DJ. "He was so sharp with setting up the sound," Lafontant said. "He'd put everything together

Courtesy of Patrick Lafontant.

and listen. After a minute, he'd point to some units and be like, 'These speakers right here are out of phase.'"

Numerous other DJs at the top of their game came on at Wild Pitch. Besides those mentioned so far, alumni include David Morales, Louie Vega, Francois K, Tony Humphries, Timmy Regisford, Tee Scott, Joey Llanos, Victor Rosado, Basil, Clark Kent, Kenny Carpenter, Naeem Johnson, Manski, French, and more.

AROUND THE WORLD

On November 20, 1989, Disciple was hanging with his friend Ralph when he got a call from Greg Daye and DJ Camacho. They wanted to know if he would spin at a Wild Pitch event. A few days later, Disciple stood behind the decks at a club called The World on the Lower East Side. It was snowing heavily that night, and the weather affected the sound system on the main floor upstairs.

"It was snowing like crazy," Biggs said. "We was like, 'Damn we're losing money tonight. Nobody's coming.' Then I looked outside the window, and the line was around the corner. I was like, 'Wow.' And the World was pretty much falling apart, too. Nothing was correct in that place. We just made do."

Daye kept everyone on the ground level while things were sorted out. When the sound system came online, everyone rushed upstairs. Disciple, Camacho, and Bobby Konders were on the bill. Disciple opened with a set of emerging and unreleased house.

"My nerves were going crazy before my set," Disciple said. "This wasn't the college circuit. This wasn't radio. This was a room full of dedicated clubbers who all had strong opinions about what records should and should not be played. They were used to hearing most of the best DJs in the world at the time play. I was shaking as I brought my milk crate full of 45s up to the booth. I put them down, looked at the setup, and thanked God to find a straightforward combo of turntables, EQ, and other basic features."

As Daye remembers it, Disciple came in hot. "Disciple helped change house music to a faster, more acceptable beat here in New York," Daye said. "When we would normally be playing downbeat, he would be up at 125 [beats per minute] at like 10:00 PM. I thought he was going to kill the crowd. But I was amazed at how he handled things. He was so mature."

Despite his nerves, Disciple kept the crowd moving—and wanting more—until he made the handoff to Konders hours later. Disciple had earned his spot in the house music underground. Much more was in store for the young house DJ.

BACK IN PLAY

Besides younger DJs like Disciple, Wild Pitch hired numerous jocks and promoters who had been out of the game.

"We brought a lot of guys out of retirement," Daye said. "Kenny Carpenter wasn't doing anything. He was lost in the source. Mike Stone—nothing. Charles Jackson—nothing. Tee Scott—I went to the roller rink where he was playing and said, 'Come on, we're getting up out of here.' He was like, 'I've got to pay rent, Greg.' So I said, 'Watch this.' I got him like $1,000 for his first gig. I said, 'Is that enough for the rent?' He just nodded and said, 'Yup, that's enough.'"

"Greg Daye, he's one of the ones who always gave the underdog a chance," said Farragut resident and DJ Kenny Carpenter. "He brought me in when no one else wanted me. I was washed out, and he said come down here and play. He gave a lot of people a break who otherwise wouldn't have had one."

Despite their growing success, a history of attracting A-list DJs, and the blessing from Levan himself, Wild Pitch wasn't without its hiccups. As an all-cash business, the crew had their fair share of encounters with various

Courtesy of Patrick Lafontant.

organizations. "Everyone had their hands out," Biggs said. "A guy would come in. He would want to know who was running the party. So we would have to give him an envelope. Then he would go on his way."

Once, the elevator got stuck while they were bringing up the sound system. Another time, they got busted for throwing a party in a building that was under construction. There would be occasional scuffles at the door, run-ins with the law, or trouble with gangs. The party wasn't immune from violence, beefing, and other drama.

"I was asked to join Wild Pitch by Monique Brooks way before I actually did," Frank Thomas said. "The reason was because I brought some of my people there, to 626 Broadway, and my boy Ozzie was stabbed in the stairwell. There were delays in getting him help. That put me off for a time. Eventually Monique got us to powwow. We joined up and made Wild Pitch the dopest gypsy party in NYC."

Sometimes the cops would show up and demand to know what was going on. The founders remember, somehow, being able to talk themselves out of most situations.

"We'd tell them we were shooting a video," Timmy Richardson said. "Sometimes it worked. I couldn't believe it. We'd have 1,500 people in there. Nothing legally ever happened to us. They didn't know about our parties, even though you could see a line going down the block."

"We wasn't stable so it was hard to catch up with us," Biggs said. "A lot of places where we were looked like office buildings. They wouldn't think anything of it."

"We had a party or two that was shut down," said Nick Jones. "Once, we had to change locations during the night. I was scheduled to DJ at a place in Midtown. I get to the spot, and we had one of our guys standing out front. He said, 'Nick, we had to move the party downtown.' I go, 'Oh god, nobody's going to be here.' I pick up all my records, head downtown, and there's like 2,000 kids partying. The audience knew the party was mobile. They expected that. So when we had to move locations, they were all set to move with us."

Throughout the late 1980s and early 1990s, hip hop was taking off and becoming a commercial success. Many believe that house suffered as a result. But Wild Pitch and other parties seemed to be immune to the trend. They kept the spirit of dance music alive.

"When hip hop got good, house changed," said Lafontant. "It's almost like it went even more underground. Most of the clubs started playing hip hop. It was a shift. The reggae changed too. And most people started moving away from both. Back then, rap was really good. It was tough competing against that."

"Things started to change around 1991 or 1992," Bobby Konders said. "Dance music got less popular. Crack was running back then. Drugs was running, money was running. A lot of the kids was going more toward hip hop."

"The underground scene was what kept everything going," Richardson said. "There was no club like the Garage that everyone was going to except for stuff like Wild Pitch."

Almost throughout, Wild Pitch was supported by Daye, Biggs, Lafontant, Jones, Richardson, Camacho, and others involved at a huge expense of time, money, and effort.

"I refused to let it die," Daye said. "I would give my whole paycheck. I was dating Monique [Brooks] at the time, and she'd give her whole paycheck too. That's enough to cover security, sound, and the DJs. I'd give each DJ like $250, $300. Everybody got paid. Everybody. Down to the people who were cleaning up. Whatever we made, we'd split. There were no fixed salaries, I couldn't afford it. I didn't know how the night was going to turn out. But God let us sustain. We were able to do a party every Friday and sometimes on Saturdays. I'd have people that would come to me and say, 'Man I need help with my rent,' or 'My girl is pregnant, we need to get an abortion.' I'd say, 'Come on, man, I'll get you half.'

"It was good times. It was all part of the struggle. Being independent versus owning a club, I'd take being independent any day."

As house and dance music declined at clubs, the DJs they previously employed found fewer and fewer opportunities to play. The underground scene became a lifeline.

"Back then, a lot of the DJs weren't playing a lot of clubs," Lafontant said. "A lot of them were making their names through the Wild Pitch parties. It was a great place to blow up. There were a lot of DJs who were with us before they got famous. We were that step that took them to the next level. After us, they were going to Japan, going to Europe."

The Just Us team was not alone in the mobile party landscape. House Nation, Save the Robots, Cafe con Leche, and others continued to sate the appetites of the Garage heads, the college kids, and everyone in between.

THE CHOICE

In the mid-1980s two New York dance heads shared a dream. Over and over in their free time, Richard Vasquez and his partner Greg Myers spoke about opening up their own club, throwing Saturday night parties, and working as promoters and resident DJs. And before long, that opportunity fell right into their laps.

Richard Vasquez had cemented a career as a successful graphic designer for some of New York's preeminent publications. Music and clubbing were among his primary afterwork pursuits. Soon, they would lead him, along with Myers and the former head of security at the Garage Joey Llanos, to take over and revamp David Mancuso's venue The Loft. Renamed The Choice, over the coming years, house legends like Robert Owens, Frankie Knuckles, David Morales, and Victor Rosado held tenures at Vasquez's Saturday events. In the short remaining years of his life, Larry Levan would also help redesign the sound system and take command of the decks.

Vazquez lived in a three-story loft—that happened to also have an excellent sound system—on 2nd in the Bowery. Like the Wild Pitch team, he made his entry into nightlife bootstrapping his own resources. "The first party that I threw at my place, they had to close off the street," Vasquez said. "It spilled out in both directions toward Second Avenue and Bowery. The party started on Saturday night, and it lasted till Monday morning. It was just a fantastic time."

This was in the mid-1980s. He continued to work his day job and make ventures into the party scene. At one point in 1987, Vasquez was recruited to join a team that was going to start a dance club in New Orleans. "I had an attorney," Vasquez said. "I had one of the most successful hairdressers in New Orleans involved, and his partner also. And I started doing parties there every couple of months to interest investors."

Greg Myers, meanwhile, had come up in high school with Larry Levan, and the two continued to collaborate into adulthood. Right before the Paradise Garage closed, Vasquez got word from him that David Mancuso, who operated The Loft, was looking for an out. "I heard that Mancuso wasn't doing too well and that there might be an opportunity for me to take over the space and give David a break," Vasquez said. "After that, I lost my interest in doing something in New Orleans."

But while Vasquez was ready to take over The Loft, The Loft was not exactly ready to be taken over. It had fallen far into disrepair. "The space was rundown," Vasquez said. "It was dirty. You couldn't clean it. Rats were running all over the place as soon as the club closed."

More importantly, the once-legendary sound system needed a serious overhaul. Vasquez, with the guidance and expertise of Larry Levan, invested significant resources to correct that. That news alone—the revamped quality of The Choice's sound system—began driving dance heads back to the venue.

"The sound system was really all I had to offer," Vasquez said. "We had the most incredible sound system after the Garage closed. There was no other club that had one like it. Larry [Levan] helped me with that. David helped me with that. David told me about tweeter arrays. For a while, Larry kind of drifted around looking for his own place. But he wound up spending most of his time at The Choice."

Not long after the Garage closed, therefore, ex-members had another club to go to that still put the music as the top priority. And with those priorities in order, a number of prominent New York DJs, including Larry Levan himself, signed on to play. Joey Llanos, who ran security at the Garage, agreed to oversee the door. He went on to join the DJ roster as well. The success of The Choice, however, was bittersweet.

"At this point, Gregory was very quickly being taken out by the AIDS virus," Vasquez said. "He only got to play one or two times. He suggested that I have Joey Llanos do the security. He did great job. But it wasn't long before Larry wanted him to play as well. So he was one of the openers for Larry and David, who was one of the openers for Larry."

Vasquez, like the Wild Pitch team and so many others, remembers Levan meticulously analyzing and calibrating the sound system. "Larry would spend a lot of time replacing speakers or putting them in various places, balancing things out," Vasquez said. "He helped me enormously to develop that sound system. That's all we had to offer—the sound system and the music."

In terms of the music, Vasquez knew (and owned) the Garage classics as well as the next clubber. And like so many dance heads, he had relationships with the good folks at Downtown Records and Vinylmania.

"The people at Vinylmania always had a pack of records for me whenever I came in," Vasquez said. "They saved them specifically for me because they would be at my party later that week and wanted to hear them on The Choice sound system. The Loft vibe had featured a lot of 1970s music. But I was also very taken by the Chicago house that Larry was playing. And house was coming out of other places as well. A lot of records were coming from the United Kingdom and from Italy. So I started playing a lot of that stuff too."

DISCIPLE'S CHOICE

By 1990, the party at The Choice had expanded to Fridays and Thursdays and drew in capacity crowds. Disciple caught Larry Levan there for the second time and began attending regularly.

"My friend Sabrina had been telling me that The Choice was where all the best dancers go, and that I'd be a great fit for the venue," Disciple said. "It was 4:00 AM and the DJ booth was center stage with a juice bar behind it. Levan was breaking two records I'd never heard, and the crowd was jumping off the walls. Like a DJ booth groupie, I asked Larry what he was playing. It would be two records that would become a signature staple of my radio show: 'I Promise' by Mark Rogers and 'Bang Bang, You're Mine' by Bang the Party."

While groups like Fingers Inc. were combining soul and R&B vocals with house beats, Bang the Party marked London's response. The group was formed by English DJ Kid Batchelor and Keith Franklin, otherwise known as DJ KCC. They were one of the first UK acts to release house records. Disciple found that playing these records would pull him to the side of Wild Pitch and The Choice's music. "When Levan played them, they were like splashes of color on a landscape," Disciple said. "But I had to get creative to work them in."

Disciple knew about some of the Garage classics from Camacho and others, but he didn't necessarily have the records to spin. At the end of the day, DJs had to keep the audience dancing far into the morning, and pushing deep cuts or unreleased tracks in the early morning was a serious gamble. Many committed dance heads judged DJs primarily on what they played hours into their set.

"I often felt like I didn't have the chops to keep up," Disciple said. All the same, he was eager for a chance to take the decks. Richard Vasquez knew Disciple from Refuge Temple, and he was a fan of *Best Kept Secret*. That resume was enough to start the conversation. But at the same time, up-and-coming boxers don't want to sign on for a fight where they'll get knocked out in the first round. Disciple knew what it took to carry off a successful night at a venue like The Choice. And he knew that it would stretch his abilities.

Once again, Farragut neighbor DJ Debonair came to the rescue. He handed Disciple numerous records from his own collection that used to get heavy play at the Garage. These, coupled with the fresh promos he received for radio play from the labels, packed out his repertoire and gave his sets a new depth. Shortly after, Disciple was chosen to alternate with Larry Levan at the Choice beginning in early 1990. DJ Basil joined them later on.

The Choice represented Disciple's biggest challenge to date. The crowd was even more discerning than Wild Pitch. Like Daye's parties, the venue pushed new music, but its audience also loved the dance classics. On top of this, Vasquez's new sound system was more complicated than anything Disciple had used before in a live context. It had a five-band EQ isolator and connected to the speaker and amp outputs via a three-way crossover.

"I was having a hard time using it to its fullest potential," Disciple said. "I got a personal tutorial from Levan on how to work it on my first night, but I was still extremely nervous I would mess up. I was terrified I was going to do something wrong that would make me look bad. Frankie Knuckles, who I often saw at the venue, made it look easy, but I kept hearing him in my head saying, 'You're good Disciple, but you got a ways to go.'"

When Disciple went live his first night at The Choice, he managed to avoid any obvious mistakes. But the crowd kept him guessing his entire set.

"My set at The World might have started out a little rocky, but a few records in, I knew I had won the crowd over, and I was in command," he said. "That never happened at The Choice. Most of the audience at the Choice showed up after midnight. If they didn't stay past 4:00 AM, something was wrong. They wanted music that would keep them going. The more parties I went to and played, the more I realized that records have different impacts based on what time they're played at. What works well to kick a set off at 11:00 PM will send dancers scattering at 2:00 AM.

"It was tough knowing where to go musically. There were also tensions with other DJs, who felt that I was playing out of my league. The atmosphere in the room made me sense that part of the audience wanted to hear music coming from the Garage, while others appreciated the other styles of house I was pushing. At 7:00 AM, I counted myself fortunate to gain any new fans. I luckily had a small but growing fan base of kids from college that heard me before and witnessed me graduate to another level. They were way more loyal and supportive."

In the end, Disciple left The Choice the next morning shivering in the cold with sweat from a nervous night drying, and satisfied. He had held his own at The Choice on a night where he shared the bill with none other than Larry Levan. The former Paradise Garage DJ continued to play at Wild Pitch and The Choice. But his time was running short.

On November 8, 1992, *The New York Times* reported that "Larry Levan, a disk jockey, producer and remixer who changed the sound of dance music, died on Sunday at Beth Israel Medical Center. He was 38 years old, and a resident of New York City."[1]

While, for a time, Levan had spiraled out of New York clubs at the hands of drug use, he'd recently gotten clean and toured Japan. It had seemed like he was making a comeback. His death shook the New York club community. Sound engineers had designed systems with Levan in mind. Promoters had cast parties in the mold of Levan's Saturday Night Masses. Now, the residents of clubland were set adrift. At the same time, Larry had given the world a gift. He had shown clubland what was possible behind the decks. Many who saw him have yet to forget his magic sound to this day.

When Disciple began to play and alternate with Levan, it proved to be a windfall for the former. With each successful party came more demand. Disciple's stint at The Choice brought him into economic stability. After the show, artist Lin Que approached Disciple about taking his talent to Queens for Friday nights at Club Mysteries at 8925 Merrick Boulevard. The venue became another stable venture for Disciple, while Wild Pitch kept him on as a monthly resident.

Que also soon became affiliated with the hip hop group X-Clan and the Blackwatch Movement. Under the name Isis, she released her album *Rebel Soul* with the group. Through this work, she found out that an affiliated Queens barbershop, Nu Tribe, was looking for the right radio exposure.

Fredro Starr, the resident barber, cut the hair of rap artists like Rakim, Jam Master Jay, and Kool G Rap. After a few conversations between Que, her business partner, and Disciple, Nu Tribe decided to sponsor *Best Kept Secret*. The barbershop's business was announced every thirty minutes while on the air. The place would be packed on Saturdays when Disciple dropped in to collect payment. Fredro was known for his designs, as was his cousin, fellow barber, and future Onyx member Sticky Fingerz.

Disciple made another ally in Fantasy (also known as Marco Berry). He was a singer-songwriter turned promoter who had success with the single "The Saga of Begging Billie." Having met Disciple at a Hunter College party, Fantasy started hiring Wild Pitch DJs for his events.

He promoted with his partner Nizer Saunders under the name Blackball. Disciple's first venture with them came later that summer when he played Greekfest at Jones Beach. He also spun later that night at the afterparty at Marquee (547 West 21st Street). The success of Greekfest and the afterparty helped build Blackball's reputation. Blackball, in turn, rewarded their DJs with more work. Disciple started playing at the Chelsea club Octagon, where he often shared the bill with DJ Camacho. Many Blackball regulars were dancers.

"Camacho and I spoiled them with our style," Disciple said. "One night when I finished my set at a Blackball party, Fantasy decided to bring in a new DJ. The crowd sat on the dance floor in protest, booing the new DJ they didn't know."

Disciple's performances got a lot of appreciation from his core fan base in New York. Promoters started sending him out for one-offs out of the city. He played Sigma parties at other colleges and events like homecoming at Howard University in Washington, DC.

The New York club scene was crumbling. Levan had passed on. Hip hop was taking over and pushing house music out. But underground parties like Wild Pitch preserved what had been born in the 1980s and kept everyone, to some extent, employed. Disciple made a name for himself on the radio. He played a handful of New York clubs. But, like many other DJs, it wasn't until he made it in the underground scene that opportunities really began to multiply.

Thurs. Mar. 22—Basil
Fri. Mar. 23—Robert Owens
Sat. Mar. 24—Joey Llanos
Thurs. Mar. 29—DJ Disciple
Fri. Mar. 30—Victor Rosado
Sat. Mar. 31—Richard Vasquez
Thurs. Apr. 5—Basil
Fri. Apr. 6—Frankie Knuckles
Sat. Apr. 7—Joey Llanos
Thrurs. Apr. 12—DJ Disciple
Fri. Apr. 13—Larry Levan
Sat. Apr. 14—Richard Vasquez
Thurs. Apr. 19—Basil
Fri. Apr. 20—Robert Owens
Sat. Apr. 21—Joey Llanos
Thurs. Apr. 26—DJ Disciple
Fri. Apr. 27—Victor Rosado
Dance Competition Playoffs
Sat. Apr. 28—Richard Vasquez
Dance Competition Finalists
Thurs. May 3—Basil
Fri. May 4—Frankie Knuckles
Sat. May 5—Joey Llanos
Thurs. May 10—DJ Disciple
Fri. May 11—Larry Levan
Sat. May 12—Richard Vasquez
Thurs. May 17—Basil
Fri. May 18—Robert Owens
Sat. May 19—Joey Llanos
Thurs. May 24—DJ Disciple
Fri. May 25—Victor Rosado
Sat. May 26—Richard Vasquez

Come on out and sow something good.

240 EAST 3 ST • 529-0271

1. DJ David Camacho appears at Dance Ritual Christmas Party at Club Deep *(courtesy of Donna Ward)*. **2.** Voodoo Ray at Wild Pitch, 1990 *(courtesy of Kim Santoro)*. **3.** Marjory Smarth and Hector 'House Nation' at Kilimanjaro *(courtesy Kim Santoro)*. **4.** DJ Disciple at Wild Pitch *(courtesy of Louis 'Loose' Kee)*. **5.** DJ Richard Vasquez in Miami *(courtesy of Donna Ward)*. **6.** The Choice Lineup, 1990 *(courtesy of Richard Vazquez)*.

EXILE

New York house DJs in the early 1990s faced a grim situation. Clubs were closing down. Other venues that once gave them reliable employment were shifting their focus to different genres. Audiences that had once flocked to dance-based parties and mixed with diverse crowds grew tribal. They began to seek out niche nightlife that catered specifically to their own identities. House music also splintered into more distinct genres, which further divided the remaining fan base.

More broadly, New York also had taken hit after hit in the second half of the twentieth century. AIDS, crack cocaine, zero-tolerance policing, mass incarceration, and broad demographic shifts shook the city to its foundations. One might reasonably question whether it has ever recovered.

The overall situation left most house DJs with two options: seek employment elsewhere or hang up their spurs. Luckily, as house music declined in popularity in the tri-state area, it exploded in other regions of the world. Raves attracted throngs of young people elsewhere in North America and Europe. Dance culture surged in certain in holiday destinations (like the island of Ibiza), as well as in East Asia. More importantly, house music found a new global capital: the United Kingdom.

The groundwork had been laid for years. Dance culture had been alive and well in the country for decades. Northern soul and reggae still held a huge influence. DJs like Kid Batchelor and "Evil" Eddie Richards set off the acid house movement and produced hits that crossed the Atlantic in the other direction. Throughout the late 1980s, a number of Chicago house records enthralled UK listeners. "Love Can't Turn Around" by Farley "Jackmaster" Funk reached number ten on the UK singles chart in 1986. A few months later, "Jack Your Body" by Steve "Silk" Hurley held the number one spot for two weeks.

American DJs began touring the United Kingdom in the late 1980s, with Frankie Knuckles, Adonis, Marshall Jefferson, and Larry Heard paving the way in 1987.[1] In the following years, artists like Larry Levan, Tony Humphries, and many others made early forays. By the early 1990s, many New York artists, including DJ Disciple, made the majority of their earnings in exile from the city that raised them.

THE ROGER SANCHEZ CONNECTION

That isn't to say that interstate and international touring came easily. For Disciple, the opportunity came through his network of connections. The first DJ that helped him decamp was Roger Sanchez.

"For DJs, selling mixed tapes in the village was a popular thing," Disciple said. "I would set up in Washington Square Park because that's where all of the dancers from nightclubs would hang out. One day in the summer of 1990, I met Roger Sanchez while he was checking in on the promotion of his record 'Ego Trip' at Downtown Records. We were around the same age and both DJs. We ended up talking for three hours in the park that afternoon when he was done selling his music. He told me about his new release on Strictly Rhythm, and his party, which he also called Ego Trip.

"We became friends. If I walk into a record store with another DJ I don't know, we're either going to be best friends or go our separate ways when we walk out because we'd be able to check out each other's taste in music. Roger's follow-up single 'Luv Dancin' became a club hit that all the DJs played. New York had fully taken notice. He'd get tons of remix work on the back of that single. Roger would listen to my radio show, and we'd fill each other in on what tracks were hot.

"Being a main supporter of his production got us closer as fellow DJs. He would invite me to sit in on recording sessions. It was one of the first times I stepped foot in a professional studio to see how the sampling of records and the use of electronic sounds were merged. With some of the latest technology at the palm of his hands, I witnessed him take multiple tracks from artists and throw in his own spin. The label would turn around and use that as the main version of the project. I'd come down to support him and hear him play. He in turn showed up at my gigs and listened to my radio show."

Sanchez also toured extensively. One day, he called Disciple and told him about his success in San Francisco and the rave scene that was growing there.

"He asked if I was interested in playing there too," Disciple said. "At the time, the farthest I'd been out of state was for a one-off gig at Club Masquerade in Atlanta.

"San Francisco as a city has long produced an eclectic tangle of music—it was the perfect environment for the rave scene to grow. House heads and ravers were different. Raving was a way of life. It wasn't just an activity enjoyed on the weekends. Ravers were open-minded toward sex, drugs, and alternative lifestyles. Even though the scene attracted people from different walks of life, it had a strong community spirit. The club scene cared what you looked like, but raves allowed you to be yourself."

Disciple was intrigued by San Francisco for another reason. In the 1990s, four budding DJs from London had chosen the city as their home away from home. DJs Markie, Garth, Jenö, and Thomas rose to prominence with Whoosh!, their psychedelic acid house party based in East London in the late 1980s, and their shared adventures with the legendary Tonka Sound System.[2] In San Francisco, the four DJs along with promoters Alan and Trish formed the Wicked Crew, a group that came to define the West Coast dance music. They began spreading UK and underground US house music throughout the Bay Area. The hundreds of lawless loft, basement, and free outdoor parties they threw set the stage for San Francisco's rave scene.

"San Francisco was thrilling and motivational," Disciple said. "The 'authentic San Francisco sound' came out of the Full Moon parties at Baker Beach, the same place where Burning Man got going before moving to Black Rock Desert. This culture was not rooted in capitalism. In fact, ravers resisted its commercialization. But they nevertheless needed funding and recognition in order to grow. Raves provided the solution."

By the time Disciple arrived in the spring of 1992, the pump was primed—raves were taking over the Bay Area. Loaded with over-the-top futuristic themes and exquisite design, the productions looked like something out of a dream. Disciple played the one-year anniversary of two parties—ToonTown and Care Free Dancing—that went down at Club Townsend. He shared the bills with Jenö, Markie, and Nikki Rivera. The flyer for the event advertised "DJ Disciple of NYC's The Shelter Club." Promoters have never been rigorous fact-checkers.

"ToonTown ravers wore sunglasses, whistles, oversized smiley face t-shirts, glow in the dark pacifiers, boiler suits, face masks, beads, whistles, ski goggles, tie-dyed clothing, track suits, and high-waisted shorts," Disciple said. "They looked like they were from the future.

"There were no anthem records in San Francisco—just a vibe. I'm used to playing a New York house sound with a touch of New Jersey. San Francisco was a long ways from the East Coast, both physically and musically. To keep the crowd engaged, I had to avoid playing vocal house music and stick to trackier music instead. The ToonTown audience did not enjoy too many breakdowns or beat disruptions. For the first twenty minutes of my set, I struggled—and then, I figured out what they wanted to hear. It was a fun challenge.

"The tunes that won the crowd over were the Danny Tenaglia remix of 'Surrender Yourself' by Daou and 'Liberty City–Some Lovin' produced by Murk. The dancers and DJs treated me like family. After my first shows in San Francisco, I got booked for return dates.

"Returning in later years, I often played at the Spundae parties. They started as underground productions in the basement of 55 Natoma Street, where I played with Roger Sanchez, but they eventually expanded to 1015 Folsom Street. I also played parties with Pete Avilla at San Francisco's version of Sound Factory. These venues and DJs were focused on music. They created the 'West Coast sound' with psychedelic grooves you couldn't find anywhere else. The producers out West always stayed one step ahead. In San Francisco, I felt at home."

GRADUATION

Though the work was a source of income and exposure, Disciple began to ease himself out of the college party scene.

"In 1992, I left WHCS, Hunter's radio station," Disciple said. "I also played my last college party with Monty and Steve. I no longer had a taste to spin open format rap and reggae with house music. If I was to develop as an artist, I had to focus on the music.

"When the trendy nightclub Mars had changed its name to the Muse later that year, Monty and Steve teamed up with Jazzy B and I to do what would be our last party together. After playing at Jones Beach with DJ Clark Kent, I came back to Muse only to find that the venue had no needles. I had to go all the way back to Brooklyn to get them while 1,000 people were outside the venue trying to get into the party. It turned out to be a disaster, and Stan Dennis, the founder of the Jones Beach parties, never hired me back again.

"Wild Pitch did shows at The Red Zone and Trax, which changed its name to Kilimanjaro. In one of my last appearances (taking place at Red Zone), I was developing a newer sound, which was tougher and rawer than I'd ever played. During the set Roger came to the DJ booth and gave me a promo record he'd just finished for Maxi Records called 'Get Up' by Soundshaft. I played it immediately, and, immediately, I got a reaction. It was clear to me that I needed to push the newer side music and lose part of my following in the process."

WNYE also made changes. They pushed *Best Kept Secret* to a later time at 7:00 to 9:00 PM on Thursday nights. Then, in 1992, Disciple forged his most important connection yet. *DJ Magazine* showed up to a New Music Seminar party at Sound Factory Bar. They took pictures of Disciple (they already knew who he was). Then Camacho came up, leading another man behind him.

It was JP Firman, who booked Camacho in the United Kingdom. He also knew Disciple through bootleg recordings of his radio show, which had sold for years in Camden Market. He offered him a gig on the spot. In the following weeks, Disciple appeared in *DJ Magazine* for the first time. Then in September 1992, he got the follow-up call from JP to play in the United Kingdom.

THE LAKOTA, STOKES CROFT, BRISTOL

"He wanted me for a gig at a club called The Lakota in Bristol," Disciple said. "For JP, it was a test run to see what the talk was about. Six milk crates of records and freshly cut acetates from a reggae dub plate factory in Brooklyn later, I was at customs in Heathrow airport."

JP picked Disciple up from the airport. The two went straight down to the record store Vinyl Solution in Ladbroke Grove, London, to see the store's owner and DJ Mark Ravenhill. DJs Phil Asher and Noel Watson were also there.

"In the car, I noticed that the radio station Kiss 100 FM was playing house music on the radio," Disciple said. "It was shocking to hear a mix show in the middle of the day like that. I realized that, while this music was dying in New York, there was excitement for it over here."

For Ravenhill, Asher, and Watson, DJ Disciple was also a known quantity. Now that they had him before them in the flesh, they wanted to see if the mixes matched the DJ. At Vinyl Solution, they took a look through Disciple's collection of promos and acetates with amazement. They barely knew of anything he had. He pulled out a record given to him by the Arista Records office right before his flight: "It's Gonna Be A Lovely Day" by S.O.U.L. System.

"JP and Mark were blown away," Disciple said. "They started salivating thinking about the upcoming show at the Lakota. Later that night, we drove the hour and a half to Bristol from London, and arrived at the club. It was filled with a mixture of university students and clubbers. The booth towered over the crowd on a balcony section looking down over them. I was wearing a royal blue

Karl Kani two-piece outfit. When I walked into the booth, I knew it would be a good show. They just had two decks and a mixer—nothing complicated. On top of that, the sound system was incredible."

Disciple was set to play on a night that would become legendary along Stokes Croft in Bristol. Known as 1 Love on a Sat, the party would bring on UK DJs like James Savage, Mike Shawe, and Ian Wilkie.

The promoters got Disciple's name wrong that first night and originally ordered flyers advertising "DJ Disable." Once they realized their mistake, they had to print stickers with the correct spelling to paste on top.

"Before my set, the crowd was acting different from what I was used to," Disciple said. "People weren't just hanging around, talking to friends—they were *excited*. I was just a kid from Farragut, but the people who met me were in awe. When I started playing, they blew the lid off the venue. I breezed through my set of freshly minted sounds and drove the crowd wild. Two hours was not enough. I hit just the right mix of old classics that the crowd knew and fresh acetates and test-pressings from labels like Strictly Rhythm, Nervous, Eightball, and East/West. After my set was done, the audience gave me an ovation for 20 minutes. They didn't want to go home. The promoter came up with the solution and had me play an afterparty."

From 3:00 AM to 8:00 AM, DJ Disciple, with nowhere left to play in New York, gave JP his best set. Firman knew he had his guy. Disciple fell in love with the Bristol crowd, but, with regret, boarded the plane and went back to New York the next day.

He got the call to come back just a few days later. Firman had booked more gigs for Disciple this time around. But customs was much stricter, and Disciple, not knowing that he needed a work permit to get into the country, was refused entry in December. It was his worst Christmas gift ever. He had to return to New York.

JP was frustrated too. For compensation, he lined up some radio play. Disciple began to send over radio mixes to London's Kiss 100 to showcase some unreleased music. Among the few but dedicated fans he'd earned in the United Kingdom, Disciple was beginning to be known as DJ Acetate.

THE FIRST UK TOUR

Despite the setback, Disciple was about to go from zero to one hundred in the UK house scene. In March 1993, Firman obtained a work permit for Disciple, flew to New York, and met up with him at the Smack Productions studios. JP was also about to launch his own label, Interstate, and he asked Disciple if he could put a track together. Disciple obliged. He called Eddie Perez and got to work. Sampling Martha Washington's vocals, Disciple came up with "People C'mon" in one session at Smack Productions.

"The quicker you can get things done, the better," Disciple said. "JP saw firsthand how I was able to work with the SP 1200. The single is built off working the vocal around the E-MU, and Perez's keyboard performance was a quick sell. Victor Simonelli edited it. Sometimes you have to detach yourself from a production you do."

With the single mixed and mastered, Disciple and JP hopped on a plane for Heathrow. On the plane, JP laid out three goals for Disciple: see gains on the radio, cut fresh tracks in the studio, and make an impact on the dance floor. Unlike today, both touring and record sales provided important sources of revenue in the music industry, while radio marked good exposure for both.

"Before the digital era, you could make money with an underground house record," Firman said. "If you had a good record, you could sell anywhere between 2,000 and 20,000 copies. So you could make money as an independent label on record sales alone. A lot of that could come from international licensing—before the internet, that was where you could make all your money. We did a lot of deals with labels in Italy and Japan.

"So you would make your record, and sell as many as you could. Then you would get licensing inquiries from all over—Italy, Japan, Holland, Belgium, all over. Then either they would release it themselves or they would remix it or, later, put it out on a compilation album. Back then, in terms of money to be made from the independent, underground music business, it was about a 50-50 split between recording and playing shows."

KISS 100 FM

Once they landed, the first order of business was radio play. And for radio play, Kiss 100 FM had established itself as the go-to British house station. Founded by Gordon "Mac" McNamee, Pyers Easton, George Power, and Tosca, Kiss took to the airwaves in 1985 as a pirate station with a focus on dance music. The outfit went legal in 1990 and set up offices in Holloway, London.

The *Zoo Experience* was a popular Kiss program hosted by DJ twins Bobby and Steve. Like many others, they were students of New York house. They had made it to the Garage to see Larry Levan and a live performance from Carolyn Harding months before it closed. Disciple came on the show for an interview and a guest set. Their radio sets were the closest he had heard to New York programming in the United Kingdom.

Disciple was set to play for the Zoo Crew's party Garage City at the Coliseum that Saturday. "Bobby and Steve wanted to give people a preview of what I was going to play at the party," Disciple said. "Commotion started happening in a good way. On the show, I broke 'Deep Inside' by Hardrive on an acetate I made from a cassette given to me by Strictly Rhythm. I also played 'Rushing' by Mood II Swing featuring Lonnie Clark from Nervous, and The Sound Of One's 'As I Am' remixed by Todd Edwards on acetate."

Disciple had previously stuck his neck out for Edwards and convinced Roger Sanchez to get him in the studio to remix the track for Sanchez's label One Record. Disciple wanted to see that remix go places, and he had some of his own reputation on the line. He also knew the young producer was headed for greatness, and UK listeners agreed. It was some of the first exposure Edwards received outside of the United States.

GARAGE CITY

Then the tour began. Firman had booked Disciple to play at clubs across the country. In doing so, he established a schedule that he would keep for the next fifteen years. Between early April and the end of May, Disciple would play once during the week, once on Friday, two sets on Saturday, and occasionally on Sunday. This would repeat again in the fall from the end of August to the end of October. These four or five shows per week would have Disciple crisscrossing the country via train and automobile.

Disciple headed to The Podium in Vauxhall, South London, that weekend to check out the Garage City party where he was on the bill. He immediately felt at home listening to Bobby and Steve warm up and party with their crowd.

"The Black/white ratio on the UK dance floors was so evened out, it made me feel like I was back at the Palladium, Tunnel, or Red Zone during my own clubbing days in New York," Disciple said. "Vinyl has no color. When people love the music, it erases race."

He was again struck by the sophistication, knowledge, and expectations of the UK crowds. "There was low tolerance for DJs who weren't critical thinkers when it came to playing in London," he said. "The music was forward thinking. People had an intellectual approach to house."

Paul "Trouble" Anderson was following Disciple that night, and by the time he was ready to come on, the crowd reached a fever pitch. Disciple's two-hour set was like a rite of passage. He felt like he had joined a family. After he finished, house heads kept coming up to him to ask what records he played and what acetates he had with him. Disciple thought about his own experience at the Palladium with Roman Ricardo. He happily spoke at length about what he played, the artists that produced them, and the producers and labels that made it all possible. "Giving music to DJs who need music is like giving water to a thirsty man," Disciple said. "It's the clearest path to building a bond." But then Paul "Trouble" Anderson took to the decks.

"I thought I was doing something special, and then Paul 'Trouble' Anderson comes on and I felt like I'm a memory," Disciple said. "The Boogie Boys came out and everyone knew 'Trouble's in the Land.' He was the UK equivalent of Frankie Knuckles or Larry Levan. Trouble's command was so strong that people were ready for whatever adventure he was going to take them on.

"As much as I was considered DJ Acetate, I'd found someone who also had a stash of acetates and unreleased music of his own that I'd have to respect and even admire. After the show, I was like all the fans who approached me. I had to ask him where he got his acetates done. The sound quality of the newly polished tracks he was playing was much crisper than mine."

FEEL REAL AT SPRING GARDENS

The week after, Disciple was up for a spot at the notorious Feel Real party at Covent Garden. At the event, he met and befriended DJs Femi B and Rob Acteson.

"Femi B, a DJ who played with a unique energy, and Rob Acteson, a talented DJ in his own right, believed in my sound and were responsible for helping JP find events for me to play at," Disciple said. "Femi B in particular gave me a taste of the future that night. While most house records drew from a range of soul, disco, funk, and more, they were surprisingly similar when it came to tempo. It would be rare to find a record outside of the range of 120–130 beats per minute. But that night, Femi B spun a faster mix. To do so, he rarely played any vocal tracks and instead favored dubs to bring the energy up."

Disciple also met Rhythm Doctor and DJ Evil Olive at the event. The two were dating at the time.

"Evil Olive is a DJ that has a unique vibe, but is also mature enough and has enough etiquette to consider the other DJs' sound and how they're going to follow her," he said. "Playing behind her feels like sailing an ocean where I can travel anywhere I'd like musically. Olive being a Black woman, I found her relationship with Rhythm Doctor (a white man) as organic as they come. Even though Spike Lee's movie *Jungle Fever* brought this issue to the forefront in 1991, interracial couples were frowned on back home. These two immediately opened my mind, seeing that culture exist in London."

The more he saw of it, the more Disciple came to understand that the racial divides common back home simply did not exist in the same way in the UK scene. The Loft, the Garage, Wild Pitch, and other New York clubs were notable for drawing mixed crowds. But in society at large, they were more of an exception than a rule.

"When house music hit Europe, I think it was more accepted than in the United States because, as a genre, it was made by artists of many different races," JP Firman said. "It was very mixed. Obviously, it's quite a wide, diverse continent, Europe is. I think that's what helped bring it out of the underground. In the 1990s, house was definitely bigger in Europe than it was in America. [Electronic dance music] changed that, but back then, even the soulful stuff, the techno from Detroit, it was bigger overseas in the sense of income and generating tours."

There was a huge demand for house DJs in the United Kingdom, but that demand did not come exclusively from the preeminent or large-capacity clubs. In some venues, fewer than one hundred people could fit on the dance floor. Disciple didn't turn down anything JP threw his way. Sometimes the intimate rooms were just as important as the big ones.

New York producers were quick to jump at the opportunity to gain a new audience overseas. Throughout the history of dance music, countless records would go down in stateside flames, but move on to achieve huge audiences, distribution, and sales across the Atlantic. Countless clubs, especially outside of London during the Northern Soul era, would play nothing but what Americans would consider Motown knock-offs.

By this time, JP was doing steady business importing New York DJs and records. He was booking Camacho, Todd Terry, and others but knew there was demand for more. Disciple started playing more and more gigs.

"UK house heads had more appreciation for what we did," Disciple said. "There were actually dance acts on Top of the Pops. House and dance records were going #1 in the country. I realized that I could press the reset button and restart my career all over again.

"Bonding with DJs like Femi B and Paul 'Trouble' Anderson, I soon made it to Music House on Holloway Road. Located at Eden Grove, it was the place where you could cut copies of records from studio masters. It was heaven and hell. Most of the jungle and the drum and bass acts pressed their music there, and it was literally two blocks away from the Kiss station. I could go and hear the next best thing coming out of London.

"DATs, cassette decks, later CDs, and everything made to cut for acetate was done the way you like it. There would be a serious queue of producers who wanted their music pressed, and I eventually learned to never go there on the weekend. With all the artists moving through the business, there were ounces of weed smoked on the premises on a weekly basis."

"It was just up the street from where Kiss 100 FM used to be," JP Firman said. "We used to go with Disciple and spend a fortune in there. He had all these exclusives, and he would let us all make copies."

MINISTRY OF SOUND

To cap off Disciple's first tour, JP lined Disciple up for another important show. The occasion was fellow DJ Bert Bevans' birthday, and the location was the Ministry of Sound. The club was designed in the spirit of the Paradise Garage. As club founder Justin Berkman told Bill Brewster and Frank Broughton, "My concept for Ministry was purely this: 100% sound system first, lights second, design third (in that order); the reverse of everyone else's idea."[3] That philosophy paid off. Within a short period of time, Ministry became London's go-to club.

The venue opened on September 21, 1991, with an all-star cast behind the decks: Larry Levan, David Morales, Roger Sanchez, Tony Humphries, and Paul Oakenfold. When Disciple came through for his first show, he played the small room. It just so happened that Tony Humphries was spinning in the main room on the same night. Disciple took the opportunity to break the track "Show Me Love" by Robin S. The crowd ate it up and kept the energy until well past sunrise. After the success of that show, the Ministry of Sound brought Disciple back twice a year until 2001.

ANGELS OF LOVE

Soon after Disciple returned from this UK trip in the early summer of 1993, Bobby Davis put out his first EP, *Street Experience,* on his label Muzik Pushers. The record featured vocals from Quamina on the track "When the Music Stops." While the record went nowhere fast in the United States, it was a different story in the United Kingdom and in Europe. *Street Experience* logged strong sales in London record shops.

The single "When the Music Stops" also became an unexpected hit in Italy. The label D:vision licensed the song for Italian distribution. Disciple's first invite to the country came from the club Angels of Love in Naples. Disciple didn't know any Italian, but on October 10, 1993, he arrived in Naples and played to a packed crowd through the night. Other invites soon followed.

"Similar to the United Kingdom, house music was heavily played on Radio Italia and the crowd at Angels of Love pioneered the idea of shaking up the Neapolitan nightlife centered around fashion and lifestyle," Disciple said. "They started featuring the best DJs in the world regardless of electronic genre. My DJ set for the outfit helped create demand at other venues in the country."

HARD TIMES

In the fall of 1993, JP brought Disciple back to the United Kingdom for another tour. This time, he sent him north. One of the first gigs was a Hard Times party at a DIY venue in West Yorkshire. The event was run by Steve Raine. He and Disciple keep in touch to this day.

"In the beginning I owned and worked on a small farm in North Yorkshire breeding sheep and horses," Raine said. "I knew nothing about dance music until a girlfriend, together with other friends, told me to ditch my suit, buy some decent clothes, and set off to the Hacienda [a Manchester venue]. That club was my inspiration for starting Hard Times. We moved into the Music Factory in Leeds where we had many a good night. I called it Hard Times because everyone was skint, facing hard times in life. On a Saturday night everyone would forget the hard times. Just for that moment everything was left behind."

While dance music was nothing new in Leeds, Hard Times was one of the first parties in the city to showcase US house and garage. Disciple made his debut in October 1993. He showed up with exclusive cuts like Roger Sanchez's mix of "Giving It Up" by Incognito and M-People's "Moving On Up" remixed by MK. Disciple found another long-term connection with Raine and his party. Like past shows, he made sure to always listen to what the resident DJ was playing and to hear where they were coming from musically. As much as Disciple was a headliner, he loved learning what the local residents played.

"That was the one thing thing about Disciple," JP Firman said. "I've *never* been in a room where's he played and I've thought, 'This isn't going to work.' Not one time. In some rooms, it might have taken longer for him to figure out the audience, or it might have taken longer for the audience to figure him out. Every time, he had them by the end of the night. He could play for any room. For me, that's what a DJ is at the end of the day. You're there to make the room rock. And different rooms have different vibes. Disciple could rock every single one."

TOP ONE HUNDRED DJs

In 1993, *DJ Magazine* put out its one hundredth issue. To celebrate, the staff polled their readership and industry leaders to create a list of the top one hundred DJs in the world. DJ Disciple found his name on page eleven. As Phil Cheesman wrote:

> Disciple is that rare breed of New York DJ—young blood on the way up. Rapidly becoming known as DJ Acetate for his unreasonable obsession with cutting himself acetates of upcoming releases from tapes obtained directly from the producers, Disciple began his career as a gospel DJ and then got his first break doing a mix show on college radio in New York. Clubwise, he managed to land a slot at New York's infamous Wild Pitch parties, and also played at Newark's Zanzibar during Tony Humphries' absence.
>
> Disciple's frequent sets in England are characterized by his intense enthusiasm for the music he's playing and precipitation of mass bugging out when he unleashes soon-to-be classics (Hardrive's "Deep Inside" was one) months before release.[4]

There were a few other familiar names in the issue: Kenny Carpenter, David Camacho, Johnny Dynell, Tony Humphries, Jazzy Jeff, Frankie Knuckles, Bobby Konders, David Morales, Junior Vasquez, and Little Louie Vega.

BACK TO THE UNITED KINGDOM, 1994

Disciple spent the winter in New York, preparing for his return to the United Kingdom the next spring.

"The buildup had been strong for me to come back to the United Kingdom, and I needed to deliver," he said. "I was getting more exclusive tracks from Strictly Rhythm's Gladys Pizzaro. She brought me in her office one week before I was set to take off. She had already handed me 'Deep Inside' the year before, and here she is, giving me a more powerful bomb with Barbara Tucker's 'Beautiful People.' It was another live debut on Kiss FM in London. I premiered the track on Bobby and Steve's show as well as exclusives from Smack Productions, Roger Sanchez, and Todd Edwards. The next week when I played at The Coliseum for Garage City, people lapped it up. *DJ Magazine* gave me a two-page feature after I played at the Zap Club in Brighton that month."

This tour would bring Disciple to clubs like Cream in Liverpool, The Empire in Middleborough, Riviera Lights in Bedford, Bakers in Birmingham, London parties like Enjoy and Junior Boys' Own, and venues like Turnmills, Maximus, and Gass Club. Disciple also spun in front of his largest audience ever: Notting Hill Carnival, which drew thirty-five thousand people that year.

The event began in 1991 when Keith Franklin and his brother Mel teamed up with the Rockin Crew sound system and became one of the biggest attractions in the region. Disciple knew KCC (the duo comprised of Keith Franklin and Kid Batchelor) from the record "Bang Bang, You're Mine" (which Larry Levan broke at The Choice following Disciple's set). They were also responsible for putting Azuli Records on the map with "Groove Thing" and "Heaven."

Keith and Disciple later bonded and became friends in a familiar setting: the Azuli Record shop. Azuli Records (a label and a record store) was started by DJ Dave Piccioni in 1991. Operating until 2009, it was for a time the United Kingdom's longest-running house label.

THE SOUL PARTY PROJECT

That summer, Disciple hit the studio again to fill out a fresh EP for Firman's Interstate Records. With "People C'mon" in the can, Disciple, Eddie Perez, Victor Simonelli, and keyboardist John Dodds cut two more tracks: "Respect" and "Your Trak." Disciple worked under the alias of The Banji Boyz, and *The Banji Boyz EP* was cut in Smack Productions studio.

JP released the *The Banji Boyz EP* a few months later as a white label record and distributed it via underground networks. This might have been an effort to avoid scrutiny from Martha Washington's management. "People C'mon" heavily samples Washington's music.

Disciple made good on his promise to Eddie Perez soon after. He headed into the studio to cut a new EP, *The Soul Party Project*. For the single, Disciple hooked up with vocalist Lemuel Blackwell for the song "On the Dancefloor." Completing three of the tracks, Disciple wanted Todd Edwards to produce another for the EP to help get his name out. Just as Roger Sanchez, Naeem, and Camacho helped Disciple in his career, he wanted to do the same for Todd Edwards. The young DJ returned to Disciple with the track "Rite Now."

The EP was first released on Zack Tom's Grassroots label. But then Mother Records, U2's Irish label, snapped up "On the Dancefloor" for UK distribution. Reaching number sixty-seven on the singles chart, it was Disciple's first hit in the country. The momentum he had built there began to reverberate out across Europe, and also back across the Atlantic. *New York's Best Kept Secret* experienced a resurgence in popularity. The legendary New Jersey label, Movin' Records run by Abigail Adams, started sponsoring the radio show. *Vibe* covered the show in the magazine's April 1994 issue. Journalist Carol Cooper wrote:

> He calls himself D.J. Disciple, and for five years he's been the best-kept secret in New York radio. Every Thursday from 7:30–9 pm retailers, musicians and fans all over the tri-state area tune into 91.5 FM, the Brooklyn-based radio station to get inside dope and unreleased tracks from the most innovative producers in dance music.[5]

More studio work in 1994 saw Disciple remixing 95 North's track featuring Phillip Ramirez's "See The Light" for Choice Records (which was run by Greg Daye from Wild Pitch). He also remixed 95 North's "Hold On" for King Street Records. JP had Disciple do two more remixes for Interstate. One by Wanda Rogers, called "Prove Your Love," contained a Hard Times remix dub, and the other was Mass Fusion's "Running Back to Me," featuring Steven Granville and produced by Booker T.

HARD TIMES AMERICAN DJ SHOWCASE EVENT

Steve Raine kicked Hard Times into overdrive in the spring of 1994 and put together his most ambitious party to date. He rented out Bagley's Studio in London and booked a who's who bill of American DJs for the UK audience.

On May 28, 1994, Disciple found himself playing in the main room at Bagley's with Roger Sanchez and Tony Humphries. Sanchez named it the Underground Solution Sound. Room two was the Chicago Vibe Sound with Maurice Joshua, Terry Hunter, and live performances from D-Bora and Loni Clark. Room three featured the Strictly Rhythm Sound with DJ Pierre, George Morel, Phil Cheesman, and Barbara Tucker live. Room four was the New York Sound with Todd Terry, Kenny "Dope" Gonzalez, Louie Vega, Benji Candelario, Dave Camacho, and CeCe Rogers live. Room five featured the UK sound delivered by Graeme Park, Miles Holloway, Elliot Eastwick, Ricky Morrison, Linden C, Phil Asher, Rob Acteson, and Bobby and Steve.

"I was in pure heaven," Disciple said. "Bagley's had a capacity of a few thousand in their main room alone. Like a legal rave, the venue was a huge multi-room warehouse club that held some of London's biggest Saturday night parties. For my set that night I broke three new tracks produced by Masters at Work: 'Bass Tone,' 'The Nervous Track,' and 'Emergency on Planet Earth.' After my set, I headed into room four to catch them [Louie Vega and Kenny 'Dope' Gonzalez] play live. It was pure pandemonium. Kenny Dope had to push people out of the way just to get on the decks. The place was so tightly packed you couldn't move."

STATE 51 STUDIOS IN LONDON

With all the time he was spending in the United Kingdom, Disciple needed a studio to be able to produce music while he was abroad. JP hooked him up with sound engineer Pete Hurst and State 51 Studios in East London. Hurst's long resume includes studio work with David Morales, the Wiggle Crew, Danny Rampling, and the Spice Girls.

"Hurst worked in the studio from 1986 to 2002. He never wasted time and knew how to work my SP 1200, along with his AKAI S3200 sampler and Juno 106 keyboard," Disciple said. "He also had an Eventide Harmonizer, a Lexicon PCM 90 reverb processor, a great mixing board, and effect modules. He ran everything through Proteus Design Suite software. For £200 you could work for eight to twelve hours on a track to your liking. We would do two in one day. Pete was that fast.

"I recorded *The Banji Boyz Part 2* EP there, as well as an EP for Roger Sanchez. I worked with vocalists like Mary Gold, Mary Pearce, and Angie Brown. Hurst would get me vocalists on a whim. He and I would come up with a groove, and by the time the singers got to the studio all we had to do was find the right hook for the singer to vibe to. After the hook we'd build verses around them if need be."

The Banji Boyz EP Vol. II was released later in 1995 on Interstate Records. Thanks to the track "Keep on Movin," it sold well. As it made its way through record stores, radio stations, and clubs over the coming months and years, house fans began to associate it both with soulful London sounds, but also with a harder, newer English sound that some were beginning to describe as UK garage.

LOS ANGELES, MARQUES WYATT, AND THE KIMCO EFFECT

During the 1995 New Music Seminar in New York, Disciple continued to expand his network. He met DJ Marques Wyatt, who became an important contact. Originally from Santa Monica, Wyatt was one of the few DJs responsible for bringing East Coast deep house vibes out west. New York clubs, meanwhile, were suffering from a dry spell. You could hear the crickets chirping.

"The New York club industry was bust," Disciple said. "Promoters started to transform The Tunnel and The Palladium into rap hot spots. Hip hop artists like Nas, Biggie Smalls, and Wu Tang Clan eventually revitalized the club scene in New York, but the revival was not house-friendly. Only a few standout clubs kept the house flame alive. Songs like 'Missing' by Everything But The Girl that Todd Terry remixed was his biggest record in Europe, but he got no support in the states.

"Jersey still had a thing where house music had a cool factor," Todd Terry said. "It had these hip hop elements to carry it through. 'Follow Me' by Aly-Us was funky, it was rich, and it was Black. I think the Jersey house held on, but in New York it just got a little bit too freaky for real brothers to mix themselves up with that crowd. They wanted to hear Biggie, Jay-Z, and Nas. It was just a manhood thing. New York lost its love for us. It got greedy. They didn't want to pay us the money that everybody else was paying.

"I had known some people for 30 years and I couldn't even get a record tested. They'd say, 'Why don't you just play it at 11:00 at night?' Or 'Oh we don't play house on radio.' I'd tell them that people are really loving this record and dancing to it in the clubs. Play it and see if people like it. Back in the days I used to get Frankie Crocker to play my music. But as the new guys got out there, they got really fickle, and just wanted to play hip hop. They didn't give house music a chance."

New scenes, however, were emerging around the United States. Marques Wyatt invited Disciple to play an afterhours party called Does Your Mama Know? in Los Angeles.

"I was fascinated by movies like *Colors*, *Boyz n the Hood*, and *Menace II Society*," Disciple said. "I arrived in LA with a fistful of money in my pockets, and the first thing I wanted to do was go to the places I'd seen in the movies—Watts, Crenshaw, Compton, Inglewood, Skid Row, wherever there was trouble. My brother Leighton had lived in Los Angeles for years. He knew where it was at.

"Leighton saw a different side of me that the family didn't know. He was involved in a twelve-step program, which meant he was in touch with former drug dealers, users, and gang bangers."

On May 27, Disciple played his first Does Your Mama Know? party at the Coconut Teaszer on Sunset Boulevard in West Hollywood. The party went from 3:00 AM to 9:00 AM on Saturdays after the rock shows wrapped up at the venue. Does Your Mama Know? had a deep, energetic feel. Wyatt taught Disciple how deep house was different from the soulful style he'd been playing. Although Wyatt's sound was inspired by New York, he threw in his own twist—he played trackier, less-anthemic music like "It's Just Another Groove" by the Mighty Dub Katz. Afterward, Wyatt and Disciple enjoyed breakfast at Roscoe's Chicken & Waffles, and Wyatt told Disciple about the DJing opportunities on the West Coast.

"He and Doc Martin were considered pioneers of house music in Los Angeles, which prompted me to ask how he got his gigs," Disciple said. "He told me he worked with Kim Benjamin, who was based in New York. My new mission was to get Kim Benjamin to manage me. Back in New York, I talked to her every time I saw her, and I begged her to put me on her DJ roster."

"I started clubbing at an early age in San Francisco," Kim Benjamin said. "Eventually I started working in them: coat check at Das Klub, cashier and coat check at Townsend, I even worked in the office and helped open Sound Factory. During this time I also met Marques Wyatt, who eventually became my first client, and our working relationship grew out of that. By the time I moved to New York I already knew many people in the club scene from my past years working in the San Francisco clubs and began doing A&R at labels and booking DJs."

Benjamin did not agree to manage Disciple immediately, to his disappointment.

"I saw how mismanagement affected my DJ gigs and studio work," Disciple said. "Robert Owens, one of the revered vocalists of Fingers Inc., and Michael Watford, who often toured with me, did a duet for Steve Raines' Hard Times label called 'Come Together.' Marshall Jefferson, the man behind 'Move Your Body,' produced it. JP brought the production to New York, called me up the same day, and told me I had eight hours to remix the track. This was my opportunity to work with living house legends, and there was no way I could turn it down. But I only had eight hours to complete it, and I couldn't do it justice.

"I hated the result. It was my first time recording in Bass Hit Studios in Chelsea. They gave it their all, but we didn't have enough time. I realized I needed a manager who could coordinate my projects. Then I'd have more time to work on my music instead of rushing to complete same-day collaborations with high-profile acts. Outside of the United Kingdom and the West Coast, I needed more of a presence."

Fortunately, Disciple continued to secure gigs around the world. Bobby Davis was good friends with promoter Shuji Hiroshii, who knew the Japanese house crowd wanted Disciple to play. They recognized him from The Choice and Wild Pitch parties. All the same, Disciple's debut in Japan didn't go perfectly.

"When I arrived, Shuji informed me that the venue wanted me to play a 10-hour set, and it was important to stick to the classics I played at the Wild Pitch parties," Disciple said. "This came as a surprise.

"Music lovers in Japan were well-versed on Black musical heritage. They knew house music, hip hop, and classics. DJs like Kenny Carpenter, Nick Jones, Francois K, Larry Levan, Camacho, and most of the Wild Pitch DJs loved playing in Japan because they shared the same musical philosophy with the fans there."

From Japan, Disciple flew to play the East Side club in Italy. However, he almost missed the gig because he got lost—he didn't realize he would have to take a train from his flight to the venue.

"In places like Italy, I flew to the country, went to the hotel, played the gig, and as soon as it was over, got on a flight back home," he continued. "No rest and no days off. No time to explore or experience the culture."

Disciple's next experience was the last straw. He flew from New York to Switzerland to play a club. When he arrived, there were only eight people in the venue. After his set, Disciple had to chase the promoter around the club to get his door fees. The promoter didn't have anything to pay Disciple, and he tried to hide instead of owning up to his mistake. At this point, Disciple knew he desperately needed a manager.

Finally, Kim decided to give Disciple a shot. "Disciple was persistent and was good friends with artists that I worked with," Benjamin said. "He was out all the time and a hard worker, which helped to turn my mind around."

Things did not get off to a good start. Benjamin's first gig for Disciple was playing a party thrown by Mystic Bill in Chicago. It turned out the Gangster Disciples, a local organization, were throwing a party downstairs. Then, as the opening DJ was getting ready to make the hand-off to Disciple, shots were heard downstairs. The dance floor cleared. Disciple packed up his records and headed back to the hotel.

SEATTLE

In quick order, Kim sent Disciple out to Seattle instead. Laurie Dragseth met him at the airport and brought him around town. She also introduced him to Mayi Picazo, who had booked him through his Tasty Productions outfit. With the explosion of Seattle grunge, music of all kinds was pouring into the city. Ivan Salavery and Laurie were pioneers in bringing DJs in from out of state.

Disciple's set at the Weathered Wall that night showcased Kenny Dope's "The Bomb," "Reach" by Lil "Mo" Ying Yang (with collaboration from Erick Morillo and Louie Vega), and the Tommy Musto–produced "I've Got Something for You" by Federal Hill.

"Desire at Victors was the first weekly house music party in Seattle," Laurie Dragseth said. "Then came Weathered Wall on Saturdays and Flammable at the Rebar on Sundays. Mayi Picazo, an independent promoter, threw raves with house DJs at NAF Studios, a huge warehouse. It had the best sound system in town.

"Victors was groundbreaking for house music in Seattle because we brought in DJs from all over the United States. Daren Monroe helped with those connections. His favorite saying was 'It's a culture, not a fad,' and it really felt that way. Our team was invested in the growth of the genre. House music isn't selective about who it loves, who it moves, or which soul it touches. Our audiences were diverse. Our efforts were largely word-of-mouth and relationship-driven. With no internet, cell phones, or email, it was tough—but we all worked together."

"For me, things started because of a girl," said Seattle promoter Mayi Picazo. "Doc Martin was playing a party at Townsend Club in San Francisco. I met a woman from Seattle at the party, and we hit it off. I was ready for a change, so I moved to Seattle to be with her.

"The clubs in Seattle mostly played top 40 hits, live music, techno, and high NRG. I saw potential to bring house music to the area. Then I met Mike Marcer, Jason Harler, and Jared Harler, three well-known club promoters in Seattle. I combined my network with theirs, and we were able to bring house DJs to play at the Seattle clubs.

"The rave scene was hardcore, but I knew the raver kids would love the soulful sound of house. I called Kim and discovered that her roster was full of club DJs, not rave DJs. But I didn't care—I decided to take a risk, and I said, 'Let's book them anyway. Seattle will love their music.' I took the opportunity to educate Seattle about the roots of electronic music and conceptualized Raveioli, the first all-house music rave in the Pacific Northwest.

"Kim Benjamin was one of the most capable professionals in the New York music industry, and she was obsessed with house music. She knew how to connect with the right people to book her DJs."

RAVES

Disciple got his first taste of raves in 1995 when Kim booked him at Lust with DJ Duke in Denver. Bobby Banks was the promoter.

"Lust mixed local talent with East Coast and Canadian DJs," Disciple said. "The show featured Peter and Tyrone from Toronto, while DJ Duke and I represented New York. Denver ravers wore uniforms, costumes, and brought glowsticks. The women wore colorful attire, drank blended energy juices, and ate candy. At raves, you could wear anything you wanted. DJs often played faster. Street drugs like ecstasy were prevalent, but undercover. There usually wasn't any alcohol, and I saw a lot of underage kids—even as young as 13—coming out to party.

"I considered San Francisco the mecca for house music on the West Coast because if you were popular there, you could play in Seattle, Vancouver, San Diego, Las Vegas, and Denver without any trouble. When I first started playing raves, I studied tapes from Doc Martin, Derrick Carter, Mark Farina, and other

DJs with big West Coast followings. Eventually, I had the pleasure of playing with them. When Raveioli came to Seattle, Mayi made sure I was one of the first DJs on board."

Raveioli would become a staple of Seattle house. Disciple shared the bill with familiar names like Marques Wyatt, Derrick Carter, Victor Simonelli, and Jay J. "During Derrick May's first visit to Seattle, I remember a conversation I had with him about the scene," Disciple said. "He had just played a gig in Israel, and he said the Israeli ravers moved and dressed like the ones in Seattle. How was that possible? It proved to me that house music really created a culture."

Shortly after Benjamin's intervention, it didn't take long for the ball to really start rolling for Disciple in the mid-1990s. As Kim's professional network grew, so did her talent. She did bookings and representation for Deep Dish, Danny Rampling, Mousse T., Pete Heller, and Murk. They drew thousands of people to their events. Disciple's fan base also expanded. In a short period, Disciple's touring through the United Kingdom and the West Coast, with frequent forays elsewhere, got him regular work and held him to an ambitious schedule. He still called Farragut home, but he was also gone most of the year. Family and friends were often surprised to learn what he was up to.

"I never knew how big my brother was until I was in Spain on a break from touring with George Benson," said Disciple's brother, Stanley Banks. "This is when I really got respect for my brother. George brought us to a beach party. You had to pay $300 to get on this beach. There were all these kids there, and they had all this champagne. They weren't drinking it. They were spraying it all over each other. They had crates and crates of champagne stacked on the beach. A DJ was playing. So I went up to him and said, 'Hey, do you know DJ Disciple?' And he goes, 'DJ Disciple? He's the man!' I just stood back like, 'Wow . . . so this is what David is doing.'"

UK GARAGE

During Disciple's first week back in London in the spring of 1994, he was doing some work in the studio when JP brought around his brother, Simon Firman, and a producer by the name of Grant Nelson. Disciple already knew Grant and Simon's work as the 24-Hour Experience. He had supported their track "I Need a Man."

Grant Nelson and Disciple hit it off immediately. Nelson had just helped George Power launch his label Nice 'N' Ripe in 1993. Power was a Kiss FM co-founder and fellow DJ who knew potential when he saw it. Nelson told him where he wanted to go musically, and Power made it happen. The work Grant recorded during this period of his career would later be heralded as part of the birth of UK garage, a new movement in house music that saw it adopt harder, faster rhythms (often borrowed from jungle and drum and bass) and develop beyond previous American influences. It coalesced into its own genre during this period, and Disciple played his part in its development. It also corresponded with one of the most productive periods in Disciple's career.

"Back in those days, everyone was basically making a US product," JP Firman said. "Even the UK DJs and producers—they were all English artists making American music. But that changed with UK garage. You had people who came from the jungle or the hardcore scene—they got into it and they started to make their version. The beats were a little tougher, a little more skippy."

Grant Nelson and Disciple quickly agreed to get to work in the studio. But before diving in, Nelson wanted to get a feel for Disciple's chops. He had him remix his and David Thackeray's track "Coming Up," which they had released as Ambassadors of Swing, for Nice 'N' Ripe.

Meanwhile, the release of *The Banji Boyz EP Vol. II* was snowballing in London. Paul "Trouble" Anderson was pushing it on his Kiss FM radio show.

"JP got a boost from our Banji Boyz tracks 'Don't Shut Me Out' and 'Keep on Movin,'" which were big on the underground scene in the United Kingdom," Disciple said. "This pushed him to have me play in more UK venues with heavy bass styled rhythms. It had an effect on New York artists, too. The productions coming from Todd Terry, Masters at Work, Roger Sanchez, Todd Edwards, Victor Simonelli, and Smack Productions suddenly had a rougher edge."

The Banji Boyz EP Vol. II set Disciple up to participate in the emerging UK garage movement. Regional identity in the country often prevails over national pride. Each country likes to support its own brand of music, regardless of the genre. Disciple's approach to DJing and producing perfectly suited this landscape. Just like Disciple could win over any club that preferred any style of music, he could also record a broad range of styles in the studio.

"UK garage was very London-centric," JP Firman said. "It didn't really export. It would kind of work in Leeds, or Birmingham, or Liverpool, but mainly London. And it didn't work abroad.

"For a lot of the early UK garage scene, DJs would take American music and speed it up. The kind of standard US soulful house is 120 [beats per minute], and the UK DJs would speed it up to 125–130 [beats per minute]. So the early

UK garage DJs, like Spoony or Matt 'Jam' Lamont, would take a Todd Edwards record, for example, and speed it up. Disciple had a record, *Banji Boyz EP Vol. II*, which was on my label. That crossed over. You could play it in clubs all over the United Kingdom, but you could also play it in UK garage clubs too."

In 2018, DJ Spoony included "Keep on Movin'" on a ten-track list charting the evolution of UK Garage for *DJ Mag*. "No self-respecting DJ would've been without this in their sets. Hailing from Brooklyn, Disciple would've had no idea from that far away how big and important this record was to the scene and sound," Spoony wrote.[6]

Throughout these early months of 1995, Nelson and Disciple developed a strong working relationship, and, similar to Disciple's agreement with Eddie Perez in New York, he and the UK garage pioneer made a pact to support each other's work. Nelson debuted his first collaboration with Disciple in 1995 with *The Klubb Vengeance EP* on Swing City records. The record featured Disciple speaking on the single "2 the Bone." Paul "Trouble" Anderson got his hands on that record too, and soon it was playing throughout London clubland.

Disciple was also collaborating more with Roger Sanchez. After playing with him at Hard Times on New Year's Eve in 1994, Sanchez had Disciple do a new EP for his label Narcotic Records. To come up with the result, *10 Steps to Heaven*, Disciple brought both Grant Nelson and Warren Clark together. The track they produced (also called "10 Steps to Heaven") charted in Belgium and was widely remixed.

Ralph Davis had helped Disciple get on the airwaves. JP had brought Disciple to the United Kingdom. Kim Benjamin had revitalized his career in the United States. In the same way, collaborating with Grant Nelson blew the doors wide open for Disciple's career in the studio. German DJs Boris Dlugosch and Mousse T., who had a hit record with "Keep Pushin'," brought Disciple to Hanover.

"After Mousse T. booked me to play at his club with Boris, I agreed to stay the week," Disciple said. "We worked on projects for his label Peppermint Jam, projects that I would later shop, and a remix I did in their studio of 'Keep Pushin.'" My remix found its way on Louie Vega's label, MAW, as well as Manifesto in the United Kingdom. I felt so locked in doing music and it gave me a bit of freedom to collaborate at a fast rate.

"I don't think people in the states will ever understand how big those records were for me in the United Kingdom. Working with Smack, Todd Edwards, Mousse T., and Grant Nelson put me in a unique position."

On tour in the United Kingdom, Disciple kept at it with his first Southport Weekender (which included Danny Rampling on the bill). Disciple made his debut in Sheffield following Pete Tong from BBC Radio 1 at the Music Factory. Tony Walker, the club's resident DJ, was picking up what Disciple was putting down that night and helped get him future gigs in the area.

Walker was the DJ behind the weekly house showcase Back to Basics at the Music Factory in Leeds (not to be confused with Sheffield's Music Factory). Once described as "the best UK midweek dance night" by *DJ Mag*, the party was legendary in its time.

"Disciple had the crowd in his hands with his energetic set," Tony Walker said. "Unlike most US DJs at the time, he brought a UK-style of energy to the dance floor, mixing often on three decks. Following Pete Tong, you would think, would be a hard task. But Disciple rocked it and had plenty of exclusives to rival the big-name UK jocks. His pure love of the music came through. He felt every beat, and this infectious energy translated to the crowd. It was at that point that I realized we were watching something very special.

"I think Disciple provided a good bridge between the slightly different clubbing cultures that had emerged within the United Kingdom. At the Sheffield party Love to Be, we championed US music along with the more uplifting UK sound. This set the north apart. The energy and the drive to lift the crowd up with the music was key up north. It led to a more electric atmosphere.

"My style came, first and foremost, from my love of house music and clubbing. I grew up in London but then moved to go to university in Leeds around the start of the house music scene. My first gig was after Carl Cox at Dream in Leeds. I then held a residency with the Utah Saints at the Gallery, also in Leeds. I still bought my music in London from Black Market and other stores and brought that sound up north. My love of music led me to manage Urban Rhythm and Eastern Bloc, two record shops in Leeds. That gave me great access to music and allowed for regular visits to the states to satisfy my love of US house. But producers like Grant Nelson, Tim Deluxe, and Joey Musaphia were bringing it on the UK scene, and I was one of the first up north to really push that sound."

A few months later, Disciple got the opportunity to do a radio show for Leeds-based Kiss 105. He invited Walker to collaborate, and the two came up with the *Transatlantic Mix*, a program that launched in early 1997. Disciple recorded his show at WNYE in Brooklyn, while Tony Walker broadcasted his part in Leeds. The program officially went on air in early 1997.

Also during this period in 1996, Disciple collaborated with Dawn Tallman on the single "That's What Life Is All About" for Joey Musaphia's newly formed label, Ulterior. During the session, he met Gerald Elms, who often produced and performed as G Club. The two shared a mutual respect for each other. When Disciple worked with Serena on the single, "Crazy," for the Love 2 Be label, the two stepped into Elms' G Club Studio to enlist his help.

Disciple's spring 1996 tour brought him back to Notting Hill, Hull, Leeds, Manchester, Newcastle, Bolton, and the Greenbelt Festival.

"Back in London in 1996, I was going through the shelves at a record shop called Release the Groove when I was approached by Omar Adimora," Disciple said. "We had a mutual friend in Eddie Perez. He started talking to me about Todd Edwards and asked if I was headed to Trouble's House, Paul 'Trouble' Anderson's party at Camden Lock. I was on the bill.

"Trouble was the first UK DJ I heard playing a Todd Edwards record and it really sent a shock to my system. On a Wednesday night, the 300-capacity venue had a similar energy to the Sound Factory Bar, but with an altogether fresh vibe and sound. Trouble's hold over the crowd was similar to the Louie Vega phenomenon. If Trouble played your record, you knew you had a hit. Not only did Trouble have the Loft on his side but, at the time, he had a Kiss FM show during London's prime-time hours of 9:00 PM to 12:00 AM.

"I met up with Omar the next week at his home near Holloway Road. I remember him saying, 'You played a great set at Trouble's last week, but see Disciple, there's another scene out here where DJs are pushing the music toward a different audience than what you see at the Loft. The Black scene in the United Kingdom has shifted from drum and bass to a more UK garage sounding of music.'

'You mean garage like Paradise Garage?' I asked.

'No, I mean garage like US-influenced house, but with more of an edge to it,' he said."

Disciple and Omar grew close. The next time they met, Disciple handed him a remix he did of "I'm Addicted" by Plutonic for Bold Records. The label had commissioned it, but then wasn't satisfied with the end result and sat on the release. That's not how Omar felt. The next day, the two hit up Trouble's House again.

"When we get to the venue, it was mobbed and the energy was high," Disciple said. "I saw Phil Asher with Bobby, Steve, and the Zoo Crew. A lot of music industry heavyweights were there. We got inside as the party was just ramping up.

"Trouble dropped another record on the turntables and, all of a sudden, I'm hearing the same beat I was recording a few months back in the studio. Those same synth riffs drop over what people would later call a classic UK garage drum track. And then the vocals kick in: 'I'm addicted. I'm addicted to your love.' Trouble was playing the DAT I gave Omar the day before. Then the crowd started screaming.

"At this point, Omar is grinning. He turns and asks, 'You're sure this isn't coming out!?'"

Over the coming months, Omar baptized Disciple in the growing UK garage movement. He introduced him to fellow DJ Matt "Jam" Lamont, who had a collaboration with Karl "Tuff Enuff" Brown known as Tuff Jam—another foundational UK garage force. Omar also brought Disciple through the party Horny's at Legend. The DJs there played the records fast, with the pitch control maxed out at +8.

"It was a style of house unlike I'd ever heard before," Disciple said. An MC (MC DT) was also on stage with a mic. He shouted, 'This is how we like it! Bumpy, sexy!' He commands the DJ to, 'REWIND MY SELECTOR!' The crowd shouted 'BO BO BO!' as the DJ spun the record back.

"Jeff John, the promoter of the night, excitedly came up to me from behind. 'Disciple! We want you here next time you're over,' he said. 'Big time, my man.' I didn't know if I could handle a crowd like this but I looked at him unfazed and said, 'Sure, anytime you want me down.'"

Jam Lamont was there that night, too, and Omar introduced him. He had been pushing "Keep on Movin'" at a party he played at Arches, another UK venue. Before Disciple left the country, he made sure Jam had a copy of "Burning Up," a new track he had cut with vocalist Angie Brown (which featured a fusion of soulful US house with dubbier UK drum and bass). He also passed Trouble Anderson a cut of "New York City Girl," a collaboration with vocalist Dawn Tallman.

"The buzz was strong in the record stores and DJs were hot for the 'I'm Addicted' remix, which was still not released," Disciple said. "It was April of 1996, and I was curious about the club Legends and what was developing there. I had witnessed MCs becoming more active on the mic. Dub versions of records began to get better reactions than the track itself. There were more rewinds, and a hell of a lot of Todd Edwards records were being played."

Less than a year later, Omar would team up with Tim Deluxe to play under many different names, including R.I.P., 10° Below, and Double 99. In short order, the two produced "RipGroove," the single off a double nine-inch EP they called *Double 99*. The track went on to become one of the most successful crossover house hits in the United Kingdom to date. It reached number one on the UK Dance charts and number fourteen on the UK Singles chart.

THE ARCHES

When Disciple had arrived in the United Kingdom the year before, he had found himself playing and recording in the middle of the emerging UK garage scene. This time around, when he came back in the fall of 1996, he was trying to understand the gravity of the changes that were rippling through British house music. One of his first gigs was playing for the jungle- and drum and bass–influenced Arches crowd.

"The party started at 5:00 PM in the afternoon and ended at 3:00 AM in the morning," Disciple said. "After being nervous going in from all the anticipation, I was able to play within the music policy to impress the promoters, but I played a couple of records that won me over with the scenesters.

"In particular Gusto's 'Disco's Revenge' and Grant Nelson with Mousse T.'s 'Everybody' made me a crowd favorite. But beyond connecting with the audience over these records, I didn't have a clue how big my own records were. I later began to understand that I only needed to be myself to play at Arches. 'I'm Addicted' and 'Keep on Movin'' had already set the table for me. They were both tracks that conferred me status in the UK garage scene.

"Playing in the United Kingdom, I began to feel divided, like I was split in three places. The crowds that loved Paul 'Trouble' Anderson's music hated the UK garage scene, yet my music crossed over to both. On top of that, my overall sound continued to grow in the north of England and the big room clubs like Ministry of Sound. I only allowed Omar to involve me in one or two more gigs in the UK garage scene, although I'll admit I was really happy to see more Black DJs make an impact. When the Arches ended its run, Omar made sure to let me play at Twice As Nice every time I came to the United Kingdom. Matt wound up taking 'New York City Girl' for his label release on Unda Vybe. Hot on the heels of their new single 'RipGroove' crossing over, I was fortunate enough to get Omar and Tim Deluxe to do a remix of 'Steal Away' for Catch 22 Recordings, my own label that I was about to launch. Omar had become like a brother to me, and we both had a passion and love for the music. The music he was starting to produce would have a profound effect on the United Kingdom.

"I was quite ambivalent but felt justified that I wasn't the only DJ that went back and forth between both scenes. Grant Nelson went down a similar path, as did Joey Musaphia."

IBIZA

The rise of the internet helped rave culture to spread via mailing lists. Both raves and the early internet attracted folks with niche interests and alternative lifestyles. People started traveling farther distances to go to raves. For ravers, the mailing lists and electronic communication cultivated a desire to connect with like-minded individuals. In the mid-1990s, Disciple continued to play shows around the world. Kim Benjamin handled Disciple's booking, mixes, and radio work in the United States, and JP Firman did the same but in the United Kingdom.

Raves became more mainstream around this time. Although the Spanish clubs never called their parties "raves," the exotic events in Ibiza left their stamp on events in the United Kingdom and, eventually, the United States. In 1987, English DJs Paul Oakenfold, Danny Rampling, Johnny Walker, and Nicky Holloway vacationed on the Spanish island. There, they found a nascent club culture and a steady supply of MDMA. And so the cultural exchange of UK and Ibiza club culture began.

World-renowned venues on the island like Pacha became party destinations for house music lovers. The biggest club nights in Ibiza attracted thousands of people every week. With crystal Mediterranean waters and white sands, it turned into a well-known destination for die-hard house fans.

The UK party brand and agency Cream brought Disciple over in the spring of 1995. The team was highly organized, and it threw extravagant parties that prioritized quality over quantity. They made superstars out of DJs. In addition to Cream, Disciple played a Ministry of Sound night at Pacha along with DJ Pippi.

With an exotic atmosphere and diverse culture, Ibiza was a destination that many DJs only dreamed of. One of the most popular parties was "F*** Me I'm Famous" with David Guetta. Swedish House Mafia, Solomun, Luciano, and Hot Since 82 also frequently played in Ibiza.

When Disciple came through, Ibiza's roster consisted of Roger Sanchez at Release Yourself on Mondays, Erick Morillo at Subliminal Sessions on Wednesdays, Ministry of Sound on Fridays, and Judgement Sundays with Judge Jules at Pacha. Amnesia and Pacha opened in the 1970s, and the Ku Club,

Space, Es Paradis, Eden, and DC 10 followed. Pacha was special because it was one of the only clubs that stayed open all year long. The party never stopped. Disciple played at Pacha two to three times per year from 1996 to 2002. He also played sets at Café del Mar every time he visited.

SHIFTING INFLUENCES

Through these diverse house movements and communities, Disciple's style began to change. He was still a New York DJ, but he grew closer to the international house vibe.

"I still loved playing deep and soulful house, but my actions were embracing more of the harder sounds of the genre," Disciple said. "I always could play harder, and did, depending on the venue. But with Kim booking me, I found myself going in that direction more often than not. Playing raves and afterhours can bring things out of you musically you never thought you had.

"I was traveling and playing at venues at a faster pace, and it was getting difficult to compartmentalize the different styles of music I'd inherited. By 1997 musical taste buds changed to listening to Armand Van Helden. DJs were playing more Rhythm Masters and Robbie Rivera.

"Guys I'd hook up with at the Winter Music Conference would always be sending me music. I'd still play the original style that brought me where I am. Playing on the *Transatlantic Mix*, on tour at gigs like the Southport Weekender, and doing Bobby & Steve events ensured that. But my taste buds were craving more music with energy.

"Eddie Amador, who was also with Kim Benjamin's management, would hang out with Willy Sanjuan and I in South Beach. Based in Los Angeles, Amador would release strong vocals over a fierce track that features bruising drums, scorching keyboards, and eerie high-pitched strings. His song 'House Music' had the catch phrase of 1997: 'Not everyone understands house music. It's a spiritual thing, a body thing, a soul thing.' It's the kind of track that's only meant for peak-time dance floor as a reminder to house heads why they are there."

AROUND THE WORLD

By this stage, DJ Disciple was a proven quantity, and he gained steam with each new region he played. In 1996 and 1997, Kim Benjamin began to send him around the world: to Ku Club, Fellini, and other venues throughout Spain; to Locomia in Portugal; to Mad Club and the Zurich Street Festival in Switzerland; to L'An-Fer in Dijon, France; to warehouse parties and Industry in Toronto with Peter, Tyrone, and Shams; to Sona, a club run by DJ Tiga, in Montreal; to Ottawa; and to the Summer of Love festival in Vancouver. Back in the United Kingdom, he and Tony Walker, off the success of their radio show, put together the Transatlantic Mix Tour. It brought the two DJs to twenty-seven dates across the United Kingdom in forty-five days. Somewhere in between, Disciple put out a compilation for Maxi Records. To promote it, he followed up the tour with Walker with twelve more dates in Miami at the Winter Music Conference, Tampa, Chicago, Denver, San Francisco, and elsewhere. After the Winter Music Conference, promoter Phillipe Nguyen booked Disciple for gigs in Hong Kong, Singapore, and Taiwan. In coming years, he would head to even more North American cities, to Belgium, Amsterdam, Germany, Greece, Poland, Russia, Morocco, Colombia, Australia, and more. Before long, this schedule began to catch up with him.

"Just imagine taking a cab from the housing projects to the airport, catching a flight to a country you've never been to before, and getting picked up by a limousine, which brings you to a five-star hotel," Disciple said. "Later that night, you play for thousands of people. Then imagine that happening every weekend. It made my head spin.

"It's also something I didn't take for granted. Every time I stepped in a place that I felt was 'high-end,' I'd say to myself, 'Earn this.' Not just as a DJ, but as a Black man. To this day, very few men of color have the opportunity to do what I do. How I represent my integrity, my character, and myself—all that matters to me. I was also representing KimCo, and if she had me play somewhere, it was important to me that her clients always had me back for repeat performances.

"I didn't have the 'Superstar DJ' tag, but I was coming over to the United Kingdom so much, people thought I was British. I was on the road constantly, with Kim checking up on me every step of the way, and that kept me happy. But oftentimes I'd see it go the other way for DJs. Once I reached a certain level of success, it definitely felt good. I was happy that I was able to take care of my dad while pursuing my passion. But I was always looking over my shoulder. I had no idea when the bottom was going to drop out from me, and I'd be looking for a job working 9:00–5:00."

Through years of international touring, surprises could come out of nowhere. One summer on the way to Marbella, Disciple boarded Iberia Airlines flight 6950 and, as usual, began to doze off. He slept through takeoff but woke up soon after to see flight attendants worriedly hurrying up and down the aisles. Other passengers were using the in-cabin phones and others were praying. He looked out the window to his left, and flames were issuing out of one of the engines.

"The pilot announced, 'this plane is being brought back to JFK,'" Disciple said. "He received no clearance to go back to the airport, but he managed to land the craft safely. As the plane was coming in, the controllers outside were trying to put out the fire. Once the plane stopped, passengers started trampling over one another to get off the plane. Many people were under the assumption that the aircraft would explode and take out a big chunk of the cabin. When I saw all of those people jumping out of the plane I just held back, remained calm, and tried to get my belongings off.

"Unfortunately, I wasn't able to get to my bags, so I jumped out and ran as fast and as far away from the plane as possible. The older people on the aircraft suffered the brunt of the injuries while the rest of us got bruises and scrapes from the landing. Confusion and chaos reigned from the time we got off the plane until we were eventually brought back to JFK.

"I was on the phone with my booking agent and my brother Larry as this was happening. My brother's confidence assured me of the one thing I needed to hear and know: that God is in control, and he spared my life that day. As people were hugging each other and crying at the sight of the horrible aftermath of flight 6950, Larry's words played in my mind again and again: 'When someone sees death staring them in the face every individual deals with it differently.'

"Scripture from the Book of John reminded me: 'If we confess our sins, He is faithful and just to forgive our sins and cleanse us from all unrighteousness.' But in the next breath, I wondered: why do I only go to God when I'm in trouble?

"I wasn't looking for God that day; God came looking for me. In that moment, I realized once again how far from my faith I had gotten. I wasn't making choices with my higher self in mind. Instead, I was responding to immediate, selfish wants. Prayer shouldn't be like stopping up the holes in your sinking ship. It should be done when times are good and when times are bad. No one goes to church because they're perfect; they need go to church because they're forgiven. If I'm DJ Disciple and claim to be a Christian (which to me means Christ-like) it should be reflected in my faith in God, as he has been faithful to me. Even though people don't forgive, God forgave me and let me live another day.

"I still didn't want to rest on my laurels. I thought maybe I could push things even farther as a DJ, and I was terrified that if I let up, I would give up before

I had reached my potential. Who knows if these fears were justified? But they drove me to never turn down work. And on the other side of the table, people in the music industry were always feeding me with more.

"For any gig, you were in and out a" quickly as possible. Missing a flight, train, or car was not an option. That often meant skipping meals or sleep. There was never time for sight-seeing. Sometimes there wasn't time to find an hour to kick back and watch television.

"Any days I had off touring, I spent in the studio, at the record press, or working on my label. Dance music and unbounded energy go hand in hand. No other genre has people dancing until the sun rises. You don't find juice bars in rock venues. You never find so much speed,"ecstasy, and MDMA at country or reggae or funk shows. The DJ and the music are the source of this energy, and they're the ones who get people moving from midnight to 6:00 AM. But while those clubbers sleep all Sunday and feel refreshed for work on Monday morning, the DJ is off doing the same thing the next night. There's never time to recoup, but there is plenty of isolation.

"Do that for any amount of years, and it will take a toll on your health, your relationships, and your mental well-being. I considered myself lucky that I had resisted the pull of drug culture. I saw a lot of DJs start out taking drugs for fun and end up using out of necessity. Sometimes this came in the form of addiction, but sometimes it was purely out of the need to have enough energy to make it through their set.

"Kim and JP were amazing to work with, and I never hesitated to tell them if something was wrong. But I knew other industry people who didn't care if they were grinding their DJs down to the bone. They focused on their bottom line first and the professionals who were making them money second or third.

"In a certain sense, this was because DJs were—and are now more than ever—expendable. Any DJ who turns down work knows that there will be three or four others who might be able to match them skill-wise who'll gladly fill in. Who knows how many DJs have been affected negatively because they never turned down work? A good many ended their career before they reached 30. Every single industry worker knows this, but it took the death of Avicii in 2018 for anyone to talk about it openly.

"In the best-case scenario, the industry will disregard your health. In the worst case, it will push you into an early grave. I feel blessed to have found JP and Kim. We cared about each other, and they never would have let anything like that happen with me. But that wasn't the case with others."

1. Keith "KCC" Franklin and DJ Disciple at Notting Hill Carnival, London, UK, 1994. **2.** DJ Disciple and Marques Wyatt at High Society, Los Angeles, California, 1996. **3.** JP Firman at Feel Real, Covent Garden, London, UK, 1994. **4.** The crowd gives Disciple a standing ovation at the Lakota in his debut, Lakota, Bristol, UK, 1992. **5.** Notting Hill Carnival in London during DJ Disciple's set in 2005. **6.** Eddie Perez and DJ Disciple at Smack studios in New Jersey, 1993. **7.** Paul "Trouble" Anderson and DJ Disciple at The Loft, London, UK, 1995. *(All photos from the author's collection.)*

1. Grant Nelson and DJ Disciple at Nice 'N' Ripe Studios, UK, 1995 *(courtesy of Si Firman)*.
2. Mousse T., DJ Disciple, and Boris Dlugosh at Peppermint Park Studios in Hanover, Germany, 1995 *(author's collection)*. **3.** DJ Disciple at Club Yellow, Japan, 1995 *(author's collection)*. **4.** Steve and Bobby Laviniere, UK founders of Zoo Groove Stereo *(courtesy of Donna Ward)*. **5.** Summer of Love in Vancouver, Canada, 1997 *(author's collection)*.

1. Pete Heller appears at the Maxi/Giant Step Winter Music Conference party in Miami, Florida, 1998 *(courtesy of Donna Ward)*. **2.** Dawn Tallman and DJ Disciple in Brooklyn, New York *(author's collection)*. **3.** Daft Punk also known as Thomas Bangalter and Guy-Manuel de Homem-Christo unmasked at Maxi/Giant Step Winter Music Conference party in Miami, Florida *(courtesy of Donna Ward)*. **4.** Kim Benjamin, Pete Heller, and Maxi Records label owner Claudia Cuseta at the Maxi/Giant Step party in Miami, Florida *(courtesy of Donna Ward)*. **5.** Tony Walker, one half of the *Transatlantic Mix* in Sheffield, UK *(author's collection)*.

REBIRTH

For a time in the 1990s, American house music was dead. Then a team of cultural and nightlife EMTs showed up with the defibrillators. They shocked the scene back into existence and gave it the heartbeat it carries today. But this second life could never be a simple replay of the first. In most cases, a capitalistic value discovery powered house culture and introduced it to advertisers, mainstream audiences, and corporate America.

It started with bottle service. With the Giuliani administration hell-bent on stamping out the consumption of illegal drugs in New York venues, clubbers embraced legal alternatives with gusto. You could still hear cutting-edge DJs play in New York through the late 1990s and early 2000s—for a price. Meanwhile, outside of the city, raves exploded in popularity, until local, state, and federal governments brought the axe down on them as well. Just as bottle service replaced clubs, festivals took the place of raves. Like bottle service, these events put an emphasis on commercialization and the sale of alcohol. With new festival audiences and new generations of college students came new music. By the mid-2000s, what we know today as electronic dance music (EDM) had taken hold. On top of all that, file sharing, MP3 players, and the internet completely reworked the dynamics of the house music community.

Still, bottle service and EDM was a whole lot better than nothing. They allowed many artists to continue to work their craft. In the meantime, a small cohort of venues and parties that drew a dedicated crowd kept underground house music alive.

CATCH 22

By 1997, Disciple had been recording music for four years. The initial motivation was to make records to get his name out there, play in more clubs, see new places, and advance his career. The plan worked, and Disciple was grateful it had.

But he also got a look inside the underground record industry, and it left him with a bad taste in his mouth. Labels typically offered house artists and producers a fifty/fifty split for initial publishing revenue, like royalties from record sales and commercial radio play. The label would take care of printing, distribution, and promotion, and they might even pay an advance. But they'd also take the copyright in perpetuity. So while artists got half the royalties from one run of the record, the label could license it for distribution in other countries, get it remixed, get it on compilation CDs, get it in commercials, and more. A total of 100 percent of the revenue from all these sources went back to the label. And especially when records crossed national borders, details could get fuzzy.

DJ Willy Sanjuan, with whom Disciple played and collaborated through the years, learned this lesson firsthand. He and two other producers, DJ Lima and DJ Elias, came up in Barcelona. They made a deal with a Spanish label to produce a record, for which they were paid an advance of three hundred dollars each. "I guess the label decided that three DJs' names on the record was too long," Sanjuan said. "DJ Lima had a successful afterhours party he was running at the time called Tijuana, and we used this cowgirl image from that party for the cover. So the label decided to just call us 'Tijuana' on the record." DJ Elias managed to get it to Danny Howells in the United Kingdom, who in turn passed it to an influential UK DJ. Both DJs were into the track, and the latter bought the universal rights from the Spanish label. He then released the track, had it remixed several times, and put it out on a number of compilation CDs. The label decided not to include the original producers in these proceedings. "We never saw a penny of it," Sanjuan said.

Even house legends like Larry Heard, Robert Owens, Adonis, and many more were exploited by early house labels. Through the decades after they were recorded, Trax—the notorious Chicago label that signed and distributed their music in the 1980s—redistributed and remixed their classic records many times without paying them or even receiving their permission. The label was founded by Larry Sherman, Jesse Saunderson, and Vince Lawrence. It was run for years by Sherman. In one egregious case, Sherman's wife Rachel Cain credited herself as songwriter on a rereleased version of Heard's "Can You Feel It." House artists tried to take Trax to court for years. Civil charges finally stuck when Larry Heard and Robert Owens teamed up and gained funding from their current publisher, Tap Music. Since Sherman had passed and Trax had been in financial difficulty for years, they didn't recoup any financial damages. But they did win back their rights to the music they created.[1]

These represent worse-case scenarios. Under normal circumstances, DJs would at least have their names (and only their names) on the tracks that they themselves produced. If it sold, that would spread their brand awareness and lead to gigs in new countries and new clubs. But you still would lose out on any further profits. In other words, as Disciple saw it, recording as a house producer was a catch-22. You could use it as a way to get your name out and earn new gigs. But once you made the record, it effectively didn't belong to you anymore. Disciple believed that rising artists deserved better. He also believed that he, himself, deserved better. So he launched his own label: Catch 22 Recordings.

In the beginning, Catch 22 releases were distributed by Shuji Hiroshi's Soundmen on Wax outfit. Soon after, Disciple prepared mixes of "Put Your Hands Up" by The Black and White Brothers and "New York City Girl" by Dawn Tallman for American distribution, along with a compilation album by Tuff Jam and his own *The Sidebar EP*.

Disciple quickly learned that the music industry wasn't for the faint of heart. Labels often charged hundreds to thousands of dollars for studio time. Vocalists charged one thousand to two thousand dollars, and producers cost even more. Then came pressing and production costs, and promotion after that. Labels usually outsourced promotion to public relations agencies. Finally, labels had to negotiate distribution deals, which often resulted in eating the costs of unsold units. Labels had to spend a high cost to give a single record a chance at selling, and before they saw a cent of revenue. "As a label owner, I had to make sure I sold enough records to cover expenses at the very least," Disciple said. "Unfortunately, not every record sold. So, when I had a new record to release, I tried to make sure the new one would sell enough to make up for the losses I took while looking for other hits."

With this on his plate, Disciple had to make another difficult decision. He was juggling the new label launch, studio work, media work for *Street Sounds* and Pseudo.com, the *Transatlantic Mix*, touring with Kimco Entertainment, and working with JP in the United Kingdom. There was little time for *New York's Best Kept Secret* on WNYE 91.5. Disciple decided to stop doing the radio show altogether. "My mindset I had was, 'If I'm not playing on *Best Kept Secret*, I'd better find an outlet to play music in New York,'" Disciple said. "I missed the local scene."

New York nightlife was splintering further in the late 1990s, even among house heads. The straight house crowd went to the Sound Factory Bar on Wednesdays, and the gay house crowd went to the Roxy. Even genres divided audiences. Lounge, electronic, and drum and bass all had distinct communities.

Disciple still managed to play parties here and there. One close collaborator emerged in the form of E Man. Disciple had known him since he was an intern for Farragut neighbor and producer Steve "Strafe" Standard. Over the years, he went to work for Tommy Boy Music, and then served as a bodyguard for Tupac Shakur. The two collaborated on a party Disciple called Lift at the Brooklyn loft space Ray Hands.

A year later, E Man was working security on the television show *New York Undercover*. Stanley Banks was recording bass for the show's score. In Brooklyn, E Man told Disciple about a new party he was running for the film crew. The two discussed collaborating further, but, typical of the time, many others involved wanted to steer clear of house music.

"E Man was very successful at the time, and I felt discouraged, although I didn't show it," Disciple said. "Even though I was making it overseas, I wanted to find more work in New York. I was earning a living as a DJ, but traveling was expensive. I wouldn't spend as much if I could work in my city instead of traveling for gigs."

MY TRUE COLORS

From the Mixer tour, and the success of "Put Your Hands Up" by The Black & White Brothers, Disciple was able to save enough to fund his first full-length LP, *My True Colors*. The ball started rolling when Disciple got in touch with Jeremy Sylvester. At Keith Franklin's suggestion, he had visited him in 1998 during a break in his UK tour. The two put out a track, "Desire," under the name X-Factor-7. The song laid some necessary groundwork for the future.

For Sylvester, studio engineering was the family business. His dad ran Eye 2 Eye Studios in Birmingham and had made a name for himself as a disco producer. Growing up, Jeremy always took the opportunity to work in the studio any time it was vacant or when a band dropped out. By the time he linked up with Disciple, he was a master behind the boards.

"Since I had begun work in the studio, I usually followed the same format," Disciple said. "I'd collaborate with other artists or producers to write the song and lay down a basic framework along with lyrics to send to the singer. They would record the vocals, I'd overlay it on the original, and then the fun began."

Disciple brought together a few familiar faces to work on the LP. The album included vocal performances from Angie Johnson, Mia Cox, Inaya Day, and

Suzy. Rhythm Masters came in to collaborate on "It's Easy," and Robbie Rivera lent his hand to "Keep It Up."

But the most successful track of the record would prove to be "Caught Up." To write the song, Disciple brought together Helen Bruner and Terry Jones. Singer Mia Cox voiced the lead. Jeremey Sylvester presided over the boards. "Helen and Terry were go-getters," Disciple said. "As songwriters they were constantly shaking things up and finding great singers to work with me or coming up with great songs quickly."

When the single was released in 2000 on Catch 22 Recordings, it made its way to the number one spot on the Billboard Dance charts. Two years later, Disciple received a letter in the mail from Contact Artist. It said that "Caught Up" had made it past the first-round level of the Grammy nomination process in the category for "Best Dance Recording." The track was licensed and redistributed around the world. It also appeared on the HBO series *Queer as Folk*, which in turn was also nominated for a Grammy in the category of "Best Compilation Album For Motion Picture, Television, or Other Visual Media."

"Caught Up" didn't win either award it was nominated for. In fact, *My True Colors* didn't sell all that well in its first run. But the album took dance floors around the world by storm. The tracks "Yes," "Caught Up," and "It's Easy" were licensed for compilations around the world, including major labels like Hed Kandi in the United Kingdom.

"There are ways to implement what you learn in the studio, while keeping the integrity of the craft," Disciple said. "I'd do harder records, and because of the people I was working with, I tried new and inventive ways to produce fresher sounds. James Preston, Eddie Perez, Michele Chiavarini, and Gerald Elms leveled the playing field for me to produce songs that implemented live musicianship. I refused to let the music I made put me in a box. There is freedom in taking chances and having a collaborative mindset."

Now that the radio show was gone, he had to prove that there were other secrets he could expose to his audience. But that proof didn't come cheap. If his living expenses weren't eating away the money he was earning, the studio was.

But some dividends paid off. Six months after its release, the Rhythm Masters collaboration "It's Easy" got picked up by Azuli Records. The track sampled the Al Jarreau song "Easy." Stanley Banks was friends with the jazz legend, and Disciple was hoping to avoid the ire of both musicians. In the end, the sample cleared, and Jeremy Sylvester teamed up again with Paul Emmanuel under the alias Club Asylum to remix the track. The two were another formative UK garage group. The same duo had earlier cut a remix for "Steal Away," one of Disciple's many collaborations with Dawn Tallman, for Tuff Jam's label UndaVybe. Ibiza DJs adopted "It's Easy" as a club favorite. The track drew the attention of the Spanish label Blanco Y Negro, which also picked up "Put Your Hands Up." *Billboard Magazine*'s Michael Paoletta wrote that the LP was "[a] sublime showcase for Disciple's gospel-splashed house productions."[2]

BOTTLES AND MODELS

In the late 1990s, New York clubland was in trouble. But necessity is the mother of invention. In an effort to keep the lights on, two Manhattan promoters were about to unleash a new club business model on the world. It would come to be known as bottle service.

Selling (and consuming) entire bottles of liquor was nothing new. Tunnel started selling bottles in 1993, offering clubgoers deals for buying in bulk. However, in the late 1990s, two things changed: the strategy and the price. In 1995, David Sarner, one of the owners of Spy Bar and Chaos, started selling bottles of Stolichnaya vodka for $195 each. This change involved a subtle mechanism. As Sarner told *New York Magazine* in 2006, "Back then, it wasn't about how much liquor we could pour down people's throats—it was about creating a barrier to entry."[3] The club world, just like any other market (and especially in the heady days of the late 1990s economy), operates by the logic of supply and demand. Sarner devised a way to concentrate and elevate the supply. It didn't take long for demand to follow.

Clubgoers with deep pockets started drinking in exclusive clubs where each table was stocked with alcohol and mixers. Spy Bar, the first club to use the new strategy, was located at 101 Greene Street in SoHo, which at the time was full of old warehouses and lofts.

"SoHo was an abandoned neighborhood for the most part," Disciple said. "You'd see sex workers walking the streets, pursuing their business just down the block from the venues. People didn't really live near the lofts and warehouses where we had the parties. SoHo had a unique vibe that Spy Bar embraced. It was cool."

As Sarner's partner, Michael Ault, told BlackBook in 2008:

The excitement of the 1990s was gone. No one was dressing up, [there was] no sense that anything could happen or would happen. The mix had evaporated, and everything was quite flat. I wanted to try something really outrageous, a synthesis of Blade Runner, a haunted house, a New Orleans Bordello, and a SoHo loft none of us could afford. That was the birth of Spy Bar.[4]

Seemingly out of nowhere, bottle service clubs completely revitalized New York nightlife. They targeted an upper-class crowd and turned away anyone who couldn't pay. For patrons, getting into the prestigious bottle service clubs required connections, good looks, or thick folds of cash on hand. Bouncers at the door had to pick and choose who could get in and who could not.

While Ault and Sarner ran Spy Bar, they selected Roger Sanchez, Disciple, and Dove as their resident DJs to play on Friday nights. Starting out, the gigs were a steal for New York DJs who were trying to stay relevant in the saturated scene. The parties provided venues for DJs to play, and they also paid well. Models, celebrities, press, and actors were all over the scene.

François Edmond was promoting for Spy Bar at the time. Hailing from France, he wanted to work with DJs who had experience playing in Europe. He wanted to bring Ibiza vibes to indoor New York venues.

"Bottle service was really at its peak when I was brought in by François, who I first met at Spy Bar," DJ Dove said. "He later brought me into the fold at Pangaea. There began my legacy in NYC. I came across great people, including celebrities like Robert Downey Jr., Bono, Sting, and Wesley Snipes. They all complimented me on my music, although my discussions with Wesley Snipes were more extensive. He was a house music fan and used to party at the Paradise Garage."

Disciple invited his brother Larry to his set one night at Spy Bar. Larry had never heard his brother play in a nightclub before, and this first time proved challenging. He brought a date, and they waited in line. When the bouncer passed by, Larry told him his brother was the DJ that night. The staff at the door were used to hearing stories like Larry's, and they wouldn't let him skip the line. It took him a while to get in.

"When I came to the place, I should have known something was wrong," Larry said. "I walked in with my girlfriend and ordered a drink. I said, 'How much?' and the bartender said, 'No, you don't pay for this one.' I said, 'What do you mean we don't pay?' He said, 'Just take the drink.'

"So we took the drink. We walked into the club. We went to sit down, and a guy said, 'Nope, you can't sit here.' I said, 'Why can't we sit here?' He said, 'This is the $500 section.' I said, 'What!?' He said, 'It costs $500 to sit here. You get a bottle, but you have to pay $500.' I didn't really like that. Then we went upstairs and another guy said, 'This is the $1,000 section.' I didn't like that at all."

Larry's experience made Disciple uneasy, but other factors also offset his feelings. The crowd at Spy Bar was very knowledgeable about music. Every time Disciple played, François called beforehand and filled him in on what to expect for the evening.

Some club owners consistently chose Disciple to play their events. More bottle service opportunities opened up, and it wasn't uncommon for promoters to jump from venue to venue. Disciple was considered François' DJ. When François left Spy Bar and started working at Pangaea, Disciple followed. (Ault opened Pangaea in 2001 as his next club after Spy Bar.)

"The bottle service gigs gave me great opportunities to play in New York," Disciple said. "But as months went by, I felt a lot of uncertainty. I couldn't trust many of the promoters. One moment, they told DJs they wanted them to be the resident every week, and the next moment, they'd fire them. No notice, no good reasoning. From what I've seen, it seems like they fired some DJs for no reason at all.

"Bottle service promoters never said the words, 'You're fired.' Instead, they'd say, 'Your set got bumped.' The explanations ranged from, 'We're having a private party tonight,' to 'We just want to try out some other DJs.' François was the only person who never gave up on me. He always told me stuff like, 'Pump it up, Disciple. No, go deep, go deep. Make it sexy, make it sexy.' He was passionate about his work, and he wanted to create an experience for the guests. And no matter what, he always believed in me.

"There were many times when François and the owners didn't see eye to eye. Some of the promoters wanted to create a European experience, similar to the clubs in Ibiza. A lot of the club owners had never seen that before. There were always too many cooks in the kitchen when a new bottle service spot opened. When the scene started to heat up, François found his way into the most exclusive clubs. Dove and I came along for the ride."

Disciple and Dove both moved to Pangaea. There, Disciple made his debut on Halloween in 2001.

"Halloween was a big success, and all the promoters agreed that I'd be a good look," Disciple said. "But one Wednesday a few weeks later, the crowd was not feeling my style at all. Sometimes, promoters clashed with one another. Gil

Traub, who was often at Pangaea on the same night as François, came up to the DJ booth. I got the impression he didn't like what I was playing.

"Gil wasn't the only one feeling this way. Other promoters came up with the same conclusion. And after that, I was never asked to play at Pangaea again. I felt like crap. When you play great music and the crowd loves you, you feel unstoppable, but when the opposite happens, it makes you want to hang up the DJ career for good. I have to admit, I was discouraged. Looking back now, I recognize that it was just the roll of the dice. In some instances, the DJ is the first to blame when things go wrong in a night.

"François decided to give me another chance. After he and Gil left Pangaea, they went right across the street and worked for Rehab, another new bottle service club. This time, I took full advantage of my opportunities. I couldn't play on the weekends because I was usually on tour. But I was always in demand when I was in town, which was usually during the week, or whenever I got a weekend off.

"Gil didn't like my music at Pangaea, but suddenly he loved it at Rehab. He and Walter Kim, his partner and host, wanted me to play for them anytime I was free. It was like Pangaea never happened. Not only did I do better DJ sets at Rehab, but it was easier for me to break in new music.

"Playing bottle service clubs felt like musical chairs. Walter Kim, who worked with Gil and François, owned many bottle service clubs over the years. I ultimately secured gigs and residencies by networking with the right people. When I moved over to Quo, I ran into celebrities like Q-Tip. His song 'Vivrant Thing' from the *Amplified* album was still tearing clubs up. He showed me love during my house music set.

"Eventually, open format DJs became trendy. They played a wide spectrum of music, from rock to hip hop to 80s to house. I stayed true to my roots and rebelled against the open format DJ trend. Gil backed me the whole way. Today, open format is considered the norm. But back then, it was house music. They gave me a platform to work and play only the music I loved. Cielo, Pacha, Vinyl, Webster Hall, Sullivan Room, and APT became the go-to spots for house music. I was a guest at most of those venues, and they never looked at me as a resident. Without Gil, Walter, and Francois, my DJ workload in the city would be little to nothing."

Through the bottle service scene, Disciple came in contact with another promoter, Jamie Mulholland. Mulholland and his business partner Jayme Cardoso were the forces behind Cain, another bottle service joint the two opened in an old taxi garage in West Chelsea. They met when they were working behind the bar at Lotus, a club in the Meatpacking District. Resolving to open their own venue, the two hustled their connections in New York nightlife, secured funding, and went on to open numerous successful clubs around North America.

Jamie Mulholland invited Disciple to play every Wednesday. On Fridays, Disciple had a residency at Quo. Outside of New York, Mulholland and Cardoso ran Cain pop-up parties all over the country. When the Winter Music Conference took place in Miami in 2003, they sent Disciple to play at The Versace Mansion with Pete Tong.

"Tons of records, artists, and tracks came out of the bottle service scene," Disciple said. "From Germany, Boris Dlugosh remixed Moloko's 'Sing It Back,' while Michael Kronenberger and Steven Sugar formed Milk & Sugar. The duo released hits like 'Love Is in the Air' featuring John Paul Young in 2001 and 'Let the Sun Shine' in 2003. In Sweden, artists like StoneBridge ('Put 'Em High'), Eric Prydz ('Call On Me'), and Axwell ('Feel The Vibe' and 'Watch The Sunrise') with Steve Edwards became the soundtracks for certain bottle service venues."

Lastly, French veterans Bob Sinclair ("Love Generation" and "World Hold On"), Daft Punk ("One More Time" and "Lady" under the alias Modjo), and David Guetta ("Love Don't Let Me Go" and "The World Is Mine") opened the door for house music with commercial appeal.

"Some of these producers transitioned to what would become EDM but helped bridge the gap between the adolescence and maturation of house music in bottle service venues. DJs like myself were always looking for the newest thing. We didn't follow a regulated music policy.

"Parties like Made in Italy, for instance, wanted music that set trends, not music that follows them. The music helped fill a void that I think people overlook. American producers like Armand Van Helden ('My My My'), Roger Sanchez ('Another Chance'), and Deep Dish ('Flashdance') got decent play and so did many UK producers like Shapeshifters ('Lola's Theme'), Tim Deluxe ('It Just Won't Do'), and Joey Negro.

"DJs like Marco Peruzzi from France, DJ Amadeus from Ukraine, and Nadav Vee and Vangee from Israel also helped change the musical landscape in New York clubs.

"Mulholland was an amazing person to work with, but as Cardoso told me, 'Disciple, you have a style, people love it, but for this venue you're going to have to be more than the one style you've been playing for us.' What worked at Quo didn't work at Cain.

"The scene was changing fast. Cain didn't have a great sound system at the time, and the lighting was automated. The club had open format nights, and the promoters were uneasy with a strictly house music policy.

"One Wednesday I got a call from the club rep, who said, 'Hey, listen Disciple, we are having a private party tonight.' I knew that was code for, 'You're fired.' Calling from a different number, I reached Jamie and got straight to the point. I told him it was great working together and that I understood the position he was in. I knew that I had become a bad fit for the party.

"'You're right,' Jamie told me. 'I appreciate you calling me and telling me that.'

"Getting fired in bottle service clubs was a reality that could happen on the drop of a dime. Sometimes, it didn't matter who you are or how you play music. If a new promoter came in with his DJ, the DJ with no promoter usually had to leave. At Cain, my style didn't always shine. I stayed true to the music I loved to play, but the crowd didn't always love it. Twenty-seventh Street does not offer cheap real estate. Bills need to be paid, so I knew exactly what the deal was. I decided to save face and keep my doors open."

Disciple was not alone on this promoter rollercoaster ride. Dove was often in the same position.

"Dove actually introduced me to many players in the bottle service scene," Disciple said. "He was well-loved at Spy Bar and Pangaea, but there were some venues he didn't vibe with. We both experienced a lot of broken promises from promoters who loved us in the moment, but dropped us when it was convenient.

"Dove made a name for himself playing Made in Italy parties. He brought me up to Manhattan and the Hamptons for a few of them. Once, during the grand opening of Greenhouse on Varick Street, the venue decided to not honor our guest lists. While we both had people showing up to see us play, we had to meet them outside and tell them they weren't allowed in. The event left a bad taste in my mouth. It wasn't fun when we couldn't get our own people to come out and hear us spin. As DJs, we experienced that often.

"Eventually, no matter how good the money was, I found drama working in the bottle service scene. There were so many other DJs willing to play, often at cheaper rates, and sometimes even for free. I had to maintain both my musical and monetary value.

"Some people said there was racism and preferential treatment in bottle service events, but I'd say the issue was more industry nepotism. For example, if I am scheduled to DJ one night, I could get canceled because a promoter, who has his own DJ, along with models and bottle-buyers, approached the owner who hired me to come in and made him a proposition to bring in more business.

"DJ Vangee, Marco Peruzzi, Nadav Vee, DJ Dove, DJ Exacta, and I rotated on different nights at the Pink Elephant. I eventually stopped regularly playing at the venue, but I maintained a good relationship with the owners. I still got to play some special events there.

"From there, I moved to Guest House, which was run by Jon Bakshi. As years went on, the bottle service scene started to go south. Promoters and club owners were constantly on the hunt to fill their venues with attractive women. More venues popped up, and more bouncers failed to check IDs at the door. If patrons fit the mold, they were in."

At the same time, more clubs did steady business selling entire bottles of liquor. New Yorkers' appetite to alter their states of conscious hadn't changed. But the vibe had. The LSD and speed of the 1960s and 1970s had slowly given way to ecstasy in the 1980s and 1990s. But with the writing clear on the wall for any venues that could be associated with drugs, legal alcohol came to reign supreme. It wasn't difficult to draw the connection between the binge drinking phenomenon, pools of vomit, and passed out partiers lining the streets on any given Thursday, Friday, or Saturday night. *New York Magazine* reported in the summer of 2005 that the bottle service industry was valued at ten billion dollars. One unnamed clubgoer described the scene as "Disneyland for drunks."[5]

Jon Bakshi, known as "Jon B," operated at the frontier of this Wild West. He was the mastermind behind Home, Guest House, and Greenhouse. He kept Home open for six nights a week, and Guest House was open for five. His bottle service operations were exclusive in price only. Many folks considered the bottle service scene to be toxic. But pushing that much liquor to that many people soon introduced a dangerous element into the mix.

The fate of Jennifer Moore exemplified this shift. On July 25, 2006, the eighteen-year-old Moore headed to New York with her friend Talia Keenan for a night out at the clubs. They were carded at Guest House, but Jennifer had her sister's ID, and they let her in. Later that night, they returned to the car to find that it had been towed. The attendants at the 12th Avenue Tow Pound refused to hand over the keys because Jennifer and Talia were so drunk. Talia soon passed out, and someone called an ambulance to take her to the hospital. Jennifer, meanwhile, went missing. Her body was found days later in a dumpster in Weehawken, New Jersey.

Disciple took the decks at Guest House a few days after the news broke. "I was incredibly conflicted, especially because the rape and murder of Jennifer Moore didn't slow down bottle service attendance in the least," Disciple said.

"The event sent me down a winding path in the moral wilderness. I was not complicit in the crime, and many didn't think Guest House was either."

Journalist and dedicated clubber Tricia Romano later voiced this perspective for the *Village Voice*, arguing how backwards nightclub policy had become in New York:

> Other deaths have been unfairly attributed to the clubs themselves, most notably the July case of 19-year-old Jennifer Moore, who is being used as the Patron Saint of Underage Drinking Legislation when she should be used as the Patron Saint of Changing the Drinking Law. If Moore had been drinking legally that night, she might not have wandered off while her friend was being taken to the hospital, which she presumably did because she was afraid of being caught. Guest House, where she'd partied much earlier that night, is still being blamed for her murder, even though she wasn't murdered there, wasn't murdered by anyone she met there, and was actually murdered in another state many hours after leaving the club, even after she came in contact with police—who could have helped her and didn't. Repeat after me: Guest House did not murder Jennifer Moore.[6]

"Still, other venues on that block catered to a younger crowd," Disciple said. "The situation was a wake-up call for me." In the 2010s, the open format formula took over New York. People opted to have their house music experience in Brooklyn, and loads of DJs followed behind them. DJ Amadeus, who played Mansion, M2, Ultralounge, Crobar, and Pink Elephant during this era, also resisted the open format phenomenon and, like Disciple, made the move to Brooklyn.

"I was never a bottle service crowd fan, but I enjoyed playing regardless," Amadeus said. "It was a huge deal for me to be a resident of such rooms. The bottle service crowd never appreciated the music, only tracks they knew, and all that commercial wave led into what we have today—open format/hip hop. That's why most of us eventually moved to Brooklyn, where people can appreciate the music. I was the resident of Tunnel, Limelight, and then Exit. That was the time. Bottle service destroyed it all. We would sometimes be able to remove tables from the dance floor. Like when I played with Offer Nissim. He got up and refused to play until all the tables were removed."

"Talk about another catch-22," Disciple said. "Bottle service turned the New York clubbing experience upside-down, and no one shed a tear when the venues closed. But for me, working in the bottle service scene was a good way to stay current if I wasn't traveling—at least for a while. I could still expose the best music in that scene, and I had an edge over the other talent I was up against.

"Bottle service didn't pay me back the way other scenes did, but I had success working in it until 2017. Later, I even convinced Roger Sanchez to play Baroque, a high-end venue in Astoria, Queens, where I had a residency. It helped me maintain relevance in a place where people have an 'out of sight, out of mind' mentality. Bottle service became a dirty word in some New York circles, and a lot of the criticism is valid. Social standing used to melt away on the dance floor. Now it was being reinforced. Still, I can't join everyone who loves to bad-mouth it to this day."

GREAT BRITISH HOUSE

All was not lost for New York house heads who didn't vibe with bottle service. A new party was about to come along and rain down on the underground savannah. It was known as Great British House, or GBH. The story of GBH started when two house fans, Alejandro Torio and Tom Dunkley, joined forces to throw Friday night parties at a Manhattan venue known as Vanity on 23rd Street between 6th and 7th Avenues.

Another friend and house fan named Karla Romero—who worked as a flight attendant—soon won them an important connection. On a flight she was working, she saw a man named Anthony Maccaroni (who DJed as Anthony Mac) scribbling down ideas on a napkin. She went over and asked what he was doing. He told Karla that he was the director of promotion at King Street Records in Manhattan and was doing a house music party in City Gardens Nightclub in Trenton, New Jersey, called Bounce.

Having something in common, Karla told Anthony that her friends Tom and Alejandro were starting a party at Vanity, but that they weren't having much luck with the DJ they had. Anthony Mac decided to go to check it out.

"There were very few people at the venue," Mac remembers. "The vibe was lousy, and the DJ was playing drum and bass. I told them that I had been DJing for over 15 years and that I grew up hanging out at NYC clubs." Mac convinced Dunkley and Torio to get him on the bill for the next GBH party. Once he started playing, the promoters were sold. They offered him the resident DJ job on the spot. "I told them I was too busy with the label," Mac said. "But I could help promote the party, fill in as DJ from time to time, and teach them a thing or two in the process."

Going forward, Mac kept Tom up to date about house music and gave suggestions to Alejandro concerning promotions. In Mac's opinion he felt that every major club was playing what some were calling New York progressive house. He sensed that most house heads were sick of this sound and would react positively to a return to basics. "After about one month with GBH I decided that we needed to draw more attention to the event," Mac said. "That's when I decided to call DJ Disciple, who had played for me a few times. We had a good, friendly relationship."

"I was playing at Spy Bar when I wasn't traveling," Disciple said. "But still, I thought this would be a great opportunity to play one more New York venue."

"I was right," Mac said. "DJ Disciple took the event to another level with not only his notoriety but also his sets. He lit the room on fire. It wasn't long before we moved from the basement of Vanity to the main floor. My assistant and partner Roman Schlepanov (DJ Little Roma) and I would rock the main floor and when Disciple would take over the decks, a special thing started to grow. The place was packed like sardines.

"We started booking other big-name guest DJs. Tom would consult me before any DJ booking to get my opinion on the DJ if he had little knowledge of their ability or style. I, on the other hand, usually knew the DJs personally, since my job was to call them every week to make sure they were playing my records. This went on for about two years until eventually Tom didn't need me to make suggestions much . . . from time to time he would consult with me but the birdie learned how to fly on his own."

In the end, GBH grew into an institution because of the promoters' attitudes. They first and foremost wanted to hear great music and put on great shows. They wanted to support artists, and they didn't want to cut corners. Fans picked up on that.

When GBH outgrew Vanity, they moved to Disciple's old stomping ground, The Sound Factory Bar, which now operated as The Cheetah. The same venue where Frankie Knuckles once spun now hosted what was considered by house heads to be the hottest party in New York. Instead of DJ Camacho playing downstairs in the funk hut, DJ Frank Delour satisfied everyone who was hungering for hip hop, reggae, R&B, and pop. If the DJ upstairs didn't play the right music, Delour would have the club to capacity in a moment's notice.

"Tom gave me the choice to either play a few spots here and there while getting paid as a guest DJ or to act like the resident," Disciple said. "I went with the second choice, because it allowed me to play more often. Suddenly I had regular monthly gigs in New York on top of bottle service spots."

The bill for one of Disciple's GBH parties advertised, ironically, "The Ministry of Sound's DJ Disciple." It turns out the secret to Disciple gaining renown in his hometown was playing for years in foreign countries.

"In house music, authority is conferred on you if you play abroad," Disciple said. "It doesn't make sense, but it's always been that way. The irony was doubled by the fact that the party was called Great British House. The house scene had come down with a bad case of reverse narcissism, preferring to import its heroes as it does. It's a dizzying phenomenon that DJs from the states are bigger in the United Kingdom and British jocks are bigger over here."

Disciple was not one to complain. He proved again that, with the right attitude, he can adapt his sound to each crowd and its collective set of expectations. After stretching to play harder in the United Kingdom and elsewhere, he recalibrated for GBH parties with more vocal, deep house.

Tom also gave Disciple the freedom to have whomever he wanted to play with him. He invited the prolific producer Robbie Rivera on for a set. He and Disciple had collaborated on a track, "Treble and Bass," which made it onto a Carl Cox mix album.

Disciple also had a few old friends over, including Tony Walker and Bobby & Steve for their American debut. The London DJ twins brought a crowd of about forty fans with them. When they landed, they were shocked to witness how publicly police brutality played out in New York.

They arrived in February of 1999, just after the shooting of Amadou Diallo. It was all over the news. The city was just recovering from the incident concerning Abner Louima, who was sexually assaulted by the police in 1997. The buzz only increased a year later when each of the four police officers, who had fired a collective forty-one shots at Diallo, were acquitted of all charges.

"As much as this took them aback, the Zoo Crew was able to leave these issues at the entrance to the club," Disciple said. "Once they started playing, everything became an afterthought. I was in awe watching Bobby Zoo bring the room up with unbridled excitement."

After a few years of continued success, Carl Kennedy and Tom decided the time had come for GBH to move on from Cheetah. They took the party to Centro-Fly.

"At Centro-Fly, it was fun playing with the likes of my mates DJ Sneak, Derrick Carter, and Donald Glaude, and sharing the bill with Tony Humphries," Disciple said. "But the biggest moment I had at the venue was when my dad came out to see me. We all learned in 2002 that he'd developed congestive heart failure, and I lost a desire to look for somewhere else to live. I decided to stay in Farragut and take care of him.

"Tom and Alejandro set up a VIP station for him, but he didn't want to sit back. He spent the whole night glued to the DJ booth looking on while the room was rocking at full capacity.

"The spirit of GBH was so refreshing. Tom and Alejandro trusted the DJs completely and they let us take control of the crowd. They also loved the music and would stay to the end of the party every time. There were some GBH resident nights where it was just Carl Kennedy, Anthony Mac, and me playing with complete freedom."

Before long, GBH took on the feel of New York dance parties from a previous era.

"I used to have a massive DJ booth and private bar with literally a prototype sound system where I would play unreleased music, filtered house tracks, vocals, and deep house to over 900 people every Friday night," Anthony Mac said. "I was always honored when guests would come to the DJ booth and ask if I was the headliner. I would set the perfect mood for the guest DJ to ensure everyone was loose, sweaty, and ready to party.

"GBH was not primarily an event to attend because of the drugs, or the scene, or the bottle service or even the women . . . the MAJOR reason people came to GBH was for the MUSIC."

A good many New York house fans responded to this spirit. The party grew and grew over the years. It provided a non–bottle service bridge for house music between the late 1990s and what would become EDM in the mid-2000s. In addition, the party showcased emerging talent. Once the founders booked a promising young French DJ duo called Justice for five hundred dollars to play a 150-person room.[7] Soon, it was time for GBH to move on again, and they selected the venue Lotus as their new spot. In their new venue, the party changed accordingly. "By 2005 GBH had moved to Lotus, and they were beginning to focus on other genres besides house music," Disciple said. "They started doing rock, electro clash, and hip hop nights. They still used me on a monthly basis to

Frankie Knuckles, DJ Disciple, Tedd Patterson, and Bobby D'Ambrosio at Centro-Fly *(courtesy of Tedd Patterson)*.

spin house music for them, but their real business transferred to other genres and other parties."

"The legacy of GBH will be that it brought back something New York was missing," Anthony Mac said. "A key ingredient of the world-renowned NYC nightlife scene that was dead at the time.... Deep, underground house music with soul, funk, and a bit of a hard edge. People from around the world came to GBH and heard quality, cutting-edge, unreleased house music that you couldn't hear anywhere else in the city. It was an event that stands with the best of them. We should hold our heads high and be proud of the music we played to thousands of enthusiasts from around the globe."

9/11

In the summer of 2001, Disciple transitioned from writing for *Mixer* to TrustTheDJ.com. A DJ-owned and -operated website, they asked Disciple to give reports of his adventures. So after playing in Ibiza in the summer of 2001 and going back to the United Kingdom, Disciple got to work. Unfortunately, one of the first things he had to speak about were the 9/11 attacks.

"They happened on a Tuesday," Disciple said. "I was in the middle of a busy schedule. I was in the United Kingdom, set to play at Milk in Belfast that Friday, head on to Pacha in Ibiza, then come back to play Ministry of Sound in London later that month. I knew the strife and the grief that New York was going through, but being removed, I didn't feel it deeply myself.

"The news played out in the United Kingdom feverishly, but in Ireland, it just felt like life moved on. No impact. Had I been in New York, I think I would have felt it harder. The main thing that immediately changed in my life was stricter security checks at the airport."

Ralph Davis, also known as Kool D, former Sound Experience Crew member and New York Police Department detective, had a different experience.

"When 9/11 happened, I was stationed at Manhattan South Narcotics," Davis said. "I was scheduled to work the late tour—from 3:00 PM to 11:00 PM. I had just moved into a new apartment after my first wife and I had divorced. I didn't have much furniture. I didn't even have a TV. So I got all my news from the radio. Every morning, I listened to 1010 WINS. So I wake up and heard the news. I called up the command, and they said just get to the nearest police precinct and pick up with them. And I guess we'll see you when we see you. That was really crazy.

"By the time I got down to the World Trade Center, it was after 1:00 PM. Both towers had fallen, and everyone was covered in this gray dust. Everybody was gray. The only building left standing was half of Building Seven. Thank God I didn't get there earlier. You know, a lot of my co-workers were in court that morning. And when they heard what was happening, they ran straight to the World Trade Center to help out. No one knew the buildings were going to collapse.

"And then a lot of my other co-workers inhaled fiberglass. A lot have been forced to retire early and go on disability. Some I know have started going through chemotherapy. Nothing has affected me yet, thank God. But it was three days before they issued us proper respirators. In that first period, we were just wearing construction dust masks. I was inhaling that crap for three days.

"Then they sent us to the Staten Island landfill for 12-hour shifts. We were combing through the wreckage they brought out, looking for body parts, ID cards, you know, personal items, police and fire department equipment. We were all working in Tyvek suits. It felt like you were being hypnotized. Some of us would nod off while they were standing, and someone had to come up and nudge them awake. For a minute after that, there was a truce between NYPD and New Yorkers. People started to trust us again."

Many remember New York coming together in the wake of the attacks. Disciple went through his own reevaluation of law enforcement.

"As I heard more about the event, 9/11 also changed the way I thought about the NYPD," Disciple said. "I remember joking with Camacho in the United Kingdom sometime in the 1990s. I asked him what he'd do if the police tried to arrest him. He said, 'What are they gonna do, hit me with a stick?' We both laughed.

"Fast forward to 2001, and I'm with Vicci Whithow, Kim's assistant, at a coffee shop in the west end of London. A young man snatched Vicci's purse and ran out of the shop. I chased him down the block, grabbing the back of his shirt. I wanted to punch him in the face, not for snatching the purse, but for reminding myself that I need to go to the gym! Straightening him up, I brought him back to the coffee shop, made him apologize for his crime, and sent him on his way. Reflecting later, I wondered what would have happened if we were in New York and the police had gotten involved. Things might have gone very differently, and not in my favor.

"The cops in the United Kingdom police by consent, not by force, which is why you don't see them with guns. I get the feeling that Brits don't want to live in a police state. That's probably one of the reasons why I initially loved staying there for more extended periods.

"But after 9/11, I wanted to be closer to home. Seeing the bravery displayed by the police officers rescuing people and trying to get them away from the towers wholly changed my way of thinking. The NYPD had a conflicted reputation in Farragut. My views about police officers were a love-hate thing. For the first time, I saw them demonstrate heroism I was proud of. The firefighters, sacrificing their lives, and people doing whatever they could to keep each other safe, it made me want to be there.

"Black lives matter, and I have supported the protests against officers who have unjustifiably taken the lives of notable Black men, practiced 'stop and frisk,' and contributed to mass incarceration for non-offensive crimes. I understand there will be people who abuse their power when in law enforcement. But

I also recognize that officers like my friends Ralph, Monty, Steve, and others have contributed to trying to making police-community relations better."

9/11 would prove to have a strong ripple effect across American music. Jay-Z, Mariah Carey, and even GBH released albums on the day of the attacks. The event triggered immediate change. Americans were both deeply saddened and on edge. Concerts, tours, and award shows were canceled. Other events were called off for fear of further attacks. The record sales in the New York metropolitan area experienced a 16.2 percent overall decline in the following week.[8] Many radio stations stopped playing music altogether to broadcast news instead. As the dust began to settle, moods began to coalesce around two foundations: supporting victims and their families, and patriotism. The 1984 country hit "God Bless America" by Lee Greenwood reached number sixteen on the Billboard Hot 100 chart. David Bowie, Destiny's Child, Jay-Z, Paul McCartney, Elton John, and Billy Joel headlined an October 20 benefit show at Madison Square Garden. Radio networks banned certain songs, while others circulated lists of tracks that were in poor taste and should be avoided. Suddenly, the last thing anyone wanted to hear was something provocative.

CDJs

Many things were changing in the early 2000s, including DJs' media and formats of choice. The compact disc had arisen during the 1980s and, by 2000, most cars were being made with CD players instead of cassette decks.

"I decided to switch from vinyl to CD and bought a Pioneer CDJ100S," Disciple said. "It was small, compact, and easier to travel with compared to records. It allowed me to keep my music from getting lost or stolen. I was touring too often to get my records taken again. Plus, the CDJ 100S had a flange that I loved.

"Some DJs looked down their noses at me for making the change. Others didn't even notice. The audiophile culture that has people spending thousands of dollars on turntable needles and filling up hard drives with FLAC files wasn't around in the 2000s the way it is now. Back then, CDs were in, and vinyl was out."

Meanwhile, the Moving Pictures Experts Group developed a new form of computer file in the early 1990s. They called it the MPEG, and the third generation of it came to be known as the MP3.[9] Saehan Information Systems developed the first MP3 player in 1997.[10] Then there was peer-to-peer file sharing from client software developers like Napster and LimeWire. Pretty soon, a lot of DJs were finding it much more convenient to leave vinyl behind in favor of newer, lighter, smaller formats.

Apple's first-generation iPod and iTunes also launched in early 2001, and Apple-sponsored dancing silhouettes were covering billboards and television screens around the world. Deep, structural changes were rumbling through the music industry. In hindsight, these changes would not turn out well for most. *CNN Money*'s Dan Goldsmith would refer to the 2000s as the music industry's "lost decade." US music sales stood at $14.6 billion in 1999. By 2010, they had tumbled down to $6.3 billion.[11] North American music sales—primarily made up today by streaming service revenue—have begun to rebound. But you have to go back to 1992 to find a year where pre-digital music sales were lower than what the industry netted in 2018.[12]

LE SOUK

While GBH was branching out from house music in 2005, Disciple made another longtime connection. Two promoters he had known for some time, Kris Graham and Corey Lane, started telling him about this great East Village venue. They did bottle service, but it had a completely different vibe. It was a Moroccan restaurant, hookah lounge, and venue fusion where one night you might see belly dancing and the next you would hear live music. The next, you would hear underground house. It was Le Souk.

"When you meet music industry people at clubs, it's kind of like your job interview," Disciple said. "If you're friendly with each other, they might try you out for a night. If the gig goes well, you get the job. With Corey and Kris, we were natural friends to begin with. I met Corey at Pink Elephant. When Gil left, I stayed on until they wanted to go back with their original residents. Kris also worked as a DJ, and I'd known him for much longer. He was a constant presence at the clubs—Nell's, Danceteria, Limelight, Tunnel, Giant Step, Soul Kitchen, all the spots.

"They were both excited about Le Souk, and when I started playing my first night there, I could see why. The club had none of the classist attitude the other notorious bottle service joints had. There were still models that would drop in, but so would a huge cast of characters that would have been immediately turned away at Spy Bar. I started playing there once a month, then once every two weeks. I kept that up for nine years."

At Le Souk, Disciple would often play with a young DJ by the name of Niki McNally. She was just nineteen at the time and had only been mixing records for two years.

"When I was first offered a spot at Le Souk, some of the best parties in NYC were taking place at that venue," McNally said. "So, on the night of my first gig, I realized that the next chapter of my career was about to begin, and it was both exciting and terrifying. Le Souk was such a special place and playing there was incredibly fun. The crowd was excellent, and cell phones weren't such a predominant force in people's lives like they are today. Everyone was focused on the music and dancing like maniacs—until they got kicked out that is! All attendees stayed until the club closed, which was ALWAYS being extended for one more song. They were fun times.

"I have to say, the best part of my experience at Le Souk was being able to learn from Disciple. He took me under his wing, and I felt blessed. I have yet to witness a DJ who can work a room the way Disciple can. He is a master at his craft. Watching him work was a valuable learning experience. Disciple doesn't falter. He owns the room. He looks up for a split second, scans the crowd, picks the perfect song for the moment, and plays it while dancing his heart out—and the crowd goes crazy. Every time.

"The most important lesson he taught me was to look up. I was shy and I was scared to look up and see people watching me. But I got over that because you need to see what's going on with the crowd in order to pick the right songs. Otherwise, you are just playing tracks you like, and that's not DJing. David also spent time with me and taught me how to pitch mix. He gave me loads of music so I was always prepared to rock the other gigs I played. Disciple had a great deal of respect for me and treated me as an equal. I loved him for that."

There were some fields, though, where Disciple did not have experience to impart, and McNally had to do her best.

"Back when I started DJing, I was a rare commodity," McNally continued. "There weren't many female DJs and unfortunately a lot of venue owners and promoters were booking me as a model/DJ because of the way I looked. But, I want to make this point clear, I was never a model nor did I want to be one. It was frustrating having people market me in that way. But, to put a nail in the model/DJ coffin, I turned down the opportunity to work for an all-female model/DJ company. I thought the idea was incredibly sexist and ridiculous. People would refer to me as a 'female DJ' and book me in all-female line-ups like I was eye candy on a dish being served up for everyone's viewing pleasure.

"In the few occasions that I took such gigs, all the DJs played different styles of music and we didn't mesh well together. But no one cared because 'Oh look! A bunch of chicks DJing!' So at first I felt I was objectified or, more specifically, booked for my looks. But, once I established myself as a serious, hardworking DJ, the objectification died down a great deal. Also, I kindly asked people to drop the gender distinction when referring to me as a DJ. I mean we don't walk around saying, 'Who was that male DJ that played last night? He was fantastic!' So why do we need to specify the gender for women in the industry? We are all just DJs. End of story. I don't think DJs who are female are being discriminated against as much these days. I am sure it exists to some degree, but there are workarounds. If you are a talented DJ and you respect yourself, others will follow suit."

THE RAVE ACT

Dance clubs were growing less popular throughout the 2000s, but some of that loss was explained by the popularity of raves. For most, they provided a safe, fun, alcohol-free venue to party as late as possible—especially for the under-twenty-one crowd. But for others—even most in some locations—they were increasingly turning into venues where kids could buy and consume drugs. Ecstasy was giving way to its cousin, MDMA.

"I remembered playing parties where kids were selling drugs in plain sight," Disciple said. "It was ugly. I'd walk by teenagers stuck in K-holes on my way to breakfast after the gig. Part of me felt hypocritical. I enjoyed playing raves. But these kids were showing up to see me play and take drugs, not necessarily in that order. I was profiting off a culture that went hand in hand with drugs, while also speaking out about the plight of the crack epidemic.

"It made me angry. The three strikes law was alive, well, and enforced in Farragut. That cut through whole communities. My neighbors were going to jail left and right, often on charges relating to marijuana. Above and below my apartment, there are few male heads of households to this day. Mandatory minimum sentencing destroyed Black communities, and it applied to dealers and users of everything from heroin to weed. Men who get caught up in the drug trade can't find public housing. The incarceration of Black men is just our latest form of slavery. Compared to Farragut, it was like raves occurred in a different country, with different laws.

"Still, raves were a great experience to be had if you loved forward-thinking music. And the message of PLUR (Peace, Love, Unity, Respect) was an amazing culture to be involved in. Drugs aside, the simplicity of people dancing, light, and positive vibes was my guilty pleasure."

Disciple wasn't the only one taking note. Drug prices were falling, concentrations were increasing, and, in too many unfortunate circumstances, kids were dying. The Illicit Drug Proliferation Act of 2003, which was signed into law by President George W. Bush, contained attached legislation that was originally known as the Reducing Americans' Vulnerability to Ecstasy (RAVE) bill. It prohibits "knowingly opening, maintaining, managing, controlling, renting, leasing, making available for use, or profiting from any place for the purpose of manufacturing, distributing or using any controlled substance."[13] In other words, if you owned a club or threw a party where people were doing drugs, you were on the hook.

"That killed all raves across the country," Disciple said. "It was the closing of a chapter and the beginning of another. Before too long, corporate America really got behind EDM festivals, and the scene changed into something else altogether. Raves just needed to be regulated. Lots of Americans were scared kids were taking too many drugs. They didn't like the look. In America, what you can't control, you criminalize."

WHEN DJing RETIRES YOU

In the late 2000s, Disciple reconnected with his neighbor and fellow DJ Kenny Carpenter. The two quickly got to talking shop.

"To be honest with you, I've always been a rebel kind of DJ," Kenny Carpenter said at the time. "I don't want to be everybody. I need to be individual. You know, when I think about these DJs today, they don't ever want to take risks. They just stay with the flow that they think is gonna make them some money or whatever, but they don't take chances. Like, throw a hip hop record on. Don't be afraid. So what you're a house DJ! Do something different. That's what I don't like about these DJs. All they do is go boom, boom, boom. They don't know how to play no vocals, or some live instruments. When I was at Bonds they wanted that obscure thing that I was doing, you know?"

In other words, tastes change, while DJs often remain true to themselves. Disciple was about to have this experience himself. During what turned out to be his last set at Sankey Soaps in Manchester, promoter David Vincent came up to him. He told him that he loved his set, but . . . There's a new wave of producers and DJs coming. "He didn't see me fitting in with them," Disciple said.

In no uncertain terms, he told Disciple that he'd be phased out soon. It was hard to hear, but Disciple was glad to get it without sugarcoating. Nic Fancculli was saying the same thing to him. Disciple had fans that respected him, but his run was over, give or take a few years.

"Sometimes you don't retire from being a DJ; sometimes being a DJ retires you," Disciple said. "The artist in me shuddered when I heard those words. I had seen it coming myself of course, but I didn't want to say it out loud. Hearing it come from David and Nic made it real. On the other hand, part of me was relieved to hear that soon I'd have a good excuse to spend more time around Farragut.

"DJing is all I've ever known. I haven't had a job that wasn't based around DJing since I worked at Godfather's Pizza. So even if I felt like I was on the way out, I wasn't going to stop. I didn't know how to."

DJ RUFF AND DAVID TORT

Disciple thought he was out. But a gig in Los Angeles planted an unlikely seed. DJ Ruff brought Disciple out to play Avalon. Out on the terrace, Disciple gave the crowd the usual treatment. That night, he was getting strong tech-house vibes in the style of artists like Âme and Dennis Ferrer. Both had recent hits out (like Âme's "Rej" on the label Innervisions and Ferrer's popular record *Fish Go Deep*). The show was a success, and DJ Ruff repeated the same cycle again the year after. During that gig, Ruff introduced Disciple to Spanish DJ David Tort. This friendship with Ruff and Tort led to Disciple's *Godfather III* moment. Just when he thought he was out, they pulled him back in.

While DJ Ruff proved that he could find gigs in Los Angeles with no problem, David Tort was a star, and Disciple could see it. The first track the trio collaborated on was "Crossroads." It was inspired by Âme and the proof was in the pudding when Innervisions licensed it from Catch 22 via Traxsource and Beatport.

Meanwhile, Dawn Tallman had made huge strides in her own career. She was becoming known as the queen of gospel energy. When Disciple and Dawn got together for another collaboration, the first idea was to do a soulful relationship record. But hearing David Tort's production made him change his mind. Disciple had Dawn lay down a vocal track and then headed into Ruff's Overbooking Studio with Tort to cut the shout-out track "Work It Out." The song combined Dawn and Disciple's vocals, along with Tort and Ruff's influence.

"Work It Out" became one of the highlight records of 2006 in Ibiza. It was Disciple's biggest record he'd done with Dawn Tallman.

"Gilbert Le Funk, David Tort, and DJ Ruff deserve credit for that," Disciple said. "Gilbert originally worked with me on the track but the way it was, it sounded too traditional. With Ruff and Tort's punch and my vocals, we turned it into a global hit. David Tort and I did most of the work in the studio, and when it was done, I sent it to Gilbert Le Funk for a remix. Gilbert's remix was more suitable for the radio. Tort agreed to engineer the record in exchange for me doing a mix on his record that he had come out on the Chus & Ceballos label. We were doing production and remix swaps. I was helping them with exposure, and they basically resurrected my career."

"Work It Out" was quickly picked up by House Trained Records in the United Kingdom, which then had Klaas from Germany do an electro house remix. Not only did Pete Tong champion "Work It Out" on his *Essential Selection*

David Tort opening for Swedish House Mafia at Pacha, Ibiza *(courtesy of David Tort)*.

Mix on BBC Radio 1, but Disciple played with him live on stage during the 2008 Winter Music Conference in Miami.

"Since the early days, the Winter Music Conference had come to draw more and more house fans through the Ultra Music Festival," Disciple said. "A lot of the event happened in hotels in those days, but most people would head straight to Ocean Drive, the main strip in South Beach. It stopped being about the actual conference; people just wanted to party. I did a brief residency at Nocturnal in Miami in 2005, but it was close to the venue Space, and couldn't compete. Rob Garcia was the person that booked me at Nocturnal and many of the high-profile events in Miami. I played with Armand Van Helden for New Year's Eve 2007 at Totem, and he thought I'd be a great fit to open up for Pete Tong at the Winter Music Conference BBC Radio 1 Pool Party.

"People didn't know who I was at first because I wasn't billed. Kris Graham and Carl Kennedy greeted me at the booth, as did Steve Angello, who later formed the trio Swedish House Mafia with Sebastian Ingrosso and Axwell. The House Trained label staff had an effective team.

"I listened to Pete Tong's *Essential Selection* and made sure that I had the etiquette not to play anything remotely close to what he touched on his mix. I wanted to show him how much my music had changed since the time we played together at The Versace Mansion back in 2005. He was the Galactus to my Fantastic Four. He played with so many DJs I'm sure my set was forgettable. To me, it was the highlight of my year.

"Getting a loud ovation, Pete encouraged the crowd to 'Give it up for DJ Disciple.' I saw Kim later, who was bummed that she missed my set. But after, David Guetta came up to congratulate me on 'Work It Out.' I was buzzing."

"Work It Out" was playlisted on BBC Radio 1, in April of 2008. The track's music video was Disciple's first to get featured on MTV. It was shot in May shortly after the Winter Music Conference, and it had a fitness workout theme. Although his DJ workload in the United Kingdom diminished, "Work It Out" kept his profile visible. Early in 2007, Disciple was at Tort's home returning the favor. Tort finished the collaboration at DJ Ruff's Los Angeles home where he co-produced and wrote the signature lyrics to "Changes," one of the most successful house records of 2007.

It stayed on the top three on the Beatport chart and hit mainstream radio in the European circuit hard. The project bought David Tort and DJ Ruff into the spotlight. Part of "Changes" was taken from Pastor Taylor's sermon at the Church of the Open Door. The lyrics go: "Is everybody listening? And I want to talk to you tonight. If time is changing it is a sign that you need to change also, you been thinking, I don't want to change, but you gonna change anyhow, you like things the way they are, well, things can't stay like they are. Change is the nature of life. We are all on the train. Are ya'll listening? The music, it changes."

"House music had changed," Disciple said. "A lot of DJs weren't using vinyl anymore. A lot of DJs weren't even using CDs anymore. For the price of a pair of turntables, you could get an all-in-one digital setup. Playing with Serato or Traktor on laptops opened up possibilities for a new generation of DJs, while record stores started shutting down. DJ styles based on where you lived were out the window. Anyone with a laptop could create a song and have their music heard online. The music became quicker and easier to make, but more disposable. I was nominated Beatport artist of the year, but it wouldn't have been possible if not for Klaas, David Tort, DJ Ruff, and Gilbert Le Funk. They saved my career."

EDM AND THE FESTIVAL GAME

For most of Disciple's career, a DJ's success depended on which clubs they could play. Advertisements promoting Disciple's gigs often said he played Wild Pitch, The Choice, Ministry of Sound, or Pacha. The promoters even invented parts of Disciple's club resume if they thought it would sell more tickets. But in the late 2000s, the requirements changed. Instead of clubs and parties, promoters began to seek out DJs with experience playing festivals. Festivals were skyrocketing in popularity, and as time went on, they only became bigger.

In the United States, the house music scene initially resisted capitalization and corporatization. DJs played house late at night and early in the morning, when most nuclear families were asleep. Old warehouses and abandoned neighborhoods hosted the parties. The house music scene drew a crowd of misfits, rebels, and dropouts. The rave scene changed things. Suddenly, events started catering to large populations of suburban white youth. With the Illicit Drug Anti-Proliferation Act on the books, the table was set. Beginning around 2004/2005, corporate America seized house music and hasn't relinquished its hold since. As *The Guardian*'s Simon Reynolds wrote in 2012:

> How did the US electronic dance scene claw its way back? Basically, by doing its best to shed the word "rave" and all its associations: drugged-up kids slumped on dance floors, hospitalizations, and the statistically rare but reputation-tarnishing deaths. Repeatedly through the

90s, governments at the state and city level enacted laws and policies designed to stamp out what concerned parents and alarmist newspapers typically called "drug supermarkets." In Chicago, people who threw a party for friends in their own loft apartment, with no paid admission and the DJing performed by the host, could find themselves ticketed for a $10,000 fine. In New Orleans, laws originally drafted to close down crack houses were used against raves and clubs where drug taking was taking place, regardless of whether the promoter or owner was involved in selling the substances.[14]

It all began with festivals. Today's electronic festivals—Tomorrowland, Electric Forest, Spring Awakening, Electric Zoo, Beyond Wonderland—all launched between 2005 and 2010. The events were characterized by increased ticket prices, strict security, twelve-dollar bottles of water, and copious insurance disclaimers inked in fine print. Much like bottle service, festivals provided good work for DJs, but it came at a price.

"Festivals were more expensive for attendees, but I always got paid well," Disciple said. "Every time I played a festival, I walked away with a good paycheck and new industry connections. The publicity was great—especially if I got a good time slot and rocked my set.

"But I never knew what to expect from the crowd. I was used to playing intimate sets in clubs, and the vibes at festivals were different. I didn't always know what the crowd wanted to hear. If I strayed too far from my usual sound, I ran the risk of disappointing the die-hard fans who showed up to hear my music. A lot of house heads viewed festivals as the mainstream takeover of the underground.

"That spirit spread to the studio. Electronic music became less about melodies and lyrics, and more about tracks and hooks. All the hit tracks started to sound the same. The lyrics were about sex encounters, narcotics, and club culture. The music was simpler—it seemed like people cared about the beat and nothing else. Artists weren't selling the song anymore. They were selling the sound."

In North America, a legitimate movement sprung out of this culture and climate. Artists like Skrillex, Bassnectar, Deadmau5, Diplo, and Steve Aoki rose to prominence with a commercialized American EDM sound. These mainstream artists started playing college jam band circuits and filling ten-thousand-seat theaters with crowds almost exclusively under age thirty. They traced their heritage to producers like Daft Punk and Justice. Another innovation: they produced three-minute songs, released them for free, and played heavily produced live shows. The American EDM movement had a heavy European counterpart, with producers like Calvin Harris, Avicii, Swedish House Mafia, Tiesto, David Guetta, and Zedd mirroring the change across the Atlantic.

In EDM, the mainstream and underground sounds can coexist. Similar to the hip hop scene, mainstream EDM artists give the up-and-coming artists more visibility, and neither side discredits the other. Rising producers learn from their predecessors and put their own spin on the classics to create fresh music.

As always, Disciple adapted to the changing scene. He played Boogie Wonderland in Venezuela in 2007 and Sneakerz Festival in 2009. He spun at the Iniesta Festival in Valencia, Spain, in 2009 in front of thirty thousand people. In 2009, he played at the Suncoast Festival in Malaga, Spain, and the Green Village Festival in Aruba. "'Work It Out,' 'Changes,' and 'Rise Up' put me in the EDM bracket," Disciple said. "I landed tons of gigs between 2007 and 2009 off those tracks."

Many house fans did not view the changes in electronic music favorably. But the more Disciple traveled and toured in the late 2000s, the more he realized that house heads' experience and love of the music was contextual—it was different everywhere he went. In Casablanca, Morocco, Choc'late resident DJ Mehdi Damir told Disciple that things hadn't necessarily changed as much as he thought.

"I learned that single tracks by a DJ does not really represent what he is," Damir said. "DJ Disciple, we know him by 'Work It Out,' but when the guy came and started playing, it was not a DJ playing like I saw too many times before from Spain or from France. We felt this New York influence on his music, with good deep house, and increase to electro but this electro was not the fake one, not easy listening monkey sonic dum, dum, dum, dum. It was good vocals; the technique was nice and people enjoyed it. When we say DJ Disciple, we think it's just a guy who plays electro, because his productions are electro music, but when you see him playing, he's a real guy that can play deep to electro. He rocked the house at Choc'late."

In Colombia, Disciple, like Willy Sanjuan before him, discovered new talent making music within Latin communities. In Medellin, he worked with Steven Kass on remixes that later showed up in Roger Sanchez's *Release Yourself* radio show. Roles were reversed. Sanchez was embracing new productions and collaborations coming from Disciple's label. Latin artists like Jesse Garcia and Christian Vila, who had little exposure at that point, found hope in their music. Roger Sanchez and Disciple later played in Bogota at the Centro de Espetaculos Autopista Norte in 2010.

These EDM festivals also exposed Disciple to a number of Dutch DJs and producers, such as Gregor Salto.

"For people in the states it might be a little hard to understand but every weekend there's so many parties going on," Salto told Disciple at the time. "There's times when you have three festivals on the same Saturday. I'll be happy when we get recognition all over the place and when we see each other on the top 10 on Beatport every week. It's just a matter of time."

Lucien Foort, another Dutch DJ, also found himself getting drawn further and further into the international scene through EDM.

"In the beginning we were a Dutch-based country, based around Dutch music, and Dutch DJs," Foort said. "What I've seen now, we're more interacting with international artists from America, Asia, former Yugoslavia, for instance. There are so many more people coming to Holland. I think it works. I've been working for 3FM, which is Dutch national radio, that not only broadcasts Dutch music, but I just like to mix it up. It might sound cliché, but there are so many good tunes out there that people want to hear, DJs that have a different insight on the dance scene. That's what I'm trying to do basically, just open things up."

In the studio, Disciple's association with Rotterdam's Bryan Dalton and Benny Royal gave him an inside look at the future Dutch hold on the EDM market. Disciple cut the track "When I Die" in Bryan Dalton's studio in Rotterdam, and Disciple also collaborated with Stefan Vilijn on "Jasmin Garden."

The Sneakerz Festivals hosted some of the best Dutch talents. Disciple played with acts like Erick E, Sidney Sampson, Chuckie, and Bart B More. He familiarized himself with the "Dirty Dutch Sound," as some people called it. Because Disciple's sound was backed by the Spanish label Blanco Y Negro, the output of Disciple's collaborations was magnified.

David Tort went on to play in bigger EDM circuits. He started sharing the stage with megastars like Avicii, Swedish House Mafia, Sander Van Doorn, and others. Musically, Disciple played both sides of the fence, but he stayed true to his roots with his personal DJ sets. When he played at certain festivals in the late 2000s, he noticed a lot of the music sounded flat and repetitive.

"I prepared my festival sets well in advance, but my club sets were more intimate and spontaneous," Disciple said. "The crowds, vibes, and expectations were different at festivals. As a DJ playing a festival, I had to make sure to play my hits and the tracks people were expecting to hear. In a club, I had more freedom to customize my set to the crowd I was playing for.

"There were still many DJs who were creating original work. But another tier of DJs sounded like they were producing cookie-cutter tracks, copying the sound that worked with little creative input. There was a lot of energy that went into the EDM surge. A lot of amazing artists and producers put out tracks that were pure expressions of who they were. But once the promoters and festivals started understanding how popular that was, they wanted more, and then things turned formulaic. It seemed like every song played was a pendulum swinging between tension and release. There was the build-up, the drop, another build-up, another drop: the casual fans loved it, the drinkers, weed smokers, and Molly heads loved it, but everyone else started looking for something else."

Social media also hit DJ culture hard. Connecting with clubbers on the dance floor wasn't enough anymore. DJs had to engage with their fans online. They had to show their personalities. They had to record their daily lives. Instead of enjoying the experience, fans began filming, editing, and posting every moment.

"EDM and electronic festivals have become an industry in themselves," Disciple said. "As a result, clubs suffered—people started spending their hard-earned cash on festival tickets instead of bottles. Promoters upped their game, trying to keep the club scene alive.

"But the shift in the electronic music industry also changed the way DJs played and made music. They're less likely to try to establish a dedicated local following. Instead, they worry about trying to look and sound good in front of hundreds of thousands of fans and music industry tycoons. The DJs who want to be 'mainstream' have to stand out, or else they won't make it.

"DJs around the world all responded differently to the changes in the electronic music industry, but gone are the days when house heads formed intimate relationships with residents and flocked to local venues for their shows."

1. DJs Roger Sanchez and Bob Sinclair at WMC Miami *(courtesy of Donna Ward)*. **2.** Kerri Chandler guest DJing at E-Man's Bang The Party *(courtesy of Donna Ward)*. **3.** DJ Disciple and Q-Tip of A Tribe Called Quest at Quo *(author's collection)*. **4.** Halloween party at Pangaea, 2001 *(author's collection)*.

1. DJ Disciple at Guest House *(courtesy of Jamall Fisher)*. **2.** DJ Disciple and DJ Dove at Pier 66, Made in Italy *(courtesy of Jamall Fisher)*. **3.** DJ Dove at Pier 66 for Made in Italy *(courtesy of Jamall Fisher)*. **4.** DJ Disciple, Tim Deluxe, Darren Emerson, and Thomas Dunkley at GBH *(author's collection)*. **5.** Thomas Dunkley of GBH with date at Centro-Fly *(courtesy of Donna Ward)*.

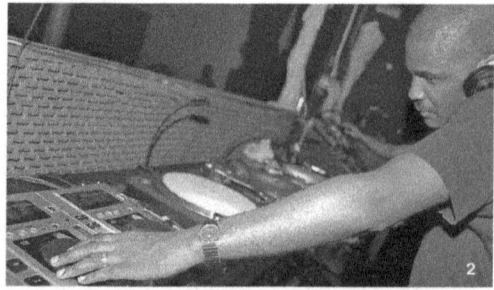

1. DJ Jaz and DJ Disciple at Le Souk *(courtesy of Jamall Fisher)*. **2.** DJ Kenny Carpenter at Vinyl *(courtesy of Donna Ward)*. **3.** DJ Disciple at Le Souk *(author's collection)*. **4.** Niki McNally at Le Souk *(courtesy of Jamall Fisher)*. **5.** DJ Disciple's Monday Night Catch 22 event at Le Souk *(courtesy of Jamall Fisher)*. **6.** Eddie Amador, DJ Disciple, and Willy Sanjuan at La Terrezza, Barcelona, Spain, 2000 *(author's collection)*. **7.** DJ Disciple in a session at Michele Chiavarini's studio, London *(author's collection)*.

1. Smokin' Jo and DJ Disciple at Skugness Festival, UK *(author's collection)*. **2.** DJ Disciple and Louie Vega at To the Manor Born, UK *(author's collection)*. **3.** Farley "Jackmaster" Funk and DJ Disciple at The Elevation Festival, Malaysia, 2003 *(author's collection)*. **4.** David Tort and DJ Disciple in LA *(author's collection)*. **5**. DJ Disciple, Todd Terry, and Doc Martin in Manhattan *(author's collection)*.

ON AND ON

As the new millennium got underway, William Banks was battling congestive heart failure. The condition brought him in and out of Brooklyn Hospital Center, but his spirit remained strong and independent. And there was no way he was going to live in a nursing home, though living in Farragut with occasional support from his sons was becoming less and less realistic. In 2009, while playing in Ibiza, Disciple heard the news. William Banks passed on the night before he was set to enter assistive care. He died as he lived: on his own terms. The Church of the Open Door sent him off. A guest minister preached:

> I found out that God will never take anyone from you, without replacing your loved ones with more of himself. He is a God who will truly fill the void in your life. Continue to cast your cares upon him simply because God cares for you.
> We commit the shell of his body to the ground from whence we came and must go. Earth to earth, ashes to ashes, dust to dust. We commit his soul and his spirit to the God that says all souls are mine. We will look for him again on the other side. The weary shall be at rest and we will be reunited with our loved ones because of the finished work of Jesus Christ on the cross.

"It was one of the greatest services that anyone can attend," Disciple said, "and that was because my father lived a righteous life. Not everyone can have a service like that; it's the way you live that determines that. Dad had sacrificed so much for all of us. I felt blessed to have been able to receive his generosity and love, and I like to think that I was able to return the favor in some small way as he grew older, and I stuck around Farragut to look after him.

"I was also proud to have been able to make a career in the music industry. I know that William would have too, if the circumstances had been right. He did the best he could with the hand that he was dealt".

"The impact he made got me thinking. My success up to that point had been self-centered. After, I started thinking about how I could serve the dance community in other ways, reconcile, redeem, and restore my way back to my family, my brothers, and God."

NEXT LEVEL

In 2006, after a couple heart-to-hearts with his longtime mentor DJ Camacho, Disciple decided to ease off touring to spend more of his time at home. Disciple wanted to play New York music in New York. For his first venture, he hooked up with E Man again. His event, Bang the Party, had attracted long lines on Friday nights at Frank's Lounge, a longtime Fort Greene mainstay. These events started as an afterwork party for the *New York Undercover* cast and film crew that E Man worked on. When Disciple and E Man first got together to collaborate, house music had been a non-starter. But something had changed in the years since. E Man started booking house DJs. The intimacy of Frank's Lounge and the spirit of the scene attracted dedicated audiences and allowed the party to grow into its own thing. It went on to achieve an underground vibe akin to what the mobile parties like Wild Pitch had during a previous era. But when Disciple came through, it had become a victim of its own success.

"With popularity came people who just heard about Frank's," E Man said. "They didn't know Bang the Party. They just heard that Frank's was banging on Friday night. There were lines around the block. That's all they knew about. Eventually, that crowd clashed with the house fans. We had guys who were not appreciating us. There's a different dynamic with someone who's coming to a party of this magnitude to do house music and people who attend bars to pick up others."

Despite differences between attendees, Disciple was able to step into the situation and launch his own event. He called it Next Level.

"E Man had something special going on," Disciple said. "Bang the Party got heavy press coverage from magazines like *Time Out* and *The Village Voice*. It was the first time I'd see a party in Brooklyn that had a great racial mixture. It got popular but it came at a cost.

"I was missing the dancers that used to come out and dance to me when I was doing with The Choice, Wild Pitch, and Blackball. With Frank's, I got that back at my debut. The reward would be just to get that feeling of playing until 5:00 AM in the morning again for people who appreciated my music and showed it in the art form of dancing that I could appreciate.

"One of the best things I loved about playing at Frank's was the end of the night, when you could be obscure with your selection. Herb Martin, another resident at Frank's, was masterful at it. People clamored for 'Twisted' by UltraNate to be the last song. After that, Ernest would have everyone come together and pose for a picture. He did that for most of the parties in New York."

As time went on, the Next Level party grew, and Disciple moved it nearby to Club Langston, which sits at Atlantic and Fulton. The venue was Brooklyn's last surviving Black-owned LGBTQ+-friendly club. Calvin Clark, the co-owner, convinced Disciple to showcase his new talent at the venue. Ruben Toro, who had a radio show on WBLS 107.5 FM, used to pack Club Langston every Sunday night. Besides Toro, Cameron Da DJ, Augie J, Herb Martin, Juwandi Barney, Troy O, Ray Vazquez, D.J.S., and DJ Sres formed the vanguard of DJs who were generating a club scene in downtown Brooklyn.

Disciple brought on up-and-coming DJs like Sabine Blaizin, Rich Medina and The Martinez Brothers. The DJ duo from the Bronx has since gone on to play long-term residencies on Ibiza and appeared at the Electric Daisy Carnival and Tomorrowland in Belgium. But when Disciple had them on Next Level, they were just cutting their teeth. Disciple knew them through photographer Ernest Newton Jr., a.k.a. Photoman.

DJs weren't the only performers. Disciple also brought poets up to give these nights a fresh flavor. In January 2008, Abiodun Oyewole took the stage. A member of The Last Poets, Oyewole has been writing for decades. His work marks some of the earliest modern spoken word. Along with his fellow Last Poets, Oyewole is credited as a foundational inspiration for early hip hop.

He was followed later that summer by Ras Baraka. Baraka had edited a volume of poetry, had been featured on Lauryn Hill's 1998 *The Miseducation of Lauryn Hill*, and recorded with the Fugees. But at the time, he was the principal of Central High School in Newark. Baraka has since risen through the ranks in local government and is now the mayor of Newark, a post he has held since 2014. Other featured poets included names like Oveous Maximus, Wunmi, and Albert Daniels, each of whom continues to create in numerous performing arts.

RELEASE 2.0

In 2010, Disciple struck up a relationship with the Sapphire Lounge down on the Lower East Side. He launched another party, Release, that went down on Tuesday nights. Paying homage to Martel and Nabiel's San Francisco venture, these events provided a throwback to the underground sounds of a previous era.

Most of the big names who played the party had shared the stage with Disciple for decades: Tony Humphries, Hex Hector, Jellybean Benitez, Kenny "Dope" Gonzalez, DJ Spinna, and Mr. V. Disciple's Release parties at Sapphire offered him and his fellow DJs an opportunity to reprise the house music they'd created a generation ago, while continuing to showcase emerging talent.

"Christopher Robinson, aka Father Chris, was instrumental in helping the Release party book talent," Disciple said. "There's no way that these DJs would have played the Release parties at Sapphire Lounge if he wasn't involved. He's promoted over 100 parties since the early 1980s and has a legendary reputation in New York nightlife.

"I hadn't played with Tony Humphries since [Great British House], but he came on at Release because of Father Chris. He gave the party pedigree. Drawing inspiration of San Francisco's Release, I also booked talents like Jihad Muhammad, AB Logic, Yuko Jikido, and Traxsource podcast host Wendy Escobar (who did her first gig ever at Release)."

At Next Level, and then Release, Disciple began to encounter a new generation of DJs and producers who had first come online listening to *The DJ Disciple Show, New York's Best Kept Secret*, or catching him at Wild Pitch or Hunter parties.

"The first time I heard house music, it was through DJ Disciple, and it moved me to the point where that's all I stuck to," said Release alum DJ Rubi, also known as RIVKA R3, NYC. "I didn't listen to anything else but just house music and I paid attention so much that I recorded all his sets. I still have the tapes to this day."

"Justin Hyppolite Jr., who now calls himself DJ AQuaBeaT, does house events all over the country with GetOpen Sessions," Disciple said. "But he discovered house music while supporting me at Hunter College. Listeners and fans of *Best Kept Secret* like Nadeeah Eshe (who works with DJ Montana for Spirits in Motion), DJ Beloved (who does various festivals in New Jersey), and Mikki Afflick were seeing their dream of being successful in the industry come to pass. Afflick even re-connected me with DJ Basil and Duce Martinez in 2012 at a Fort Greene Park event called Afflickted in the Park. I returned the favor, having her spin with Kenny Dope and Sres at Release."

Kim "Redness" Hayes was also a notorious promoter who lent her hand to Release. Red, as she's called, has promoted some of the biggest events in Gotham. She made a breakthrough collaborating with Ejoe Wilson and Brian Coxx at Soulgasm, a Wednesday night party located at Sin-Sin on the Lower East Side. In 2019 she collaborated with Lil Ray to bring house music to Negril,

Jamaica, and she's worked Timmy Regisford and Louie Vega events at Doux in Chelsea. "DJ Disciple for me is legendary and I don't throw that word around," Redness said. "Those who know, know. It was a privilege for me to be invited to work with him. The atmosphere, the parties, the energy, it's just a good thing."

In the mid-2010s, the owners of Sapphire Lounge changed things up and rebranded as The Rumpus Room. After some downtime, Disciple launched another Tuesday night party at the venue, Feel Real, in homage to the legendary London party that used to go down in Covent Garden. E Man still frequently came by to collaborate.

Becky Nuñez and Disciple's old radio secretary, India Lawson (ND), also lent their hands to the event. Nuñez has since become one of New York's most sought-after house promoters. Guest DJs have included Danny Krivit, Josh Milan, and Oveous. Ejoe Wilson, who'd made a name for himself as a dancer, became one of Disciple's resident DJs. As the party grew, Disciple added Veronica Evans and Fred Milan to the team to take care of things on the promotion side. That allowed Disciple to focus on breaking new talent.

"Doing my own events meant that I don't have to play events where I don't fit in, or booking me, not for the music I play or for the attention it can get," Disciple said. "I can do something different where people can feel my music. Where you can 'feel real' with that experience."

COLLABORATING WITH DANCERS

Disciple always sought to create a motivated, inclusive environment. When he started playing bottle service clubs like the Pink Elephant and the Guest House outside of the promoter circuit, he had to fill in a couple more pieces of the puzzle. He wanted to bring that Paradise Garage, Choice, and Wild Pitch vibe into the twenty-first century. And to do that, he needed some motivated dancers. Advertising on Craigslist, he hired dancers and performers to join him on stage and get the party going.

Like the poets, promoters, actors, musicians, and fellow DJs who have worked with Disciple in the past, his party motivators hailed from all around the world. Each had their own unique styles and impressive resumes. Some have gone on to win further fame and acclaim while branching out into other art forms and initiatives as well.

Disciple first met Collette McLafferty when she responded to his Craigslist post. Besides being able to work a crowd, she was also a skilled vocalist. One thing led to another, and she ended up recording the vocals for Disciple's 2017 single "Birdseye View." She then went on to help him out on stage at Le Souk, Webster Hall, and Cielo.

"I was going through some hard times when I first got here," said Sarah Fritz, another dancer who worked with Disciple. "The first night I danced for Disciple, it was like going to church. Everybody was together, just partying, and celebrating. Feeling in the spirit uplifted me from what I was going through, so it meant a lot. Especially at Frank's, it's like a family and a community of people. Everybody's there for the right reason, nobody's there to try to pick somebody up, and you just want to dance."

Joy Villa, another performer who responded to Disciple's Craigslist ad, danced with him at clubs like Le Souk, the Coffee Cave in Jersey, and at the Sapphire Lounge during the Release days. In 2017, she attended the Grammy Awards in a dress designed by Andre Soriano. It was colored red, white, and blue, and on the back bore the words "Make America Great Again." After the event, Joy Villa's EP, *I Make the Static*, climbed to number one on Amazon and iTunes for downloads in the United States. It sold over fifteen thousand copies in the next two days and premiered on Billboard charts the following week at number twelve.

Disciple has also performed alongside Princess Lockeroo, Magnolia Nunez, and Ljuba Castot who have gone on to appear on television, win awards, and hold high-level choreography positions. "I'd get a kick out of hiring dancers at my Next Level or Release parties, since the people that party at those events are already seasoned dancers," Disciple said. "It was like this powder keg of energy."

THE MUSIC . . . IT CHANGES

In 2019 DJ Spoony took a Garage Classical show to the Royal Albert Hall in London. In Dublin, Jeff Mills performed with the Montpelier Philharmonic Orchestra. Luca Parmitano from Italy became the first DJ in space. MIXMSTR—a DJ app that focuses on improving your DJ skills—went live. Boiler Room and Mixmag live sets can be found on YouTube. Through it all, house music has continued to shift.

Brooklyn emerged as the clubbing capital of New York in the 2010s. House of Yes, Elsewhere, Good Room, Nowadays, TBA, Bossa Nova Civic Club, and later, 3 Dollar Bill, were some of the exciting venues that brought Williamsburg and Bushwick to life. Former Le Souk DJ Niki McNally rode the wave.

"Playing in Brooklyn is completely different from playing in Manhattan, and I think that's partly because Williamsburg was a newly gentrified hotspot with more music-minded venues," McNally said. "I preferred playing in Brooklyn because I liked what was happening there. There was a long-overdue revival taking place when I was a resident at Verboten, and it was exciting to be a part of that movement."

"Niki tried her hardest to get me to come to Williamsburg to spin," Disciple said. "She was right—Williamsburg nightclubs were the future. House music was disco's revenge, but techno was Brooklyn's next chapter, as the genre continued to thrive. Every few years, you get new clubbers, new DJs, and parties that shake up the establishment. By 2013, there were more DJs than ever before.

"But at the same time, some of the DJs and nightclubs of my generation are still going. Todd Edwards' collaboration with Daft Punk on the song 'Fragments of Time' from their album *Random Access Memories* won a Grammy. Dawn Tallman went number one in the Billboard Dance chart when she worked with Bob Sinclair on 'Feel the Vibe.' Roger Sanchez, David Morales, Kenny Carpenter, Tony Humphries, and Derrick Carter travel and play religiously. That gives me confidence that the music will never die."

Foundational New York DJ Todd Terry has also continued to produce house music. "[Electronic dance music (EDM)] was a big lesson for us," he said. "A lot of us got lost in it. I was kind of confused for the first seven years of EDM, but I stuck to my house. I stuck to my roots, and I kept on doing my thing, and now EDM guys want to play house. It just shows you that real music is just gonna last forever."

As he settled back into New York life, Disciple started playing afternoon and evening shows. He played with DJs like Kervyn Mark and DJ Erv on the boardwalk at Coney Island and out in Fort Greene Park with Mikki Afflick and Duce Martinez.

These gigs, along with his regular parties, showed that house music was heading back to the community. The genre was no longer the soundtrack of underground clubs or high-end bottle service joints. Mainstream acts like Swedish House Mafia, David Guetta, and Avicii were making house music familiar. You no longer had to explain to unseasoned listeners what it was all about.

In 2021, the South African house DJ Black Coffee won the Best Dance/Electronic Album Grammy for his record *Subconsciously*. The following year, Drake brought him into the studio to co-write and co-produce three tracks for *Honestly, Nevermind*. Shortly after, Beyoncé released *Renaissance*,

Black Coffee performs at Summer Stage on Rumsey Playfield in Central Park, 2014 (courtesy of Donna Ward).

a front-to-back dance record that pays homage to dozens of different house music sub-genres, scenes, and traditions. It is recorded to sound like a DJ mix, with subsequent tracks matching the beats of previous ones. It features collaborations with DJs Honey Dijon, Skrillex, and dozens of others with ties to house music. Those releases, along with others from Lizzo and Megan Thee Stallion, led some critics to call the warm months of 2022 the summer of house. In reality, house has been coming back around for years. Mainstream electronic artists like Lady Gaga, Tiesto, Calvin Harris, and Charlie XCX have been as popular as ever.

This mainstream success has begun to reverse another trend as well. House music and hip hop had developed alongside one another, but then split completely in the 1990s. In the 2010s, however, with both genres producing mainstream acts, they began to cross over again. JP Firman witnessed this firsthand. Since running labels and booking shows in the United Kingdom, he had transitioned to tour management. His clients are well known: Black Eyed Peas, Rihanna, Drake, Young Thug, and many more.

"On one of the tours I ran, Calvin Harris came to support Rihanna," Firman said. "Things have really come back around. If you look at hip hop and house now, it's all DJ-based. Most of the hip hop guys tour with a DJ.

"Hip hop obviously blew up before house, but now, they're kind of on the same level. They can make the same money. It used to be that all the underground DJ stuff was hip hop's poor cousin. That isn't true anymore."

On the other hand, Disciple has seen New York hip hop enter a lull.

"New York hip hip is not dead, but when hip hop in general evolved into trap music, the southern music movement greatly impacted the clubs in New York," Disciple said. "In time New York hip hop will have its revival. I can only hope that nightclubs in Manhattan have a similar revival as well.

"Producers can make electronic music tracks sitting at home on their laptops. Within seconds, they can upload their work to SoundCloud and share it with the world without having to spend a dime. There are thousands of other producers who are creating their own sounds and making their mark on the industry. The highest paid DJs in the world make millions of dollars per year. With America being the catalyst for the mainstream popularity of EDM. DJs like Diplo, Marshmello, and Zedd have all held Las Vegas residencies.

"There's a platform for DJs who want to hustle, play music, rock your party, and do it again the week after. Why? Because people still love house music. People still love the DJ, the artist, the dancer. They love the quality of what we do."

REUNIONS, GOODBYES, AND INTRODUCTIONS

As the 2010s progressed, many of Disciple's long-time relationships in the industry came to an end. Disciple played together with KCC, DJ Spoony, and Paul "Trouble" Anderson in August 2010 at a Carnival after-party. It would be the last time Disciple would see Trouble. He passed in 2018. "It hurt me to my heart," Disciple said. "Too often, you don't realize you've seen someone for the last time until it's too late to say goodbye."

Back in New York, Disciple was also able to spend more time with his mentor, DJ Camacho. But unfortunately, their time together was short-lived. David Camacho passed on July 28, 2011. He was one of the undisputed pioneers of house music. He and promoter Greg Daye were the first to bring Disciple out of the radio station to play Wild Pitch parties. Camacho helped Disciple make the leap from college radio to the forefront of house music. He positively influenced everything from Disciple's record collection to his reputation as a DJ.

"Young DJs like Ameer Brooks and Just The DJ (at 17 years old) from New Jersey have maintained the soulful energy that came from DJ Camacho's, Naeem Johnson's, and Hippie Torrales' family tree of house music," Disciple said. "That also includes Rissa Garcia, DJ Rimarkable, and Eli Escobar in Brooklyn to Seth Troxler, Jamie Jones, and Solomun overseas. They all share an independent sound that kids love about house music, the same way, kids loved Camacho.

"In an era where some artists today just care about the bag, Camacho's investment and legacy to the culture can never be denied. He had the real, raw personality walks, personality talks, personality smiles love for his music. He mixed cassettes like hot wings on a grill."

While Disciple had been touring internationally in house music exile, the long-time Wild Pitch promoter and dancer Voodoo Ray had been doing his thing in New York. He and Disciple reconnected in 2009 at the Sullivan Room. Ray was putting on a party called Funkbox. After the event he filled in his old friend from Wild Pitch on what he missed in New York along with his collaborator, rapper, and producer Tony Touch. "Our room on Sunday night is almost the closest that you can get to an old-school Wild Pitch party," Ray said. "We're not the Garage, we're not Choice but we're pretty close as far as the energy with people loving each other, a young crowd and a lot of schooling."

In 2015, Voodoo Ray brought Disciple on to another Funkbox party at Le Passion Rouge to observe a milestone. Disciple had been spinning for thirty years. It was the party of a lifetime. But Disciple and Ray weren't able to collaborate again; Ray passed two years later in 2017. Ray's legacy and the scene he helped develop lives on. Disciple continues to celebrate and honor others who have passed before their times, like David Mancuso, Frankie Knuckles, Boyd Jarvis, and Colonel Abrams by playing their music.

In 2011, Disciple found another reason to stay off the road, stay at home, and connect with his community: his daughter was born.

"After my daughter Julia was born in 2011, I went once to Washington, DC, to spin for Sam Burns at the 18th Street Lounge. I never traveled out of state again. Raising a family and no longer playing in high-profile clubs was tough. I still remember the call I got from Kim Benjamin in 2013 confirming I wouldn't be touring any more. I thanked her for being the best manager I could have had. I didn't want to announce to the world that I'm retiring, and I didn't want another manager. I'd given it all I could."

"He was always good at recreating himself or making himself relevant," Kim Benjamin said. "He stepped away more to be a good father to his children. If he had remained single, I am sure he would have kept moving forward. Priorities change, and the DJ life is grueling."

HEALING OLD WOUNDS

When Disciple was growing up, Brooklyn was territorial and dangerous to say the least. But in recent years, many Brooklynites who've stuck around have tried to rebuild those burned bridges. Rusty Taylor, Shannon's former bass player and long-time Farragut resident, began throwing Farragut and Fort Greene reunions at the nearby Commodore Barry Park. People from both communities began to come down in August for a celebration of fellowship between the two housing projects. DJ Debonair helped champion this cause and also liked to organize Farragut–Fort Greene boat ride events on the Hudson.

"We used to fight each other back in the day," Debonair said. "There was just a whole lot of ignorance. But here's the silver lining: when we fought, we fought with our hands. So years later, as we got smarter, became adults, got responsibility, got wise, got kids, we said, 'What the hell? What are we fighting for?'

"So we started getting together, we started playing basketball. We got schools together. We started dating each other. We started coming together as a community. And today we tell the kids, 'We were smart enough to fight with our hands. Today, we're the best of friends. We embrace each other.'"

The annual Afropunk festival, which seeks to foster artistic communities among Black Americans and has attracted huge crowds in recent years, also moved to Commodore Barry Park and forged even stronger connections. Beginning in 2010, Disciple himself played for stretches at Fort Greene's Club Tamboril on 527 Myrtle Avenue with DJ Sadiq. With his partners DJ Tabu and Jeff Mendoza, the three organized the Soul Summit collective, which puts on Sunday afternoon park events that draw thousands to Fort Greene Park for the house music fellowship.

But at the same time, DJing in Farragut and Fort Greene had changed drastically since the 1980s and 1990s. For one thing, impromptu park jams had practically become a non-starter.

"When we started getting drug infested, that changed a whole lot of things as far as being able to just come out and play music on a whim," Debonair said. "We didn't have a schedule; we didn't have any flyers. It used to be word of mouth that DJ Shah D was playing around his way and people would gather around and listen to some good music. The music was free. We still have the passion for the music to the fullest.

"All it takes is one shooting, and then no more jams, no more this, no more that. The guns started to come out. One guy would see another guy that he was after at a jam. . . . Us DJs who had half a brain stopped playing park jams. We were scared to put people in that situation."

DJ 2 Nice voiced similar thoughts, as did DJ DLS, who grew up in Farragut in building 192.

"It's just not the same anymore," DJ DLS said. "Cops don't want you there because they're scared they can't control the crowd, and they only want you out there at a certain time. They don't want you doing what you need to do to have a good time, so they're not giving out the permits. When the music is on, they're shutting you down; they're making you cut it off. You ask for permits, and they're not even giving it to you. It's just not the same anymore."

THE FARRAGUT CULTURE

The Farragut Houses have weathered New York's mid-century development boom, the closure of the Brooklyn Navy Yard, the crack cocaine epidemic, Reagan's War on Drugs, Giuliani's zero tolerance policing, decades of crime and violence, and countless other conflicts and crises.

But in the 2020s, gentrification still poses a threat to the neighborhood. While more and more stores and businesses serving the more affluent residents of Dumbo, Vinegar Hill, and Brooklyn Heights move in, more and more Farragut community institutions move out.

The Dr. White Community Center closed long ago. Farragut's Children Day Care Center also closed in 2010. But in 2019, the Church of the Open Door managed to open a new one. As Pastor Taylor liked to say, "The sign of a dead church is when there are no young people in it."

When Disciple entered school, he was among a generation of students who were bussed into other districts in an effort to end segregation in public education. Despite these commendable efforts, New York City public education remains both the largest and among the most segregated school systems in the United States. "I initially had reservations about having my daughter at PS 307," Disciple said. "I found out that Deborah Isom, my mentor at Dr. White

Community Center, was the vice principal at the school. Although she's since moved on, she inspired hundreds of students under her care."

Disciple himself began to look for ways to give back to the community. During Thanksgiving, he began pausing his Next Level party to throw an annual DJs Against Hunger event along with Fort Greene native Eric Blackwell. The benefit show went down at Frank's Lounge. Proceeds were donated to Brooklyn Community Housing and Services, a group that provides housing and resources to Brooklynites in need.

"Homeless people are shipped around the city," said event collaborator Eric Blackwell. "We've got people in Fort Greene who are not from Fort Greene who are living in Fort Greene just off of homelessness. Every community has a role to play. Our community is only as strong as the thread that holds it together. That thread is only as strong as the fabric we put on."

Blackwell is an urbanist, an educator, a real estate finance consultant, and an adjunct professor at Long Island University. He met Disciple at Frank's Lounge. The two ran the event for ten years until the venue closed in 2020.

Disciple also began to reach out to the younger generation. Every October, he began hosting the King in Me event at PS 287. Sponsored by the Church of the Open Door, the conference brings together boys aged five to fifteen to empower, raise self-awareness, and talk about what it takes to become a DJ. Disciple has also put together aid efforts for the fallout of Hurricane Sandy and the 2010 earthquake in Haiti.

Meanwhile, Farragut's look has completely changed. Dumbo's reputation made it the go-to place in terms of Brooklyn real estate. In 2016, the average household income in Dumbo was $191,188. Practically across the street in Farragut, the figure stood at $61,570.[1] This income disparity has played out in multiple ways. For one, Farragut residents have had increasingly limited access to affordable fresh produce and groceries. Throughout the 2010s, the only nearby options were a handful of bodegas and a single small grocery store with one aisle of fresh produce.

But change came in 2019 when the Fort Greene & Farragut Fresh Pantry, operated in collaboration with City Harvest, began providing nearly ten thousand pounds of free fresh produce to residents of the Farragut, Ingersoll, and Whitman Houses each month. Additionally, a development deal for a supermarket in the former Brooklyn Navy Yard finally came to fruition in 2019. A large Wegmans grocery store opened across the street from Disciple. Employment opportunities for Farragut residents were first on their list.

What's more, drug trafficking has diminished in Farragut. But it hasn't left completely. In 2017, authorities began to notice a spike in violent crime in Farragut. A few months later, the New York Police Department and the Brooklyn North Narcotics Squad broke up a heroin and crack trafficking ring operating out of a Farragut building.[2]

And, finally, both the Farragut Houses themselves and most of New York City Housing Authority (NYCHA) buildings are in terrible condition. Issues of mold, lead, broken elevators, plumbing, electrical systems, and delayed regular maintenance have plagued NYCHA residencies for years. In 2018, it was estimated that it would cost roughly $31.8 billion to repair all the existing issues in New York's public housing.[3]

In 2019, NYCHA appointed a new chair and chief executive officer, Gregory Russ, who had seen success as the head of Minneapolis' public housing. Progress has been slow but promising. In the summer of 2022, he, the city council, and Mayor Eric Adams managed to create a trust that would redevelop twenty-five thousand NYCHA units. Mayor Adams wants to recapitalize another sixty-two thousand by 2028.[4]

Farragut's continued existence is not in question, but the neighborhood has changed drastically since the 1960s. While it's not easy to measure, recurring maintenance and infrastructure issues, a long-time lack of nearby groceries and produce, and continuing crime take a toll on its residents. Farragut has a rich musical and DJ history, but who knows if that will carry forward into the future?

"I'm proud of being from Farragut," Disciple said. "Some of the greatest people in the world are from the projects. Plenty of my friends and neighbors went to jail, but eventually, most of them got on the right path and realized what's important in life by not reinforcing stereotypes. Distraction is the enemy of purpose.

"The future of Farragut is always going to be in question, but not its history. *Project Girl*, a book by Janet McDonald, speaks openly about Farragut. Candida Alvarez is a painter from Farragut and now a tenured professor at the School of the Art Institute of Chicago. Tracy Wilkins-Dickerson, who lived in 177 Sands Street, inspired countless girls in the neighborhood with the Diamonds cheerleading squad while all of her kids attended PS 307. I can't even touch on half of the achievements that other residents have made in Farragut, but there are plenty of unspoken heroes here.

"I wouldn't have what I have unless the people from Farragut and other NYCHA buildings continued to fight against unfair practices. Whether it be the Church of the Open Door, which fought against the development of a pollution-heavy incinerator in the Brooklyn Navy Yard, or Mary Andrews, president of the Farragut tenants association, who fought for heat and boiler issues to be addressed. Regardless of any picture painted of us from the media, our stories, and the activism that has protected us, will always be valued.

"Attorney General Letitia James, NY State Assemblyman Walter T. Mosley, Mayor Eric Adams, Congressman Hakeem Jeffries, Council Member Laurie Cumbo, and State Committeewoman Olanike Alabi are strong elected officials in leadership that have protected and led the way to secure Farragut's future."

AND THEN CAME COVID-19

At the end of 2019, many people around the world looked forward to the beginning of a new decade, hoping that it would at least be better than the last. They had no idea what was around the corner.

In March 2020, Disciple had been playing his resident parties at Rumpus Room. He remembered seeing a group of Air France workers at the party one Wednesday night.

Later that week, the manager of Rumpus Room fell ill with COVID-19. The hospital would not take him because he was asymptomatic. On March 15, Ejoe Wilson was supposed to celebrate his fiftieth birthday. But two days before, Wilson texted Disciple, "You need to rethink this party, seriously." He showed Disciple an article from *The New York Times* describing the risks of gathering in public. That following Sunday, New York City officials announced that all bars, restaurants, and nightclubs were required to close.

"There were many days I'd wake up and wonder if I had symptoms," Disciple said. "It was something that kept me up at night. I kept hearing information that was perplexing, confusing, and contradictory. It was incredibly stressful. Living in the housing projects meant that I was at a higher risk of contracting the virus.

"A fellow DJ had it. He called me up at 6:00 in the morning, telling me that he had to quarantine himself. I felt like I was watching *The Walking Dead* movie, seeing New York's streets scaled down to nothing. Todd Terry's manager Gary Saltzman and Detroit's Mike Huckaby died from the disease. I was hit hard by all the lives that were lost.

"There was no way I could see my brother Larry, who had his bout with diabetes. I started avoiding Facebook in fear of finding out who died next. Wearing a mask and gloves, I got on the drums, played the Church of the Open Door service with Pastor Taylor in a church with only 10 people. I practiced social distancing and uploaded YouTube videos of the sermons that many people looked forward to. It was like therapy for me. The hysteria, nervousness, insomnia, and anxiety wouldn't fix the situation. I found peace by holding on to my faith.

"I also uploaded 114 archived mixes from the last thirty-five years to Mixcloud. I decided to compile a playlist full of old mixes I created to share with my fans. Since I couldn't work during the pandemic, I wanted to give them a way to enjoy my music from home. I hoped to touch their hearts and bring up good memories, even though they can't physically come to one of my sets.

"The coronavirus pandemic dealt a terrible blow to the music industry. Artists could no longer connect with their fans in person. Because concerts and festivals did not return to normal for a long time, livestreams were a brilliant way for people around the world to party together and enjoy the music they know and love.

"Events like Ultra Music Festival, Electric Daisy Carnival, SXSW, Coachella, and Tomorrowland were forced to cancel or postpone as a result of the pandemic. To adapt, many started hosting virtual festivals and livestreams on platforms like Twitch, Discord, Facebook, and Instagram.

"Events play an important role in the EDM industry. The experiences are paramount, second only to the music. It's difficult to convey the same human connection and audiovisual experiences over the internet, but music industry professionals did everything they could to make the best of the situation.

"In an attempt to engage with their fans from a distance, DJs worldwide have started hosting livestreams. Since many people are spending more time online, livestreams help them enjoy music from home.

"DJ Dove had been telling me about Live Spin at The Funktion House where DJs get a chance to showcase their skills online. I caught a glimpse of his set in November that year. There were plenty of venues that were fundraising to keep themselves afloat. Eventually I decided to follow Dove and started doing my own livestreams at The Funktion House. Partners Anthony Vitale and Michael Gentile lived by the mantra 'If you treat DJing like a hobby, you will never be paid like a business.'"

Disciple had spent more time in the studio through the 2010s. But when lockdowns came, they proved to be his most productive period as a recording artist in his career. In 2020 and 2021 alone, he collaborated with dozens of other vocalists, artists, and producers on numerous singles, remixes, EPs, compilations, and two full-length records, *Full Circle* and *Grateful 24/7/365*.

The 2020s have moved along from those initial lockdowns, but COVID-19 has and will cast a long shadow on Farragut, New York, and house music. Only time will tell how it all plays out. One change has already become apparent. If you walk through Commodore Barry Park in the summer, you'll hear something that hasn't been heard in years. "The park has become a weekly hub for DJs," Disciple said. "The mobile DJ movement is back in a big way."

In the 2021 mayoral election, New Yorkers sent Eric Adams to City Hall. A moderate democrat, he campaigned on a platform to focus policy toward the long-neglected NYCHA system, police and safety in the city, and public health initiatives. He also came in with another goal: support New York nightlife. Not only does he regularly attend jams in Commodore Barry Park and Coney Island, but he has also begun to lift previous limitations, allowing DJs to play later into the night.

PEACE

Since Disciple returned to New York, he's shared the stage with a truly diverse crowd of performers. His collaborators have gone on to star in movies, record Billboard hits, and become successful activists, choreographers, dancers, live performers, and even elected officials. More than a few are no longer with us.

It's been a long time since he was spinning gospel records for WBMB at Baruch College. Disciple still remembers the early days when Monty and Steve, David Camacho, Joey Llanos, Richard Vasquez, and Terrence O'Driscoll saw something in him and gave him a platform.

"In the past decade, I've found peace," Disciple said. "The drive that pushed me to travel the world and make my contribution to house music is still with me, but it now manifests in different ways. While I'm proud to have been able to help up-and-coming artists, the most rewarding collaboration I've been a part of yet is my family."

That work has hardly been easy. He is currently the sole provider for his daughter, who despite everything is thriving at home, at school, and in her community. Medical issues, however, have continued to dog the Banks brothers. Larry began to suffer kidney failure in 2006. He was told by doctors that he wasn't going to make it. He refused to believe them.

Larry managed to fight back and, while he has lost his sight, he continues to direct the Walter Johnson Choir. Disciple joins Larry on the drums every Sunday at the Church of the Open Door along with Rusty Taylor on bass.

Though going blind and living on dialysis, Larry Banks has continued his work with his community and the Walter Johnson Choir. "Let the work I do, speak for me! It was in that vein that Larry was living his life," Disciple said. "He lost his sight, was on dialysis, but was still faithful to the church; working with at-risk kids at Von King Park in Bed-Stuy, Brooklyn for ten years. He also wrote and published the family's first book, a novel called *Drowning in a River Called Time*."

Meanwhile, Sherman retired from his construction job, is a happy bike collector, and has fallen in love. On May 9, 2018, Stanley was inducted into the Brooklyn Jazz Hall of Fame and Museum, which he celebrated with his daughter Deanna Greene and his granddaughter, Amaya Graves. He continues to tour with George Benson while being instrumental in spreading the good message about juicing and body cleansing.

"Stanley came to a few of my events and we finally did something in the same building on March 16 in 2018," Disciple said. "While Stanley was having a jam session upstairs at the Williamsburg Music Center, I was downstairs spinning with DJs in the wee hours of the morning. The ultimate fulfillment was having me, Stanley, and Larry bringing in 2019 at the Church of the Open Door.

"I knew it would be a moment our parents would have been so proud of. Having children in my life meant giving the same sacrifice my parents gave me. I understand that musical movements come and go. My daughter Julia might never know who DJ Disciple really was. I'm okay with that. I will cherish house music for the rest of my life. I've been able to give much to the music industry. Now it's time to turn that focus to my family and community.

"There was a time when I struggled to square my career and passion with my faith. Those days are gone. It's been a while since I've been caught up over calling myself DJ Disciple. Now, with every mention of that name, the gospel verse rings in my ears: 'Only what you do for Christ shall last.'"

1. DJ Disciple Release NYC party with Tony Humphries at Release, Sapphire Lounge. **2.** Voodoo Ray and DJ Disciple at Funkbox. **3.** Ejoe Wilson at Release, Sapphire Lounge. **4.** RUBI aka RIVKA R3 NYC, DJ AQuaBeaT, Mikki Afflick, and DJ Disciple at Release, Sapphire Lounge. **5.** DJ Disciple and Jellybean Benitez at Release, Sapphire Lounge. **6.** Al, Father Chris, Hex Hector, DJ Disciple at Release, Sapphire Lounge. *(All images from the author's collection.)*

1. The Next Level party *(courtesy of Ernest Newton Jr., also known as Photoman)*. **2.** DJ Disciple with The Martinez Brothers at Club Langstons *(courtesy of Ernest Newton Jr., also known as Photoman)*. **3.** Julia Banks, 2022 *(author's collection)*.

ENDNOTES

THE HOUSES

1. "Funds Okayed for Farragut Housing Units." *The Brooklyn Daily Eagle*, September 1, 1949.
2. "First Farragut Tenants Move In Tuesday." *The Brooklyn Daily Eagle*, March 25, 1951.
3. Maloney, Thomas. "African Americans in the Twentieth Century." EH.Net Encyclopedia, edited by Robert Whaples. January 14, 2002. URL http://eh.net/encyclopedia/african-americans-in-the-twentieth-century/
4. Pritchett, Wendell. *Brownsville, Brooklyn: Blacks, Jews, and the Changing Face of the Ghetto*. Chicago: University of Chicago Press, 2002.
5. Clark, Alfred. "Gang Wars Upset Area in Brooklyn." *New York Times*, May 2, 1961.
6. US Census Bureau. "New York – Race and Hispanic Origin for Selected Large Cities and Other Places: Earliest Census to 1990." July 13, 2005. https://www2.census.gov/library/working-papers/2005/demo/pop-twps0076/nytab.pdf
7. Gardiner, Sean. "Heroin: From the Civil War to the 70s and Beyond." *City Limits*, July 5, 2009. https://citylimits.org/2009/07/05/heroin-from-the-civil-war-to-the-70s-and-beyond/
8. Musto, David F. "Illicit Price of Cocaine in Two Eras: 1908-14 and 1982-89." *Pharmacy in History* 33, no. 1 (1991): 3–10.
9. Drug Enforcement Agency. "1985-1990." *History of the DEA*, University of Minnesota, 2008. https://web.archive.org/web/20060823024931/http://www.usdoj.gov/dea/pubs/history/1985-1990.html
10. Vagins, Deborah, and McCurdy, Jesselyn. *Cracks in the System: 20 Years of Unjust Federal Crack Cocaine Law*. American Civil Liberties Union. October 2006. https://www.aclu.org/other/cracks-system-20-years-unjust-federal-crack-cocaine-law

THE AIRWAVES

1. US Census Bureau. "20th Century Statistics Statistical Abstract of the United States: 1999." https://www.census.gov/history/pdf/radioownership1920-1998.pdf

2. Ankosko, Bob. "The Mighty Technics SL-1200." *Sound and Vision*, February 18, 2021. https://www.soundandvision.com/content/mighty-technics-sl-1200

3. "Tested in the Home." *High Fidelity Magazine*, October 1955. https://worldradiohistory.com/Archive-All-Audio/Archive-High-Fidelity/50s/High-Fidelity-1955-10.pdf

4. Armano, Alessandro. "Francis Grasso, The Pioneer of Beatmatching." *House of Frankie*, November 6, 2017. https://www.houseoffrankie.com/francis-grasso-pioneer-beatmatching/

5. Reichert, Herb. "Gramophone Dreams #3." *Stereophile*, March 11, 2015. https://www.stereophile.com/content/gramophone-dreams-4

6. Commandeur, Jordan. "Ultramagnetic MC's Ced-Gee Reveals He Produced Most of BDP's *Criminal Minded*." *Ambrosia for Heads*, October 11, 2018. https://ambrosiaforheads.com/2018/10/ced-gee-boogie-down-productions-criminal-minded-bpd/

7. Batey, Angus. "UltraMagnetic MC's–Critical Breakdown: An Oral History." http://www.angusbatey.com/index.php?id=589&category=features

8. Batey, Angus. "Enter the Golden Age: BDP, Public Enemy, Eric B and Rakim 30 Years On." *The Quietus*, February 27, 2017. https://thequietus.com/articles/21877-public-enemy-eric-b-rakim-paid-in-full-bdp-hip-hop-golden-age-anniversary-review

9. Beta, Andy. "Fingers Inc.: *Another* Side." *Pitchfork*, January 12, 2016. https://pitchfork.com/reviews/albums/21391-fingers-inc-another-side/

10. Lal, Kish. "How Hip Hop Learned to Embrace Dance Music." *Red Bull Music*, October 16, 2018. https://www.redbull.com/au-en/hip-hop-house-music-history

THE CLUBS

1. McKinley, James, Jr. "Dinkins Reduces Task Force on Safety of Social Clubs." *The New York Times*, June 30, 1990. https://www.nytimes.com/1990/06/30/nyregion/dinkins-reduces-task-force-on-safety-of-social-clubs.html

2. Pinker, Steven. "Decivilization in the 1960s." *The Better Angels of Our Nature: Why Crime Has Declined*. New York: Viking, October 4, 2011.

3. Rubinstein, Jonathan. *City Police*. New York: Farrar, Straus and Giroux, 1980.

4. Flood, Joe. "Why the Bronx Burned." *New York Post*, May 16, 2010. https://nypost.com/2010/05/16/why-the-bronx-burned/

5. Brewster, Bill, and Broughton, Frank. *Last Night a DJ Saved My Life*. New York: Grove Press, 2006, 226.

6. Kolata, Gina. "Boy's 1969 Death Suggests AIDS Invaded U.S. Several Times." *New York Times*, October 28, 1987.

7. Weinstein, Steve. "Why Clubbing Was Crucial for Gay Men During the AIDS Crisis." *Vice*, December 1, 2015. https://www.vice.com/en/article/qkak87/why-clubbing-was-crucial-for-gay-men-during-the-aids-crisis

8. Golderberg, Paul. "An Appraisal; The Palladium: An Architecturally Dramatic New Discotheque." *New York Times*, May 20, 1985.

9. Siano, Nicky. "Nicky Siano on The Gallery, Larry Levan, and Life After Music." *Red Bull Music Academy*, May 13, 2016. https://www.youtube.com/watch?v=KR6pHVkzuew&ab_channel=RedBullMusicAcademy

10. Ibid.

11. DM. "A Look Inside the Hi-Fi Equipment Behind Paradise Garage." *In Sheep's Clothing Hi-Fi*, December 4, 2020. https://insheepsclothinghifi.com/a-look-inside-the-hi-fi-equipment-behind-paradise-garage/

12. Lawrence, Tim. *Life and Death on the New York Dance Floor, 1980–1983*. Durham, NC: Duke University Press, 2016.

13. Shapiro, Peter. "Saturday Mass: Larry Levan and the Paradise Garage." *Red Bull Music Academy Daily*, April 22, 2014. https://daily.redbullmusicacademy.com/2014/04/larry-levan-feature

14. Markman, Alex. "Interview: The Loft Founder David Mancuso." *Red Bull Music*, June 2016. https://daily.redbullmusicacademy.com/2016/06/david-mancuso-interview

15. Grimes, William. "David Mancuso, Whose New York Loft Was a Hub of '70s Night Life, Dies at 72." *New York Times*, November 18, 2016. https://www.nytimes.com/2016/11/19/nyregion/david-mancuso-dead-the-loft.html

16. https://www.diyaudio.com/community/threads/big-bertha.232565/

17. Beta, Andy. "Magic Touch: Richard Long's Life-Changing Soundsystems." *Red Bull Music*, May 20, 2016. https://daily.redbullmusicacademy.com/2016/05/richard-long-feature

18. Ibid.

19. "Studio 54." *Internet Broadway Database*, 2019. https://www.ibdb.com/theatre/studio-54-1165

20. Locker, Melissa. "Bianca Jagger Finally Sets the Record Straight About That Night at Studio 54." *Vanity Fair*, April 25, 2015. https://www.vanityfair.com/hollywood/2015/04/bianca-jagger-studio-54

21. Weber, Bruce. "Robert Isabell, Who Turned Events Into Wondrous Occasions, Dies at 57." *The New York Times*, July 10, 2009. https://www.nytimes.com/2009/07/11/nyregion/11isabell.html

22. Warren, Emma. "Todd Edwards." *Red Bull Music Academy*, 2013. https://www.redbullmusicacademy.com/lectures/todd-edwards

23. Blumenthal, Ralph. "Fire in the Bronx; 87 Die in Blaze at Illegal Club; Police Arrest Ejected Patron; Worst New York Fire Since 1911." *The New York Times*, March 26, 1990. https://www.nytimes.com/1990/03/26/nyregion/fire-bronx-87-die-blaze-illegal-club-police-arrest-ejected-patron-worst-new-york.html

24. McKinley, James, Jr. "Dinkins Reduces Task Force on Safety of Social Clubs." *The New York Times*, June 30, 1990. https://www.nytimes.com/1990/06/30/nyregion/dinkins-reduces-task-force-on-safety-of-social-clubs.html

25. Oder, Ufi. "How the 1994 Crime Bill Fed the Mass Incarceration Crisis." *ACLU Blog*, June 4, 2019. https://www.aclu.org/blog/smart-justice/mass-incarceration/how-1994-crime-bill-fed-mass-incarceration-crisis

26. Purdum, Todd. "The 1993 Elections: Mayor; Giuliani Ousts Dinkins by a Thin Margin; Whitman Is an Upset Winner Over Florio." *The New York Times*, November 3, 1993. https://www.nytimes.com/1993/11/03/nyregion/1993-elections-mayor-giuliani-ousts-dinkins-thin-margin-whitman-upset-winner.html

27. Taylor, Clarence. *Fight the Power*. New York: New York University Press, 2019.

28. Powell, Michael. "Another Look at the Dinkins Administration, and Not By Giuliani." *The New York Times*, October 25, 2009. https://www.nytimes.com/2009/10/26/nyregion/26dinkins.html

29. Kelling, George, and Wilson, James. "Broken Windows." *The Atlantic*, March 1982. https://www.theatlantic.com/magazine/archive/1982/03/broken-windows/304465/

30. Giuliani, Rudy. "'Freedom Is About Authority': Excerpts from Giuliani Speech on Crime." *The New York Times*, March 20, 1994. https://www.nytimes.com/1994/03/20/nyregion/freedom-is-about-authority-excerpts-from-giuliani-speech-on-crime.html

31. *Muchmore's Cafe LLC vs. The City of New York*. US District Court Eastern District of New York. https://www.govinfo.gov/content/pkg/USCOURTS-nyed-1_14-cv-05668/pdf/USCOURTS-nyed-1_14-cv-05668-0.pdf

32. Bumiller, Elisabeth. "Can Clubland Live in Quality-of-Life Era?" *New York Times*, August 4, 1996.

33. James, George. "Limelight Goes Dark as Crackdown on Drugs Reaches Major Clubs." *New York Times*, October 5, 1994. https://www.nytimes.com/1995/10/05/nyregion/limelight-goes-dark-as-crackdown-on-drugs-reaches-major-clubs.html

34. Gatien, Peter. *The Club King: My Rise, Reign, and Fall in New York Nightlife*. New York: Little A, 2020.

35. Ibid.

36. Musto, Michael. "How Mayor Giuliani Decimated New York Nightlife." *Vice*, March 6, 2017. https://www.vice.com/en_us/article/bjjdzq/how-mayor-giuliani-decimated-new-york-city-nightlife

THE UNDERGROUND

1. Pareles, John. "Larry Levan, 38; His Tastes Shaped Dance-Club Music." *New York Times*, November 11, 1992. https://www.nytimes.com/1992/11/11/arts/larry-levan-38-his-tastes-shaped-dance-club-music.html

EXILE

1. Smith, Phil. "How DJ International Took Chicago House Around the World." *uDiscoverMusic*, November 21, 2019. https://www.udiscovermusic.com/stories/dj-international-chicago-house/
2. Garber, David. "Meet the Renegade DJ Crew Who Helped Bring Rave Culture to the West Coast." *Vice*, October 18, 2016. https://www.vice.com/en_us/article/4x88gq/wicked-san-fransisco-anniversary-feature
3. Brewster, Bill, and Broughton, Frank. *The Manual: The Who, the Where, the Why of Clubland*. London: Headline Book Publishing, 1998, 95.
4. Cheeseman, Phil. "DJ Disciple." *DJ Magazine*, October 21, 1993, 11.
5. Cooper, Carol. "Sounds of the Underground." *Vibe*, April 1994, 24.
6. Spoony, DJ. "10 Tracks that Chart the Evolution of U.K. Garage, According to DJ Spoony." *DJ Mag*, September 7, 2018. https://djmag.com/content/10-tracks-chart-evolution-uk-garage-according-dj-spoony

REBIRTH

1. Lauren Martin. "'It Gives Me Peace.' House Legends Larry Heard and Robert Owens on Winning Their Trax Legal Battle." *The Guardian*, August 25, 2022. https://www.theguardian.com/music/2022/aug/25/ihouse-legends-larry-heard-robert-owens-trax-legal-battle-copyright.
2. Paoletta, Michael. "DJ Disciple, Minus 8, Others Provide Essential New Sets." *Billboard Magazine*, July 1, 2000, 27.
3. Milzoff, Rebecca. "Taking the Fifth." *New York Magazine*, October 13, 2006. http://nymag.com/news/intelligencer/22834/
4. BlackBook Staff. "Industry Insiders: Michael Ault, International Spy." *BlackBook*, October 16, 2008. https://bbook.com/nightlife/industry-insiders-michael-ault-international-spy/
5. Wilner, Isaiah. "The Short, Drunken Life of Club Row." *New York Magazine*, February 19, 2007. http://nymag.com/nymag/features/27845/index3.html
6. Romano, Tricia. "You're Fired." *The Village Voice*, January 23, 2007. https://www.villagevoice.com/2007/01/23/youre-fired/
7. BlackBook Staff. "The Party Moves: GBH's Tom Dunkley & Alejandro Torio." *BlackBook*, August 24, 2009. https://bbook.com/good-night-mr-lewis-1-109/the-party-moves-gbhs-tom-dunkley-alejandro-torio/

8. Christman, Ed. "The Music Business Remembers 9/11." *Billboard*, September 11, 2011. https://www.billboard.com/music/music-news/the-music-business-remembers-911-467518/

9. Chiariglione, Leonardo. "MPEG's First Steps." *Riding the Media Bits*, August 21, 2011. https://web.archive.org/web/20111101091827/http://ride.chiariglione.org/MPEG%27s_1st_steps.php

10. Smith, Tony. "Ten Years Old: The World's First MP3 Player." *The Register*, March 10, 2008. https://www.theregister.co.uk/2008/03/10/ft_first_mp3_player/

11. Goldman, David. "Music's Lost Decade: Sales Cut in Half." *CNN Money*, February 3, 2010. https://money.cnn.com/2010/02/02/news/companies/napster_music_industry/

12. "U.S. Sales Database." *Recording Industry Association of America*, 2018. https://www.riaa.com/u-s-sales-database/

13. Illicit Drug Anti-Proliferation Act of 2003. 21 U.S.C. 843 and 856. https://www.govinfo.gov/app/details/BILLS-108s226is

14. Reynolds, Simon. "How Rave Music Conquered America." *The Guardian*, August 2, 2012. https://www.theguardian.com/music/2012/aug/02/how-rave-music-conquered-america

ON AND ON

1. "Brooklyn, New York Neighborhood Map–Income, House Prices, Occupations, Boundaries." *City-Data*. http://www.city-data.com/nbmaps/neigh-Brooklyn-New-York.html#N51

2. Tran, Elliott. "Ten Indicted Following More than 70 Sales of Narcotics at Brooklyn's Farragut Houses." *Office of the Special Narcotics Prosecutor for the City of New York*, October 25, 2018. http://www.snpnyc.org/ten-indicted-narcotics-farragut-houses/

3. Hicks, Nolan. "NYCHA Repair Bill Estimated to Reach $31.8 Billion." *New York Post*, July 2, 2018. https://nypost.com/2018/07/02/nycha-repair-bill-estimated-at-31-8-billion/

4. Rash, Natalie. "NYCHA CEO Outlines Next Steps for Recently Passed Preservation Trust." *Gotham Gazette*, July 15, 2022. https://www.gothamgazette.com/city/11456-nycha-ceo-russ-preservation-trust

LIST OF INTERVIEWS

Anderson, Jerome (DJ Jaz). Phone interview, 2019.
Anderson, Randy. Phone interview, 2020.
Banks, Larry. Phone interview, 2019.
Banks, Stanley. Phone interview, 2019.
Benjamin, Kim. Email interview, 2020.
Berry, Glenn. Email interview, 2020.
Blackwell, Eric. Video conference interview, 2010.
Biggs, Trevor. In-person interview, 2020.
Bobby and Steve. Video conference interview, 2009.
Carpenter, Kenny. Phone interview, 2007.
Davis, Ralph. Phone interview, 2019.
Daye, Greg. Phone interview, 2020.
DJ Amadeus. Web message interview, 2020.
DJ Debonair. Phone interview, 2019.
DJ DLS. Video conference interview, 2008.
DJ Dove. Email interview, 2009.
DJ Keoki. Phone interview, 2022.
DJ Mehdi Damir. Video conference interview, 2009.
DJ Romain. Phone interview, 2022.
DJ Rubi. Video conference interview, 2008.
Dragseth, Laurie. Email interview, 2020.
E Man. Email interview, 2019.
Firman, JP. Phone interview, 2019.
Foort, Lucien. Video conference interview, 2008.
Fritz, Sarah. Web message interview, 2020.
Green, Brian "Footwork." Email interview, 2020.
Hayes, Kim "Redness." Video conference interview, 2008.
Jones, Nick. Phone interview, 2020.
Konders, Bobby. Phone interview, 2020.

Lafontant, Patrick. In-person interview, 2020.
Mac, Anthony. Email interview, 2019.
McNally, Niki. Email interview, 2018.
Picazo, Mayi. Web message interview, 2020.
Raine, Steve. Web message interview, 2019.
Richardson, Timmy. Phone interview, 2020.
Salto, Gregor. Video conference interview, 2008.
Sanjuan, Willy. Phone interview, 2022.
Santoro, Kim. Email interview, 2020.
Terry, Todd. Phone interview, 2021.
Thomas, Frank. Email interview, 2020.
Vasquez, Richard. Phone interviews, 2020, 2021, and 2022.
Voodoo Ray. Video conference interview, 2009.
Walker, Tony. Email interview, 2020.

SELECTED BIBLIOGRAPHY

Brewster, Bill, and Broughton, Frank. *Last Night a DJ Saved My Life: The History of the Disc Jockey*. New York: Grove Press, 2000.

Gatien, Peter. *The Club King: My Rise, Reign, and Fall in New York Nightlife*. Seattle: Little A, 2020.

Goodman, Lizzy. *Meet Me in the Bathroom: Rebirth and Rock and Roll in New York City 2001-2011*. New York: Dey Street Books, 2017.

Lawrence, Tim. *Life and Death on the New York Dance Floor, 1980–1983*. Durham: Duke University Press, 2016.

Lawrence, Tim. *Love Saves the Day: A History of American Dance Music Culture, 1970–1979*. Durham: Duke University Press, 2004.

Matos, Michaelangelo. *The Underground Is Massive: How Electronic Dance Music Conquered America*. New York: Dey Street Books, 2016.

Pinker, Steven. *The Better Angels of Our Nature: Why Crime Has Declined*. New York: Viking, 2011.

Pritchett, Wendell. *Brownsville, Brooklyn: Blacks, Jews, and the Changing Face of the Ghetto*. Chicago: University of Chicago Press, 2002.

Taylor, Clarence. *Fight the Power: African Americans and the Long History of Police Brutality in New York City*. New York: New York University Press, 2019.

INDEX

Adimora, Omar, 136–38
Adonis, 6, 47, 111, 148
Alig, Michael, 86–88
Anderson, Jerome "Jaz," 41–47, 60, 62, 67, 69, 80, 83
Anderson, Paul "Trouble," 119, 121, 133–34, 136–38, 193

Banks, Julia, 13–14, 17, 19, 22, 41, 51, 80
Banks, Larry, 14, 18, 21–22, 29–30, 153–54, 201–2
Banks, Leighton, 14, 21, 81, 128
Banks, Sherman, 14, 27, 202
Banks, Stanley, 14, 17–18, 27–29, 132, 202
Banks, William, 13–14, 40–41, 70, 80, 163, 185
Baruch College, 6–7, 27, 35, 44–46, 63–65
Benjamin, Kim, 128–132, 134, 139–140, 194–95
Big Bob, 9–12, 40
Biggs, Trevor, 91–103
Bobby and Steve, 117–18, 124, 126, 162
bottle service, 7, 147, 152–60, 168, 189–90
Brooks, Monique, 92, 98, 102–103

Camacho, DJ David, 5, 73, 77, 91–103, 106, 108, 115, 126, 129, 166, 186, 193–94

Carpenter, Kenny, 5, 7, 15–16, 100–1, 171, 191
Catch 22 Recordings, 138, 147–49, 151, 172
Choice, The, ix, 97, 103–108, 128
Civil Rights Movement, The, 13; school desegregation, 16–17
COVID-19, 199–201
Crash Crew, The, 34–35
crossover (device), 10–11, 40, 61, 106

Davis, Ralph "Kool D," 33–37, 42–43, 45, 49–50, 67, 70, 81, 165–67
Davis, Bobby, 77–78, 122, 129
Daye, Greg, 91–103, 125, 193
Debonair, DJ, 9, 11–12, 16, 61, 66, 69, 106, 195
DJing: as a career, 70–71, 75, 77, 129–30, 132, 171–72, 194–95; mobile DJs, 9–12, 15–16, 24–25, 34, 39, 43, 196; technique, 10–11, 37–40, 59, 123, 133, 140–43
DJ Dove, 74, 76, 80, 153–54, 157–58, 200
DJ Keoki, 84–87, 89
DJ Ruff, 172–75
DJ Magazine, 71, 78, 115, 123–24
Dynell, Johnny, 63–65, 123

E Man, 150, 186, 189
Edmond, François, 153–55

215

Edwards, Todd, 78, 118, 124–25, 133–37, 191

Farragut Houses, The, 9, 12, 14–16, 19–20, 22, 24, 80–81, 196–99
faith and religion, 21–22, 25–26, 41, 43–44, 142-3. *See also*: Church of the Open Door, 21–22, 30, 80, 185, 197, 201; crossover with club culture, 58–59; Five-Percent Nation, 21–22; Greater Refuge Temple, 22, 25–26, 37, 43, 106
Feel Real, 119–20, 189
Firmin, JP, 49, 72, 115–23, 125–26, 129, 132–34, 143, 192–93
Flowers, Grandmaster, 5, 9–12, 16, 24–25, 39, 77
Funk, Farley "Jackmaster," 4, 111

Gatien, Peter, 86–89
gospel (musical genre), 21, 25–26, 39–40
Great British House (GBH), 160–64, 167
Green, Brian 'Footwork,' 66, 97–98

Happy Land Fire, The, 55, 79, 82–83
Hard Times, 122–23, 126, 129
Heard, Larry, 6, 43, 46–47, 95, 111, 148
HIV/AIDS, 8, 56–57, 64, 83, 92, 105, 111
house music: community, 48, 56, 58, 91–108, 120–21, 147–50, 175–79, 190–93; crossover with hip hop, 43, 46–50, 192–93; dance, 4, 47, 66, 98; divergence from hip hop, 82–83, 127; origins, 3–4, 41–43; popularity overseas, 111, 120–21
Hunter College, 64–68, 114
Humphries, Tony, 50, 71–72, 74
Hurley, Steve "Silk," 4, 44

Ibiza, 139–40, 152–54, 165, 173, 187

Jefferson, Marshall, 4, 7, 43, 45, 60, 95, 111, 129
Johnson, Naeem, 73, 76, 194
Jones, DJ Nick, 91–103

Knuckles, Frankie, 3–5, 43, 51–52, 58–60, 82, 104, 111
Konders, Bobby, 52, 91–103

Lafontant, Patrick, 91–103
Lakota, The, 115–16
Levan, Larry, 5, 43, 58–62, 65, 95, 99–100, 104–8, 111, 121, 129
Loft, The, 5, 56, 58–59, 61–62, 96, 104, 120
Long, Richard, 5, 10–11, 40, 58–59, 61–62, 65, 67, 72

Mancuso, David, 5, 58, 61–62, 67, 96, 104, 194
Martinez, Duce, 72–73, 188, 191
McNally, Niki, 169–70, 190–91
Melendez, Angel, 87–88
Ministry of Sound, 74, 121, 138, 162, 165
Mixmag, 71, 190
Mulholland, Jamie, 156–57
My True Colors, 150–152

Nelson, Grant, 132–35, 138
New York City: 9/11, 165–67; clubs, 55–57, 79, 85, 89. *See also*: bottle service; crime, 2–3, 19, 23–24, 55–56, 80–82, 162, 195; Dinkins, Mayor David, 79, 83; fires, 56, 79; Giuliani, Mayor Rudolph, 6, 83–86, 88–89, 147, 196; policing, 82–89, 166–67, 195

Owens, Robert, 46–47, 52–53, 73, 92, 129, 148

Palladium, The, 47–48, 50, 57–58, 62–63, 67, 86, 119
Paradise Garage, 5, 40, 44, 50, 55–56, 58–62, 68, 91–96, 121, 153, 189
Perez, Eddie, 78, 117, 124–25, 136
Phi Beta Sigmas, 35, 64–69, 108

radio: Kiss 100 FM, 117–18; mass communication, 33; *New York's Best Kept Secret*, ix, 50–53, 76–77, 108, 115, 149, 186; New York radio DJs, 34, 43, 50, 60; *Transatlantic Mix,* 135, 141; WBMB 590 AM, 35, 38–39
raves, 111–13, 131–32, 170–71, 175–76
Ray, Voodoo, 92, 98, 194
record promos, 52–53, 74, 124
Ricardo, Roman, 47–48, 63
Richardson, DJ Timmy, 91–103
Robinson, Christopher "Father Chris," 66, 188
Rosner, Alex, 62, 67

Sanchez, Roger, 74, 76–78, 112, 114, 118, 121, 126, 133–34, 139, 153, 160, 177
San Francisco, 112–114, 128–29, 131
Sanjuan, Willy, 140, 148
Siano, Nicky, 5, 59
Smarth, Marjory, 73, 92, 98
Souk, Le, 168–70, 190,
Sound Experience Crew, 44–48, 66–67
Sound Factory Bar, 76–77, 115, 149, 161
Strafe, 15, 27, 150
Studio 16, 55, 65, 68–69

Taylor, Rusty, 16, 195, 201
Tallman, Dawn, 135, 137, 149, 152, 172–73, 191
Terry, Todd, 7, 47–48, 50, 76–77, 126–27, 133, 191
Thomas, Frank, 66, 96, 98, 102
Torrales, Hippie, 72–73, 194
Tort, David, 172–75, 178
Tucker, Barbara, ix, 76–77, 124, 126
Tunnel, 55, 57–58, 63, 86, 89, 118, 152, 159

Ultra Magnetic MCs, 37, 45–46
UK garage, 127, 132–38, 152
underground parties: House Nation, 103; Save the Robots, 84–85, 103; Wild Pitch, 91–103

Vasquez, Richard, ix, 26, 58, 79, 103–8, 201
Vega, Louie, 5, 76–7, 92, 126, 130, 134, 136

Walker, Tony, 1, 135, 141, 162
Warehouse, The, 3–4, 40, 42, 59
Wicked Crew (DJs Markie, Garth, Jeno, and Thomas), 113–14
Wilson, Ejoe, 73, 98, 188–89, 199
Wyatt, DJ Marques, 127–28, 132

Zanzibar, ix, 40, 70–76, 123

ABOUT THE AUTHORS

David Banks, also known as DJ Disciple, is a Black artist, DJ, radio host, producer, and community advocate based in Brooklyn, New York. He has toured the world over a forty-year career, playing for audiences on five continents, including Studio 54 in New York, Ministry of Sound in London, and Cream in Ibiza. His Grammy-nominated track "Caught Up" reached number one on the US Billboard Hot Dance Club Play chart in 2002 and was later featured in the Showtime series *Queer as Folk*. His music has landed on scores of top music charts around the world. He won an ARIA music award for his remix of Stephen Allkins' "The Bass Has Got Me Movin.'"

Henry Kronk is a journalist who has covered a range of subjects over the course of his career. His reporting has appeared in *OPIS, Greenbiz, Exclaim!,* the *Burlington Free Press, International DJ, Vallum: Contemporary Poetry*, and more. His creative fiction and poetry have appeared in *The Wrath-Bearing Tree, Ricky's Backyard, The Veg,* and *Omega*. In 2018, he produced the investigative radio program and podcast *Code Burst*, which explores a coding bootcamp that sought to train out-of-work coal miners for jobs in tech. He lives in Burlington, Vermont.

www.ingramcontent.com/pod-product-compliance
Ingram Content Group UK Ltd.
Pitfield, Milton Keynes, MK11 3LW, UK
UKHW022228230426
12048UKWH00016BA/1122